STRUGGLERS INTO STRIVERS

HUGH B. PRICE

INTO
STRIVERS

What the Military Can Teach Us About
How Young People Learn and Grow

Small Batch Books
Amherst, Massachusetts

ISBN 978-1-937650-45-2
Library of Congress Control Number: 2014948504

Designed by Simon Sullivan

SMALL
BATCH
BOOKS

493 SOUTH PLEASANT STREET
AMHERST, MASSACHUSETTS 01002
413.230.3943
SMALLBATCHBOOKS.COM

Contents

Prologue

EXPERIENCES DURING OUR FORMATIVE YEARS often make enduring impressions that indelibly shape our personal and professional lives. This book stems from the confluence of three such experiences—one when I was growing up, the second while I was in law school, and the third early in my marriage.

The first dates back to my childhood in Washington, D.C., during the 1950s. Some of my male classmates simply weren't into school. Eventually they dropped out of school and out of sight. When I encountered a few of them several years later, they had joined—or been drafted into—the Army. These guys were ramrod straight in their crisp uniforms, purposeful and polite. In other words, the Army had virtually reinvented them.

Since I never served in the military, exactly how the Army accomplished this turnaround was a mystery to me. But I was struck back then by the transformative power of the experience that these guys had undergone. Either the Army possessed a magic potion, or, more likely, it operated a potent training and educational regimen that worked wonders with these tough young men who were utterly turned off to school. Beyond the legendary discipline imposed by the Pentagon, my strong hunch was that the intricate system of incentives and ranks helped motivate boys who have little help, let alone hope. Years later, I became fixated on this question: Can the way the military educates and trains troubled and troublesome recruits be adapted to serve youngsters who are struggling in school and in life?

The second formative experience occurred while I was in law school. I was married and a father by the middle of my second year. To earn extra money, I served in the local antipoverty program as a social group worker and mentor for a half-dozen inner-city teenage boys who were constantly in scrapes with the law. These kids qualified as bad actors by the standards of those days. They robbed parking meters, tossed lit matches into the gas tanks of cars, and engaged in other hell-raising. They were a huge headache for the courts and on course to become gangbangers and hardened criminals. The idea behind hiring me was to connect them with a caring adult who might be able to steer them back on the right track before they permanently ruined their lives, or worse.

I worked three afternoons a week at the old Prince Street School in the Hill neighborhood of New Haven, Connecticut. It took awhile to break the ice with these teens and gain their trust. After all, they were street toughs, and I, a Yalie, was anything but. They greeted me with skepticism, and I initially felt insecure dealing with them. Yet eventually, we bonded. We hung out together and talked about everything and nothing. We shot hoops and even formed a basketball team that competed in the municipal park-recreation league. That was important because it introduced structure and teamwork into their aimless lives. I took them to New York City to see the sights and ride the Staten Island Ferry. They visited our apartment, where my wife taught them to bake cakes. I dropped by their homes to get acquainted with their families, usually a mother or grandmother with several siblings, but seldom a father in sight.

I met with these fellows several days a week, three to four hours per day. I did not realize how much our relationship had come to mean to them until I showed up late one afternoon because a law school class had run long. Speaking on behalf of his buddies, one of the youngsters said something that has stuck with me ever since. "Mr. Price," he began, "being together with you and the guys at three o'clock has become the most important thing in our lives. If we're going to keep this going, we need to know that being here at three o'clock with us is also the most important thing in your life. If you're ever late again, we'll know it isn't and that'll be the end of it for us."

During our two years together, the guys had nary another encounter with the cops or the courts. They stayed completely out of trouble and persevered through school, although admittedly it was a struggle. In short, we really bonded, and some of the guidance and support I had hoped to provide apparently actually penetrated. I discovered from this experience the power of mentors who are a reliable presence in the lives of youngsters with few other caring adults they can look to and trust.

Reflecting on this experience, I can attest that troubled boys aren't necessarily lost causes to be consigned to the human dumpsters we call prisons. In other words, I gained an early understanding of the wisdom of one of the key ideas advanced in this book, namely the critical importance of fostering the academic and social development of youngsters who are teetering on the brink of disconnecting from school and society.

The third experience that made a lasting impression occurred in the late 1960s when my wife and I lived in a New Haven neighborhood known as Newhallville. We enrolled our daughter in one of the first public schools—Martin Luther King Elementary School—where James Comer, the renowned child psychiatrist at the Yale Child Study Center, had recently initiated his School Development Program (SDP). The SDP emphasizes the academic and social development of youngsters, particularly low-income and minority children. It engages educators and parents in deep collaboration to foster the success of students.

While I would like to think my wife and I provided ample doses of social and emotional development for our daughter, the reality is that most of her classmates came from low- and moderate-income families that were coping with many stresses. Newhallville was a predominantly black, inner-city neighborhood with many single-parent households and families on public assistance. Plus, there was plenty of crime. In fact, our home was burglarized a half dozen times in four years.

Yet MLK School, with its emphasis on academic and social development along with abundant parent participation, worked well for our child and for the other students. It posted gratifying scholastic gains. Dr. Comer went on to become the preeminent national exponent of academic and social development, and many "Comer" schools have registered impressive results.

Three lessons from these formative experiences roughly a half century ago resonate to this day:

• The critical importance of academic and social development

- The power of consistent and intensive mentoring

- The potential of military educational and training methods to transform young people on the precipice of failing in school and in life

When I served as vice president of the Rockefeller Foundation in the late 1980s and early 1990s, I was instrumental in spawning an innovative approach to turning around the lives of high school dropouts. The National Guard embraced and subsequently implemented my proposal that it create a quasi-military youth corps for dropouts. Known since its inception in 1993 as the National Guard Youth ChalleNGe Program, this initiative has achieved impressive results, as documented by a long-term evaluation conducted by the social policy research organization MDRC utilizing random assignment, and as further validated by a cost-benefit analysis undertaken by the RAND Corporation. Among the many surprises embedded in ChalleNGe is the fact that, contrary to the military's prevailing image, this program espouses the development of the whole person.

Cumulatively, these lessons derived from my formative experiences and from ChalleNGe, coupled with nearly a half century of witnessing public schools, especially urban ones, wrestle with the burdens of educating children who present significant academic, motivational, and behavioral challenges, have made a profound impression on me. Indeed, they have utterly convinced me that the conventional model of schooling that concentrates exclusively, or even primarily, on academic instruction and high-stakes testing is off the mark and will not work with many youngsters who are barely getting by or dropping out of school.

We urgently need a new paradigm. We need to create public schools—actually, for the sake of differentiation I much prefer calling them academies—whose overt mission is to advance the academic and social development of youngsters who clearly are struggling in school and in life. The purpose of this book is to make the case for this new paradigm and articulate what it might look like.

Let me alert readers that the design and implications of the National Guard Youth ChalleNGe Program feature prominently in this book. I know from years of exploring this avenue of school reform that allusions to the military are off-putting to some educators, parents, and policymakers. I ask skeptics and naysayers to indulge me and read on. By invoking and examining ChalleNGe, my goal is to glean lessons from this demonstrably effective intervention for disengaged adolescents that might be applied in a strictly civilian context.

This book is not a brief for militarizing public schools. Nothing could be farther from my purpose in writing it. My sole mission is to look outside the proverbial box for ideas, experiences, and evidence that might help us imagine a robust intervention with the potential to rescue adolescents who are chronically disengaged from school before they become hopelessly disconnected from society.

1

The Perennial Quest to Improve America's Schools

In 1983, a panel appointed by U.S. Secretary of Education Terrell Bell issued a report that jolted the country. In *A Nation at Risk: The Imperative for Educational Reform*, the National Commission on Excellence in Education castigated American education by declaring:

> If an unfriendly foreign power had attempted to impose on America the mediocre educational performance that exists today, we might well have viewed it as an act of war. As it stands, we have allowed this to happen to ourselves. . . . We have, in effect, been committing an act of unthinking, unilateral educational disarmament.[1]

The educational challenges spotlighted in that report persist to this day, as do equally dire warnings about the consequences. In 2012, a task force convened by the Council on Foreign Relations and cochaired by former U.S. secretary of state Condoleezza Rice and former New York City Schools chancellor Joel Klein bemoaned the fact that only 22 percent of American high school students were deemed "college ready" in their core subjects.[2] The ratios were even worse for African-American and Latino students.

As Rice and Klein warned in their report, "The lack of preparedness poses threats on five national security fronts: economic growth and competitiveness, physical safety, intellectual property, U.S. global awareness, and U.S. unity and cohesion. . . . Too many young people are not employable in an increasingly high-skilled and global economy, and too many are not qualified to join the military because they are physically unfit, have criminal records, or have an inadequate level of education. . . ."[3]

Rice and Klein contend that human capital will determine power in the current century, and the failure to produce that capital will undermine America's security. "Large, underdeveloped swaths of the population," they continue, "damage the ability of the United States to physically defend itself, protect its secure information, conduct diplomacy, and grow its economy."[4]

A Nation at Risk helped start a torrent of school reform measures aimed at improving America's schools, closing the achievement gap along ethnic and economic lines, and thus boosting the performance of youngsters who are bringing up the rear academically. These reform initiatives have targeted public education from every conceivable angle—from on high by the federal government to ground up in the classroom and local communities. Reforms have been imposed consecutively, concurrently, even at cross-purposes. It is a gross understatement to characterize the last 30 years of school reform as a fertile era in public education. Still, the jury remains out on how productive this profusion of policies and interventions has been, especially when viewed through the prism of students who are persistently faltering in school.

A Dizzying Array of School Reform Initiatives

The roster of school reform initiatives over the years is imposing. Little point is served by listing them all. Let me summarize a cross-section of the more noteworthy policies and interventions.

No Child Left Behind—President George W. Bush championed this aggressive federal law that was enacted in 2001 with bipartisan congressional support. The legislation set lofty—many educators and experts would say unattainable—goals for America's schools and schoolchildren. It imposed an unprecedented federal oversight regime on local public schools by calling for pervasive testing, grading of schools according to their "average yearly progress," disaggregation of achievement data by socioeconomic group, and transparent reporting of individual school results to the media, parents, and the general public. The law remains in force, albeit under mounting fiscal and political pressure and modified in recent years by waivers granted to states.

Higher Academic Standards—For years, state education agencies and local school districts promulgated their own academic standards that set forth what students should know and be able to do to advance from one grade to the next and ultimately graduate from high school. In response to charges that the standards were lax, especially compared with the academic norms of nations whose students routinely outperform ours, many states have stiffened their standards and aligned the tests accordingly.

Common Core—Since these standards vary by state, it has been difficult to gauge whether and to what extent American students overall, as opposed to those in individual states, are progressing vis-à-vis commonly accepted norms of achievement. That is why, with the encouragement of the U.S. Department of Education and funding from large foundations, most states and the District of Columbia so far have coalesced around an effort to define common core standards they all will implement in their jurisdictions.

High-Stakes Tests—Spurred by No Child Left Behind and the get-tough atmosphere generated by the law, state education agencies and public schools embarked on a testing binge. High-stakes tests are taken by all students—typically at the conclusion of the fourth, eighth, and eleventh grades—to determine whether they have sufficiently mastered the required course material to be allowed to progress from grade to grade and to graduate from high school. Pupils who do not fare well may be held back in grade as part of the crackdown on so-called social promotion. With their tenure, ratings, and salaries increasingly dependent on the results, teachers often teach to the tests in an effort to boost their students' performance. Since principals' jobs may also be on the line, they too obsess about test results. So do school superintendents and everyone else on the education totem pole. The fixation these days on testing carries a price. Teachers, parents, and students—just about everyone except politicians—complain bitterly about regimented instruction, loss of creativity, and, sacrifice of arts and physical education classes in favor of extended courses and supplemental instruction in core subjects that are tested.

State Takeover—Exasperated governors and state education agencies occasionally seize operating control of entire school districts that are wracked with educational or fiscal failure (or, quite likely, both) and seemingly clueless about how to improve student performance. High-profile examples include St. Louis, Oakland, Philadelphia, and Newark, New Jersey. State officials typically appoint a superintendent or oversight board to run the district. Yet state takeover seldom proves to be the antidote for low performance, and local politicians and parents bitterly oppose the negation of home rule.

Few states dare to take over entire districts any longer. However, variations on this intervention still crop up these days with the establishment by states of special districts that incorporate, in the case of the Achievement School District in Tennessee, the lowest 5 percent of schools in the state. This collection of schools is overseen by a state-appointed commissioner or superintendent. Another example of this approach is the Education Achievement Authority in Michigan, which mainly oversees faltering Detroit public schools but also includes others around the state.

Mayoral Control—Some venturesome mayors have wrested policy, operating, and fiscal control of school systems from local boards of education. Prominent examples include Michael Bloomberg in New York City and Adrian Fenty, the former mayor of Washington, D.C. These "education" mayors then appoint superintendents or chancellors who report directly to them and impose the mayors' own reform agendas. While mayoral takeovers capture headlines and potentially can be game changers because of the consolidation of power, they are not a commonplace approach to school reform.

Teacher Accountability, Tenure, and Merit Pay—The accountability movement in education extends beyond testing and transparency to the performance of principals and teachers. In politically fraught legislative and labor negotiations across the country, elected officials and local school boards in many districts have managed to introduce policies that take students' academic performance into account in the hiring, retention, promotion, and compensation of teachers and principals.

Public School Choice—In the past, children routinely attended the school that served their neighborhood or, in education-speak, their zone. If these schools performed reasonably well and parents were pretty satisfied, they basically went about their business year after year. However, if these schools were lousy, chaotic, and unsafe, parents who could not afford private or even parochial school tuition had no alternative but to stick it out. Enterprising parents traditionally have exercised public school choice in a variety of ways. Families with enough money move to neighborhoods or towns with solid, perhaps even superb, public schools. Or if their youngsters are high achievers, they may enroll them in selective public schools like Boston Latin or Bronx High School of Science in New York City. That was then. The school choice game is radically different now. Many local districts allow vastly more parents and children to play, sometimes whether they want to or not, by offering a growing range of choices, including:

• Assignment to customary neighborhood schools

• Limited competition for slots in magnet, charter, or alternative schools

• Widespread choice, with neighborhood schools as the fallback for parents who do not make a selection[5]

Choice may even be universal in some districts and at certain grade levels. For instance, New York City conducts open enrollment for all high school students, requiring that they submit a list of preferred schools without any assurance they can attend their neighborhood school if their other selections fail to materialize. A computer matches students with their first choice, which works for close to half of them. Assuming the assignment system works as expected, if that preferred school is filled, the matching system moves on to the second choice and so forth until the youngster is placed.

Magnet Schools—Since the late 1960s, school districts have established so-called magnet schools with a distinctive theme or focus designed explicitly to attract an ethnically and economically diverse student body. Magnets grew during the 1970s and '80s. By the turn of this century, there were just over 3,000 such schools in the U.S.[6] Most choose their students by lottery, but many use merit or talent as the basis for selection. When it comes to creating alternatives to traditional schools, however, the momentum has shifted away from magnets to small public schools and charter schools. These days, those magnets that exist are part of the menu of choices available to parents.

Small Public Schools—Choice is fueled and facilitated by a major change in the local education landscape—the advent of small public schools. Traditional zoned schools still exist, but they no longer hold a monopoly on students. Small schools have blossomed all across the country. They typically are organized around a curricular theme, such as science or the arts, and enroll roughly 100 pupils per grade. The small school movement has taken root with varying degrees of robustness around the country. Quite often these small schools, as well as charter schools, are actually schools-within-schools. In other words, they share space in larger buildings with other small schools, charter schools, or what remains of traditional ones. In New York and elsewhere, they primarily serve minority and disadvantaged students.

Charter Schools—Another formidable player in the school choice game is charter schools, which are publicly financed but typically operated by nonprofit or for-profit groups instead of school systems. Nationally, charter school enrollment has surged as states encourage expansion by relaxing legislated limits on the number of charters allowed. This is a sure sign of their popularity among parents and politicians seeking alternatives to traditional public schools for educational and, in some cases, ideological reasons. Charter schools operate by different rules than regular schools. They tend to be about the same size as small public schools. Charters usually are exempt from some bureaucratic regulations and they enjoy more leeway than regular schools when it comes to hiring and firing teachers and deciding how their budgets will be spent. Charter schools spring from many impulses and points of origin. They may be:

- Conceived and operated in a number of cities by highly resourceful national nonprofit outfits like the Knowledge Is Power Program (a.k.a. KIPP);

- Founded by entrepreneurial nonprofit charter entities, like Harlem Village Academies, that operate a portfolio of elementary through high schools in a particular city;

- Formed by parents, teachers, and community members with a specific philosophy about educating children;

- Created by the local school district; and/or

• Established by for-profit charter management companies.

School Vouchers—Parents use vouchers to help pay tuition for their children at nonpublic schools. In essence, some of the tax money collected for education ends up at private, parochial, and other religious schools instead of all of it going to public schools. Vouchers subsidize the ability of parents to exercise school choice. Aside from the notable examples of Milwaukee and Washington, D.C., vouchers are seldom offered. Not surprisingly, school districts vehemently resist them out of fear they will drain public resources from public schools.

School Turnaround—The economic stimulus package advanced by President Barack Obama and enacted by Congress in 2009 designated roughly $3 billion for so-called School Improvement Grants (SIG). Local districts competed for these grants, which are aimed at turning around woefully underperforming schools. The districts were obliged to choose among several courses of action, such as (a) closing the school, (b) removing the principal and half of the teachers, or (c) implementing a less traumatic transformation plan that might entail replacing the principal, extending learning time, and instituting a new teacher evaluation system.[7] There are roughly 1,200 SIG-funded turnaround efforts underway.[8]

Student Performance: the State of Play

Glimmers of progress can be spotted through the pervasive haze generated by all this reform. The National Assessment of Educational Progress (NAEP) serves as the nation's report card for public and private school students. NAEP, which is taken by 50,000 students each year, is overseen by the National Assessment Governing Board, a bipartisan panel created by Congress in 1988 whose members, appointed by the U.S. secretary of education, include state school officials, governors, educators, businesspeople, and public representatives. In addition to issuing annual reports of student achievement, NAEP's governing board occasionally publishes long-term trend assessments, most recently covering the span from 1973 through 2012.[9]

According to the 2012 report, 9- and 13-year-olds scored higher in reading and math in 2012 than did their counterparts in the early 1970s. Yet academic gains for 17-year-olds have stagnated over that lengthy time span. The achievement gaps between white and black students and between white and Hispanic students have closed significantly over the course of four generations due to larger academic gains registered by minority versus white youngsters.[10] As Kati Haycock, president of a leading advocacy group known as the Education Trust, observed, "While it might have seemed impossible 25 years ago for black and Latino nine-year-olds to reach the proficiency levels that white students then held, they have indeed reached those levels in math."[11]

This encouraging news notwithstanding, the long-term assessment also paints a sobering picture. With the exception of 13-year-old Hispanic youngsters, who continued to gain in math, the achievement gaps in reading and math that plague black and Hispanic youngsters have barely budged since 2008. As Haycock warns, "If we have a crisis in American education, it is this: that we aren't yet moving fast enough to educate the 'minorities' who will soon comprise a 'new majority.' At best, students of color are just now performing at the level of white students a generation ago."[12]

Let's turn specifically to urban districts. The Council of the Great City Schools (CGCS) is a national organization comprising nearly 70 of the largest districts. These school systems contain roughly 16 percent of the nation's public school students, one-third of the black, limited-English-proficient, and Hispanic students, and about a quarter of all economically disadvantaged students in this country.[13] A 2011 report by CGCS indicated that, in general, students in its member districts continue to make important gains in math and reading scores on state assessments.[14] Although achievement in these urban districts still falls below the averages on state tests, the gaps appear to be narrowing. The trend lines do vary by school district, and elementary school gains generally outshine those in middle schools.

The picture gets murkier, however, when student performance in member districts is measured against national norms embodied in NAEP. The council found that students in large cities and those in public schools across the nation made significant gains from 2005 through 2009 on NAEP math assessments in grades four and eight, whereas notable progress in reading was recorded only at the fourth-grade level.[15]

While some students in these districts outperformed their peers nationally in reading and math, few urban districts eclipsed public schools nationwide on NAEP.[16]

Turning next to small public schools, one large, random-assignment study, which is considered the gold standard in evaluation, reported impressive results for those schools located in New York City. MDRC, the esteemed evaluation outfit that conducted the study, contrasted the outcomes for pupils in these schools with a control group of comparable students who did not attend them. The evaluation found that:

- Participants were more likely than nonparticipants to earn 10 or more high school credits;

- They also were less likely to fail more than one core subject;

- 58.5 percent of participants were on track to graduate in four years versus 48.5 percent of controls;

- Small schools increased overall graduation rates by 6.8 percentage points, from 61.9 percent for students who attended traditional schools to 68.7 percent for those who went to small schools; and

- Higher proportions of students in small schools passed the English Regents exam administered by New York State.[17]

Several things stuck out in this study. First, the students in these small schools were genuinely disadvantaged by any accepted definition. Ninety-three percent were black or Hispanic, 83 percent qualified for free or reduced lunch, and virtually all of them resided in inner-city neighborhoods. These students typically entered the ninth grade performing below grade level. They usually had labored in school and seldom graduated on time. Second, minority boys as well as girls profited from the robust benefits of these small schools. Lastly, this wasn't a smattering of pilot schools. Taken together, the enrollment of the small schools in MDRC's study equaled that of the high schools in all of Houston. School reform initiatives rarely achieve comparably strong results on this scale.

The welcome findings in New York City notwithstanding, the story

nationally for small schools is more equivocal. Some research continues to suggest that small schools outperform large schools in critical
ways.[18] Yet the pace of new school formation has slowed markedly. One
reason stems from the withdrawal of the Bill & Melinda Gates Foundation from further bankrolling the expansion of small schools in favor
of focusing on broad policy reforms like common core standards and
teacher accountability.[19]

As my graduate students at Princeton reported after surveying the
research landscape, there is empirical support for social benefits con-
ferred by school size, but inconclusive evidence regarding academic
gains.[20] They noted that since the height of the small-schools movement in the mid-'90s, mixed evidence has led to a reconsideration of the
role of school size in secondary school reform.[21] As their report concluded, "Advocates of small schools agree that size is not a sufficient
criterion for success, but there is disagreement among proponents about
whether small size is necessary for, or simply conducive to, success. Op-
ponents argue that some features of small schools are detrimental, with
most of their objections focusing on issues of equity."[22]

When it comes to evidence, charter schools also present a mixed picture. A random assignment evaluation of KIPP Academies conducted
by Mathematica found that for the vast majority of their schools, the
impacts on KIPP students' math and reading scores on state assessments
were positive, statistically significant, and educationally substantial.[23]
KIPP's students are overwhelmingly black or Hispanic and most qualify
for free or reduced lunch. In fact, their student bodies have higher concentrations of poor and minority youngsters than the public schools
they previously attended. But their proportions of special education and
ESL (English as a second language) youngsters are lower.[24]

KIPP schools experience high rates of student attrition, especially
among African-American boys.[25] These patterns lead some observers
to attribute KIPP's success to admission—and expulsion—practices
that yield enrollments composed of youngsters who will benefit from
attending school with peers who are engaged, have supportive families,
and are willing and able to work hard in school.[26]

As with small public schools, the national picture of charter school
performance is best captured by the phrase "It all depends." A
meta-analysis of the literature published in October 2011 identified

positive academic effects compared with traditional public schools in some locales, subjects, and grade levels, but negative effects in others.[27] The authors found larger effects for charter schools in inner-city neighborhoods compared with those serving wider areas. To this point, they particularly cited KIPP Academies as well as charter schools in New York City and Boston.

In 2013, the Center for Research on Education Outcomes (CREDO) issued the most recent analysis of charter school performance nationally, namely in 25 states, the District of Columbia, and New York City.[28] This study built on CREDO's earlier assessment entitled "Multiple Choice; Charter School Performance in 16 States," which was released in 2009.[29] In their 2013 study, the researchers found that charter schools are educating more disadvantaged youngsters compared with 2009. Also, charter school quality remains uneven across states and schools.

When it comes to academic performance, "charter schools now advance the learning gains of their students more than traditional public schools in reading, and academic growth in math is now comparable to peers in traditional schools."[30] The CREDO researchers acknowledge that they cannot ascertain whether charter schools manage recruitment to enroll academically stronger students. That said, the biggest leap was registered among Hispanic students who are English language learners; they gained 50 days of learning in reading and 43 days in math. Black students living in poverty progressed, gaining 29 days in reading and 36 in math. Special education students also benefitted. Yet white students in charters regressed in both reading and math, while Asian students slipped in math.[31]

The jury remains out on school vouchers. After a review of the evidence, Lisa Barrow and Cecilia Rouse concluded that: "The best research to date finds relatively small achievement gains for students offered vouchers, most of which are not statistically different from zero. . . . Many questions remain unanswered, however, including whether vouchers have longer-run impacts on outcomes such as graduation rates, college enrollment, or even future wages. . . ."[32]

A study of the New York School Choice Scholarship Fund, which provides vouchers or tuition aid for youngsters to attend private schools, picked up on this point about longer-run impacts. Receiving a voucher generally did not increase the likelihood that most recipients would attend college. On the bright side, however, African-American beneficiaries of vouchers were 24 percent more likely to attend selective private universities than their peers who sought but did not receive vouchers.[33]

The early returns on the federal SIG initiative aimed at turning around the lowest-performing schools are murky, albeit with some encouraging signs.[34] Disputes have arisen about the adequacy of data collection. The U.S. Department of Education preliminarily reported that during the first year of the initiative, two-thirds of the schools registered gains in reading and math, while roughly a third slipped backwards academically.[35] Some schools that have yet to register achievement gains nonetheless report improvements in discipline and attendance. Students say their schools are calmer and more challenging academically.[36]

Even so, Education Secretary Arne Duncan cautions that it is far too early to draw any reliable conclusions about the impact of SIG. One among many open questions about these early returns is how the SIG schools that were not covered by the department's report are faring. More importantly, what enduring impact, if any, will SIG have on struggling students and schools once federal funding provided under the 2009 federal economic stimulus package expires?

Looking beyond the impact of specific reform initiatives, there is heartening news on the school dropout front. According to the Research Center of Editorial Projects in Education (publisher of *Education Week*), the nation's high school graduation rate climbed to 74.7 percent for the class of 2010, the most recent year for which statistics are available.[37] This represents a 2 percent improvement in a year and an 8-point gain in the past decade. It falls just shy of the previous high-water mark of 77.1 percent back in 1973. Among minority groups that traditionally bring up the rear, the graduation rate for Latino students soared 16 percentage points to 68 percent over the past decade. The rate for black students climbed 13 percentage points to 62 percent. The Latino-white gap shrank by half, while the black-white gap closed by almost 30 percent. Only Native Americans have slipped backwards.

According to Robert Balfanz, the nation's leading expert on this phenomenon, the number of "dropout factories," i.e., high schools with graduation rates below 50 percent, and the number of students attending them declined by 23 percent in the last decade. Better yet, the rate of decline is accelerating.[38]

Though modest, these gains thankfully extend to black males, who routinely suffer the lowest graduation rates among all racial, ethnic, and gender groups. As the Schott Foundation concluded in a report aptly titled *The Urgency of Now*, over the past nine years there has been progress in the national graduation rate for male students across the board. The rate for black males has increased by 10 percentage points, from 42 percent in 2001–02 to 52 percent in 2009–10.[39] Schott celebrated the fact that for the first time, more than half of the nation's black males in grade nine graduated with regular diplomas four years later. What's more, the Latino graduation rate has increased by 12 percentage points, from approximately 46 percent to 58 percent, and the white, non-Latino graduation rate has increased by seven percentage points, from 71 percent to 78 percent.[40]

Taking stock of a sweeping law like No Child Left Behind is daunting because it contains so many components, sets such aggressive targets, impacts so many facets of public education, ricochets in so many directions, and potentially generates so many intended and unintended consequences. Dan Goldhaber, director of the Center for Education Data and Research at the University of Washington/Bothell, contends that NCLB deserves credit for shedding light on how public schools are performing and for ratcheting up pressure on them to improve. I agree. The annual publication of students' test scores—school by school, grade by grade, group by group—enables, indeed empowers, parents to hold their schools to greater account and, when disappointed with the results, to seek out alternatives like small schools and charter schools. Transparency and the resulting pressure provided the impetus for the Obama administration to launch the SIG initiative aimed at turning around woefully low-performing schools.

The Downside of High-Stakes Tests

The national obsession with testing and accountability continues to roil public education and arguably is even counterproductive. So says a blue ribbon committee established by the National Research Council

(NRC) of the National Academy of Sciences.[41] The 17-member panel reviewed and synthesized research from economics, psychology, education, and related fields about how incentives work in educational accountability systems such as NCLB, as well as test-based teacher incentive pay systems and high school exit exams. The committee reached two sobering conclusions:

- "Test-based incentive programs . . . have not increased student achievement enough to bring the United States close to the levels of the highest achieving countries."[42]

- "The evidence we have reviewed suggests that high school exit exam programs, as currently implemented in the United States, decrease the rate of high school graduation without increasing achievement. The best available estimate suggests a decrease of two percentage points when averaged of the population."[43]

The NRC panel's scan of the literature raised other warning flags when it comes to students who are struggling in school. It noted, for instance, that when performance incentives for educators and schools are pegged to the number of "proficient" students, the result is extra attention to those who are just below the threshold of proficiency, and may even trigger competition for proficient students, who do not pose a threat of negative consequences.[44] Furthermore, the panel found evidence of attempts to increase scores in ways that are completely unrelated to improving learning, such as teaching test-taking skills, excluding low-performing students from tests, feeding students high-caloric meals on testing days, providing help to students during a test, and even changing student answers on tests after they were finished."[45]

Cheating scandals attributable to the pressure to produce better test results erupt periodically in school districts. Indeed, the former superintendent of the El Paso, Texas, schools was convicted and imprisoned for forcing some students out of school and otherwise manipulating test results to improve the district's ratings. In Atlanta, the high-profile superintendent and nearly three dozen former principals, teachers, and administrators stand indicted on charges of erasing and then upping pupils' test scores.

Daniel Koretz, a member of the NRC panel and professor at Harvard

Graduate School of Education, summed up the worrisome findings: "We have put a lot into these programs over a period of many years, and the positive effects when we can find them have been pretty disappointing."[46]

Thus, when it comes to low-income and minority students, the bottom line, after all these years, all the interventions, all the tough love, and all the investment, is intermittently encouraging but still underwhelming. Improving how these youngsters perform in school and equipping them for adulthood thereafter remains a work in progress. America's schools have made modest progress. But more arduous work and innovative thinking lie ahead.

2

Children Still Left Way Behind

IN 1996, THE NATIONAL COMMISSION on Teaching and America's Future issued a trenchant warning in its report titled *What Matters Most*:

> There has been no previous time in history when the success, indeed the survival, of nations and people has been tied so tightly to their ability to learn. Today's society has little room for those who cannot read, write, and compute proficiently; find and use resources; frame and solve problems; and continually learn new technologies, skills, and occupations. . . . [1]

In contrast to 20 years ago, the commission continued, individuals who falter in school have little chance of finding a job or contributing to society—and societies that do not succeed at education have little chance of success in a global economy.[2] A senior executive of the U.S. Chamber of Commerce put it even more bluntly: "If you want a real job, even a blue-collar job, you're probably going to need some postsecondary education, but at the very least you've got to get those skills in high school."[3]

These stark assessments predated the implosion of the U.S. economy in 2008. Compounding the difficulties facing poorly educated young people, the slack labor market these days places heightened pressure on them due to competition from better educated applicants who are desperate to land jobs they would have shunned in the past. Youngsters at risk of being left behind face—and present—an array of challenges that must be addressed if they are ever to succeed in school and in life.

Weak Academic Achievement

Demographic trends indicate that the U.S. economy will rely increasingly on Latinos and African Americans because they, and especially the former, will comprise a steadily growing proportion of the adult workforce. Yet despite glimmers of progress in student achievement, these economically indispensable groups, along with the overlapping population of low-income youngsters, consistently lag farthest behind academically.

NAEP test results officially sort students into three levels of academic competence:

• Advanced — "signifies superior performance"

• Proficient — "represents solid academic performance for each grade assessed"

• Basic — "denotes partial mastery of prerequisite knowledge and skills that are fundamental for proficient work at each grade"[4]

Actually, there is a fourth tier of achievement on NAEP that is a national embarrassment. I refer to "Below Basic," where an alarmingly high proportion of American youngsters have languished for years. As recently as 2013, 50 percent of African-American fourth graders and 47 percent of Latino fourth-graders scored Below Basic—roughly two notches under grade level—in reading, according to NAEP. That is certainly a welcome contrast to 2002, when 68 percent of black youngsters and 61 percent of Latino students, respectively, scored Below Basic at the same grade level.

Yet as Table 1 depicts, the trend in NAEP results since 1992 hardly provides a reason for school reformers to proclaim "Mission Accomplished."

Thus in spite of all the reform initiatives and investments over the years, roughly half of African-American, Latino, and Native American fourth graders continue to languish way below grade level. In fact, the imperative of boosting youngsters from Below Basic to Basic and beyond transcends ethnicity, even though the proportions of low-achieving youngsters are most pronounced among black, Latino, and Native American students. White students far outnumber those from other ethnic groups, and they constitute 37.6 percent of all young-

Table 1: Fourth-grade reading achievement level results by race/ethnicity (1992–2013)[5]

Year	Below Basic	Basic	Proficient	Advanced
WHITE				
1992	29%	36%	27%	8%
2002	25%	35%	31%	10%
2013	21%	34%	34%	12%
Year	**Below Basic**	**Basic**	**Proficient**	**Advanced**
BLACK				
1992	68%	24%	8%	1%
2002	60%	28%	11%	2%
2013	50%	33%	15%	2%
HISPANIC				
1992	61%	28%	10%	2%
2002	56%	29%	13%	2%
2013	47%	33%	17%	3%
ASIAN/PACIFIC ISLANDERS				
1992	40%	35%	20%	5%
2002	30%	33%	27%	10%
2013	20%	28%	34%	18%
AMERICAN INDIAN/ALASKA NATIVE				
1994	41%	28%	24%	6%
2002	49%	29%	17%	5%
2013	49%	29%	17%	4%

sters scoring in the lowest quintile, according to NAEP.[6]

Notwithstanding the modest gains in student achievement and the narrowed gaps between white and minority youngsters in some places, the pace of progress remains utterly unacceptable and obviously contrary to the national interest. What's even more disturbing, a study by the Center on Education Policy projects that it could take decades for minority and low-income students to catch up with their better-performing peers.[7] The center even offered the astonishing projection that in the state of Washington, for example, it will take 105 years to close the black-white gap in fourth-grade reading![8]

Youngsters who can barely read by the fourth grade face a steep climb uphill in school and in life. They will struggle with the reading assignments in social studies, the writing assignments in English class, and the word problems in algebra. They probably will not pass the exams imposed by states for moving from grade to grade and for graduating from high school. Community colleges and four-year colleges will be off limits to young people with lousy educations. The same goes for the good jobs that provide a solid living for those who are well prepared academically.

Once states embrace so-called common core academic standards, the task of progressing in school may get tougher, not easier. Interestingly enough, that's not the case thus far in Washington, D.C., where the school system quickly incorporated common core into its curriculum and administered annual exams in 2013 that were aligned with the national norms.[9] The students registered strong gains in English and math. In 2013, New York State instituted new tests aligned with the common core even though New York City and other districts had not yet synchronized their curricula and instruction with the new standards. Scores cratered statewide, and at one East Harlem middle school that serves mostly poor children, the proportion of students rated proficient in reading plunged from 31 percent to 6.8 percent and in math from 44 percent to 9.5 percent.[10]

The price of low achievement persists beyond high school. According to Charles Kolb, CEO of the Committee for Economic Development, only 20 percent of black students and 16 percent of Latinos graduate from high school adequately prepared for college.[11] The picture was even bleaker in Washington, D.C., where a 2006 study commissioned by city and school officials reported that only 9 percent of ninth graders in the public schools will complete college within five years after graduating from high school.[12] Furthermore, the report found that nine out of ten freshmen in the D.C. schools will be confined to low-paying jobs because they never began college or else failed to complete it.

Suspension From School

Compounding pervasive low achievement is the problem of rampant school suspensions. Of course, not all low achievers face suspension. However, the demographic profile of low achievers roughly mirrors that of youngsters who are disproportionately suspended. In a study entitled "Opportunities Suspended: The Disparate Impact of Disciplinary Exclusion from School," the Civil Rights Project/Proyecto Derechos Civiles at UCLA analyzed approximately three million suspensions reported to the U.S. Department of Education.[13] The UCLA study revealed yawning disparities in disciplinary actions and grade retention imposed on African-American students. For example, nearly one in six black students was suspended during the 2009–10 academic year, more than three times the rate of white youngsters.[14]

Suspension rates vary by state and by school district. The proportions in Texas border on astonishing. According to a recent report by the Council of State Governments Justice Center and the Public Policy Research Institute at Texas A&M University, more than half of all students in Texas were suspended or expelled at least once between the seventh and twelfth grades.[15] Three-quarters of black students were expelled or suspended compared with 50 percent of white students. Roughly 200 school districts suspended 20 percent of their students during the course of the school year. Black students are more likely to be suspended than any other ethnic group, followed by Latino and Native American youngsters. According to the UCLA study, Hartford, Connecticut, registered the highest suspension rate for Latino students at 44.2 percent. Fifty-six percent of black students in Fort Wayne, Indiana, were suspended at least once.

The high incidence of suspensions extends to students with disabilities (defined below). Nationally, 13 percent of disabled students from kindergarten through twelfth grade were suspended during 2009–10, as opposed to 7 percent of those who are not disabled.[16] The rate among black students with disabilities that year was worse—one out of four. Texas is even tougher on disabled students. In that state, 75 percent of these students were suspended or expelled compared with 55 percent of those who were not deemed disabled. The Chicago school system suspended nearly 63 percent of black students with disabilities. In

Memphis, a majority-black district, nearly 53 percent of all black males with disabilities were suspended that year.

The term "disability" typically evokes images of physical infirmities or mental retardation. Yet for purposes of education law and disciplinary policy, "disability" also encompasses learning difficulties. That phrase, of course, covers a potentially wide spectrum of student circumstances, from youngsters who are lagging behind academically to those who are faltering because their teachers do not know how to reach or teach them.

Parsing what is behind the suspension disparities turns up many explanations, some of which may be counterintuitive. While some people suggest that inappropriate classroom behavior by minority students explains why they bear the brunt of suspensions, Russell Skiba, a professor at the Center for Evaluation and Education Policy at Indiana University, contends that research does not substantiate this hypothesis.[17] Not surprisingly, many educators on the ground disagree. As Karen Lewis, president of Chicago Teachers Union, put it: "What most teachers complain about is that they have problem children and nobody helps them."[18] It may be tempting to attribute the disparities to the social and experiential distance between minority students and white teachers. But Russlyn H. Ali, assistant secretary for civil rights in the U.S. Department of Education, does not buy that argument either. "In lots of these urban districts," he says, "the leadership and faculty are also people of color. So it certainly doesn't fit into the color-coded boxes of the 'ism' that we've used historically."[19]

In a telling commentary on the disconnect between youngsters who pose challenges and educators who are ill-prepared to address them, a spokeswoman for the Fort Wayne school district observed: "We certainly realize that when kids come into our schools, they often don't come with the same background and home experiences that our teachers and our staff may have come from."[20] Indeed, this disconnect leads advocates like Maisie Chin, executive director of Community Asset Development Re-defining Education (CADRE), to charge that schools use zero-tolerance policies toward disciplinary problems to "push out" students whom they consider difficult to deal with.[21]

Whatever the reason for the disparities, there is no disputing that they spell big trouble for students. As the authors of "Opportunities

Suspended" noted, "suspensions matter because they are among the leading indicators of whether a child will drop out of school and because out-of-school suspension increases a child's risk for future incarceration."[22]

Like the proverbial canary in the coal mine that warns of danger lurking below, disproportionate suspension rates signal other serious academic troubles for students and schools. Districts with high suspension rates tend to suffer lower student achievement.[23] According to Daniel Losen, coauthor of "Opportunities Suspended," "Kids with disabilities make up a very large proportion of the kids who are in the juvenile justice system.. . ."[24]

Retention in Grade

Sadly but not surprisingly, the picture when it comes to grade retention basically resembles that for suspensions. Nationwide data compiled by the U.S. Department of Education's civil rights office reveals that black and Hispanic students are far more likely to repeat a grade, especially in elementary and middle school.[25] Overall, 4.2 percent of black youngsters were retained. This compares with 2.9 percent of Hispanics, 1.9 percent of Native Americans, and 1.5 percent of white students.

Viewed from a different angle, the racial disparities are even starker. An analysis by *Education Week* indicates that even though African-American youngsters constitute less than one-fifth of all students nationwide, 56 percent of fourth graders retained at the end of the 2009–10 school year were black.[26] Third grade was not much better; 49 percent of those held back were black. The rate hovers in the high 40s through much of elementary and middle schools. Across all grades, *Education Week* found, African-American pupils were 3½ times more likely than whites to be retained in grade. Hispanics fared a little better; they were twice as likely to be held back. As with suspension, retention in grade can be a harbinger of dropping out of school entirely.

Grade retention rates soar in secondary school. As Craig Jerold, an education consultant, commented: "We've always seen the highest retention rates among ninth graders. A lot of students enter high school completely unprepared, so ninth grade is a very difficult transition year. . . . When students arrive in high school, they're expected to take a lot more personal responsibility for their learning than in middle school."[27]

Interestingly enough, the retention gap along racial lines tends to shrink in secondary school.[28] By the ninth grade, 35 percent of students retained in grade were black, 31 percent were Hispanic, and 31 percent were white. Three years later, white students hold the dubious distinction of registering the highest retention rate at 40 percent. This contrasts with 25 percent for blacks and 31 percent for Hispanics. Some experts attribute the shift to the fact that more black and Hispanic students drop out in high school, leaving fewer low achievers who are vulnerable to being held back.

Less publicized than suspension and retention but closely related is the phenomenon of student disengagement. According to Robert Balfanz and Nettie Legters of Johns Hopkins University, many students in low-performing high schools start out poorly prepared for academic success and rarely (or barely) make it out of the ninth grade. They typically disengage from school, attend infrequently, flunk too many courses to be promoted to the tenth grade, try again with no better results, and ultimately drop out. In school systems that Balfanz and Legters studied, 20 to 40 percent of students repeat the ninth grade, but only 10 to 15 percent of repeaters go on to graduate.[29]

Dropping Out

Distressingly large numbers of Latino and African-American youngsters give up and drop out of high school. Unfortunately for them, many of these youngsters attend lousy high schools, labeled "dropout factories," where fewer than half of the students reach senior year on time and where graduation is not the norm.[30] Balfanz and Legters note that many cities have large numbers of high schools with weak promoting power. In half of the nearly 100 largest cities, at least half, and often more, youngsters enrolled in regular or vocational high schools with more than 300 students attend schools with weak promoting power.[31] In some cities, the Hopkins researchers found, students have virtually no other choice but to attend a school with weak promoting power.[32]

The dropout phenomenon is concentrated ethnically, socioeconomically, and geographically. Balfanz and Legters report that as of the mid-2000s, nearly half of the nation's African-American and Latino students attended high schools with high poverty rates and low graduation rates. High schools where minority students constitute the majority are five times more likely to have weak promoting power than majority-white schools.[33] As might be expected, low-income students tend to end up in lousy schools. High schools where minorities constitute the majority yet the schools have more resources, such as academically selective programs, higher per-pupil expenditures, and suburban locations, successfully promote students at the same rate as majority-white schools.[34]

Despite the welcome progress among youngsters who are dropout prone, the ever-vigilant Schott Foundation views the glass as only slightly more than half full. It found that nationally, 52 percent of black males and 58 percent of Latino males graduate from high school within four years, while 78 percent of white, non-Latino males graduate in four years.[35] According to the foundation, the progress over the past nine years toward closure of the black vs. white, non-Latino male graduation gap has achieved only a three percentage point gain, from a 29 percentage point gap to 26 percentage points.[36] Based on its analysis, Schott ventured the alarming projection that "at the current pace of progress for both, it would take nearly 50 years for black males to secure the same high school graduation rates as the white male peers."[37]

Balfanz frets about the pace of progress as well and offers an equally disturbing projection. If the rate of progress during the first decade of this century persists during the second, he estimates there will still be more than 1,000 high schools in the U.S. in which the odds of graduating are about 50-50.[38]

Disconnection

For far too many young people who drop out of school, the next stage of their lives is disconnection from society. "Disconnected" refers to those in their late teens and early 20s who are neither in school nor working. The problem is particularly acute among young black and

Latino adults, up to 40 percent of whom qualify as disconnected, according to some estimates.[39] The disconnected give up hope, partly because in a depressed labor market, they face stiff competition even for low-skill positions from better-educated job seekers and thus are pushed farther back in the applicant queue. In the view of Phillip Jackson, executive director of Chicago's Black Star Project, this leads to violence, broken families, and "hyperincarceration."[40]

The profile of the disconnected should come as no surprise. Nearly 40 percent live in poor households, and 35 percent are women with children. One-third dropped out of high school. Racially, 22.5 percent are black, 18.5 percent Latino, nearly 12 percent white, and 8 percent Asian-American. Disconnection ensnares millions of young adults. By some estimates, nearly six million teenagers and young adults between the ages of 16 and 24 neither work nor attend school. That accounts for roughly one-seventh of this age cohort.[41] During the Great Recession, the ranks of the disconnected swelled by 800,000 people between 2007 and 2010.

Rampant disconnection among young adults costs them—and society—dearly. According to Sarah Burd-Sharps and Kristen Lewis, "Rather than laying the foundation for a productive life of choice and value, these disconnected youth find themselves adrift at society's margins, unmoored from the systems and structures that confer knowledge, skills, identity, and purpose."[42] Taxpayers ultimately foot a hefty bill for disconnection. As Sharps and Lewis note, "[D]irect support costs and lost tax revenues associated with adrift young people set U.S. taxpayers back by more than $93 billion in 2011 alone. And this bill compounds as time goes on."[43]

Poor Children Left Farthest Behind

Typically we view educational disparities, from achievement levels to dropout rates, through an ethnic prism. That certainly has been my propensity. Yet recently, some scholars have placed greater emphasis on the economic profile of low achievers. As Sean Reardon of Stanford University School of Education observes, the achievement gap between poor and rich children has widened significantly in the last three decades and is now nearly twice as large as the black-white achievement gap.[44] For instance, Reardon found that the gap in average math scores between high- and low-income students grew by one-third between 1978 and 2008.[45] As Leslie Maxwell writes in *Education Week*, some scholars argue that until policymakers and educators confront America's deepening economic and social disparities, upward social mobility will increasingly elude poor children.[46]

There are dueling visions in education advocacy circles about whether and to what extent schools can lift children out of poverty. Educators, experts, and advocates who call for a "Broader, Bolder Approach to Education" contend that schools alone cannot erase the effects of poverty and instead should be considered one component of a larger strategy to address health, housing, parenting, and out-of-school time, among other issues, to improve the well-being of children.[47] Another group, known as the Education Equality Project, advocates a less holistic approach and calls for dramatically changing the teaching profession by instituting performance pay, ending tenure, and creating more rigorous evaluations that hold teachers accountable for their students' performance.[48]

The sharp ideological schisms and dysfunctional politics in this country leave me deeply skeptical that policymakers at the federal, state, or local level have the appetite, inclination, or fiscal capacity for confronting the severe economic and social disparities that keep families mired in poverty. Income supports and other measures that help low-income families risk being scaled back as part of a comprehensive effort to address the federal government's long-term deficit challenges. I foresee no expansion in federally financed job creation or income support programs explicitly aimed at lifting low-income families out of poverty. What's more, for the foreseeable future, policymakers seem likely to focus on shoring up the middle class and working families, namely, the most favored constituency of politicians. The needs of poor people scarcely appeared on the radar screens of the major party candidates during the 2012 election season.

While the quest for an intensified government effort to lift families and children out of poverty must continue, it is folly to pine for the second coming of a federal War on Poverty. In the view of Andres Alonso, the pragmatic former CEO of the Baltimore city schools, "It's been so unproductive to somehow pit competing theories of what accounts for failures of schools. To say that poverty doesn't matter is something that teachers and people in schools feel trivializes their reality. You potentially sacrifice credibility to not say that poverty matters at the same time that you must assert that [poverty] should not determine what schools do in response."[49]

The enduring challenge, then, is to create schools that equip children to climb the ladder of opportunity out of poverty. While this certainly is a daunting challenge, research, pilot programs, and the everyday experiences of dedicated educators affirm that the cause is not hopeless. A smattering of high-performing/high-poverty public schools indeed exist, as do plenty of effective small public schools and charter schools serving disadvantaged youngsters.

Even so, there is little hope of dramatically improving those dropout factories and other woefully low-performing schools so long as we cling resolutely to the idea that, as currently conceived and structured, these schools can reach the large cohorts of youngsters who, while technically enrolled, have disengaged and dialed out, as a prelude to dropping out. I refer to youngsters who, as things now stand, are chronically way behind in school with little hope of catching up, let alone acquiring the requisite knowledge, skills, and habits needed to become self-reliant and law-abiding citizens, parents, and providers. The presence of these youngsters in schools that are struggling to improve stymies the recovery of these troubled schools and impedes the academic growth of children who regularly come to school in a frame of mind to learn.

Requiring deeply disengaged youngsters to attend schools that are palpably ill-designed and out of synch vis-à-vis their needs does them no favor. Conventional public schools focused exclusively or predominantly on strictly scholastic objectives clearly are not attuned to their needs and do not work for them, much less serve their best interests. As Balfanz and Legters argue, until dropout factories are replaced or reformed, the promise of the American high school as an engine of economic growth and social transformation will not be met.[50] The balance of this book is devoted to imagining and advancing a new paradigm for children who continue to be left far behind.

3

Why Youngsters Dial Out of School

THEORIES AND EXPLANATIONS ABOUND about why students, especially low-income and minority youngsters, disengage from school and eventually drop out. Disengagement and disconnection are not new phenomena among adolescents. Nearly a half century ago, sociologists wrote about anomie among teenagers. The persistence of juvenile delinquency in cities provided much of the impetus for the federal War on Poverty in the 1960s. In the '70s, economists agonized about the dual labor market that seemed to lock young black males into alarmingly high rates of structural unemployment.

So we have seen this movie before. But the picture today seems bleaker and the problems more intractable. In the search for explanations, the customary practice is to cite recognized scholars. Yet I want to turn first to some youthful amateur ethnographers who are closest to the phenomenon. The perspectives of young people can be illuminating and compelling. In their own way, these youngsters are experts on why they and their peers disengage and drop out of school.

Phi Delta Kappan magazine teamed up with *Education Week* to publish the results of a survey that asked young black males what obstacles and attitudes stand in the way of their academic success.[1] Consider the sophistication, explanatory power—and programmatic implications—of their responses. One youngster, now in college, commented that black boys lack enough positive role models, often having only "the drug rats on the street." Children, he said, need someone to ensure that they do their homework and do the right thing at school. Another teenager observed that boys drop out of school because they are "following what they see," and they do not see black males who are traditionally successful.

A 21-year-old commented that children are "products of their environment." Life outside of schools is your main life, he said, and you adapt to that. "All you see is all you know." Yet another youngster noted that the biggest factor in determining what will make black males successful academically is "who they hang out with." If the people they hang out with are bad and do wrong things, he said, they will try to be like their friends, and they will start being off task in school.

Several interviewees took rap-music culture to task. According to one youngster, rap culture teaches young black males to live a life on the street and not worry about education. Another noted that young black men are influenced negatively by rap music and its messages about the desirability of material things. "White kids listen to rap for entertainment," he commented. "Black kids are living it. That leads to many bad choices that interfere with educational success. . . ."

Some of those surveyed zeroed in on the role of parents. One astute youngster mentioned that school success starts at home. "We don't even need better parenting, we just need adequate parenting. Many black kids don't have a sense of belonging, and 'the streets accept anyone.'"[2] According to a 15-year-old, "Parents are the biggest factor in black males' success because it means they will be in a good environment and off the streets. If a parent had a bad childhood, then it's passed down generations. Their parent might not be there for them, and they'll have no one to express their feelings to, and they'll get in fights." An even younger interviewee added that a good family life and home environment are important for success in school. Yet their parents are not doing right. "They see their parents and friends cursing and smoking. They do the same thing. They want to be just like their friends." Some respondents cited the need to drop out and earn money to help their parents. Another said he did so because he desired material things here and now.

Finally, one interviewee pointed to deep-seated skepticism and self-doubt as factors. Said another, boys drop out because "they think they can't make it. They think they won't amount to anything because they think whites are going to be higher than blacks." In his neighborhood, most of "the guys around here, they went to jail," or "they drop out of school, for drugs and everything. They don't really care. We think because we are from the 'hood' we don't have a chance to do something with ourselves. They don't got nobody to support them at home. They need a role model."

Other surveys of young people point to additional reasons for disengaging and dropping out. A report prepared for the Bill & Melinda Gates Foundation gathered the perspectives of a racially diverse group of 16- to 24-year-olds who did not complete high school.[3] Roughly seven in ten of those surveyed said they were not motivated or inspired to work hard in school. Nearly half of them mentioned uninteresting classes as the major reason they dropped out. Forty-five percent said they were poorly prepared at the outset of high school, and roughly a third cited the fact they were failing in school as a major factor in dropping out. Close to 30 percent of the respondents doubted they could have met the high school graduation requirements even if they had expended the effort.

The dropouts interviewed for the Gates Foundation cited several other reasons for leaving school. Some indicated that they spent time with people who were not interested in school. Nearly 40 percent believed they had too much freedom and not enough rules in school. The interviewees' comments about the availability of caring adults in their schools were instructive. Roughly two-thirds of the youngsters said there was a staff member or teacher who cared about their success. Yet only 56 percent felt they could go to someone on staff for help with a school-related problem. Fewer still—merely 41 percent—said there was someone in school whom they could talk to about personal problems.

A 1986 study of dropouts' attitudes cited self-doubt as another reason for leaving school.[4] When asked if they were satisfied with themselves or if they had much to be proud of, dropouts were significantly more likely than those who stayed in school to display lower self-concept. Dropouts were more alienated from school and more inclined to believe that their destiny is out of their hands. As early as their sophomore year, future dropouts expected to get less education than those who ended up completing high school. In addition, males were more than twice as likely as females to say they left because of behavioral problems, such as not getting along with teachers or being expelled or suspended.

The authors of the 1986 study concluded that there is no single underlying cause of dropping out. The decision may be driven by academic, behavioral, economic, and/or personal factors. Clearly, behavioral problems and poor grades are major determinants of dropping out. According to the authors, "Students exhibiting behavior problems, such as cutting classes and having disciplinary problems, during their sophomore year tended to be males with low verbal ability . . . and with a sense that they had little control over their lives. . . ."[5] The authors added that the dropouts' mothers had low educational aspirations for these students and the parents were not involved in helping the student select a high school curriculum."[6]

Balfanz argues that dropouts basically fall into four categories.[7] Some leave school because of what he calls life events, such as pregnancy or an arrest, that fundamentally alter their lives. Other youngsters fade out of school because, despite being promoted on time, they become frustrated or bored and see little point in coming to school. The third type is what Balfanz calls push-outs. These youngsters are viewed as difficult, even dangerous, or a detriment to the success of the school. Officials subtly or overtly encourage them to withdraw or transfer. School officials may even remove them from the rolls if they flunk too many courses, miss too many days, or remain past the legal dropout age.

Finally, there are youngsters who fail academically or else attend schools that do not provide the climate and supports they need to succeed. Balfanz notes that for some of these youngsters, failure results from poor academic preparation. But for others, he argues, their failure in school is rooted in social and emotional needs that go unaddressed.[8] According to him, most students who drop out do so for a combination of academic and social-emotional reasons. "[E]ven the best instruction in the world will have limited impact if students do not attend school on a regular basis, try to succeed, and behave."[9]

Balfanz's research and experience working in dropout factories have exposed him to the depth and pervasiveness of youngsters' social and emotional needs. He suggests that four out of five students need substantial and sustained supports to succeed at all, let alone in a high-standards, high-stakes testing environment. Middle schools serving large concentrations of poor children encounter similar needs. As

Balfanz writes, "Here you can have 25 sixth graders with attendance problems, a different 25 with behavior problems, and an additional 50 students failing either math or English, with each group needing different levels of different interventions."[10] He adds that middle school students in poor neighborhoods face greater dangers and temptations than when they are younger and are often recruited into roles that interfere with school attendance and involvement.[11]

The social and emotional needs of these children, Balfanz argues, require more than short doses of support. The academic and behavioral problems that surface early in middle school do not self-correct, he notes, at least in urban schools serving high-poverty populations.[12] Balfanz's long experience in dropout factories leads him to issue a grim warning that educators and policymakers should heed:

> A common response to students who struggle in sixth grade is to wait and hope they grow out of it or adapt, to attribute early struggles to the natural commotion of early adolescence and to temporary difficulties in adapting to new organizational structures of schools, more challenging curricula and assessment, and less personalized attention. Our evidence clearly indicates that, at least in high-poverty urban schools, sixth graders who are missing 20 percent or more of the days, exhibiting poor behavior, or failing math or English do not recover. On the contrary, they drop out.[13]

According to Balfanz, the stark reality, seldom reflected in education policy or reform proposals, is that in some schools more than 80 percent of students are either repeating grades for a second or third time, assigned to special education, performing two years or more below grade level, or missing a month or more of school.[14] Only one out of five students in these schools, he estimates, would be considered the typical students that traditional high schools were designed to educate, who attend school faithfully, who are not in special education classes, and who perform on grade level or better in reading and math.[15] Another pernicious characteristic of schools serving these kids, he finds, is a climate that appears on the surface to be orderly, but in reality is languid and undemanding. A school climate infected with low expectations can be ruinous.[16] Nor, he adds, does it fool even struggling students who know they are not being challenged.

Traditional public schools that serve high proportions of low-income minority students are often ill-designed and under-resourced to address the academic, social, and emotional needs of the bulk of their student body. In Balfanz's view, schools need to devise and implement comprehensive plans to get and keep students on track for graduation. He calls for school-wide initiatives that serve the needs of most students, augmented by more targeted interventions for the 15 to 20 percent of youngsters who require increased attention. He further estimates that 5 to 10 percent of youngsters will need intensive, sustained one-on-one attention and problem solving, supplemented by appropriate social service or community supports.[17]

On this very point, Balfanz's research and experience in dropout factories suggest that an effective strategy for reaching an unresponsive student typically requires assigning a specific adult, usually one of the student's main teachers.[18] This means shepherding that youngster through school by building a closer, more personal relationship with the student, understanding the sources of disengagement from school, checking in daily with the student, and providing immediate feedback. If the student is chronically absent, shepherding might even necessitate calling each day that he or she is unaccounted for.[19]

The feedback that dropouts provided to the Gates Foundation survey pinpointed additional strategies that might improve the odds of future dropouts staying in school. For starters, they called for improvements in teaching and curricula that would make school more relevant, provide real-world learning opportunities, and enhance the connection between school and work.[20] They urged more support for struggling students, more classroom discipline, and increased measures to make students feel safe from violence. The dropouts said they craved more one-on-one attention from teachers and stronger adult-student relationships in school. They also advocated better communication between parents and school, heightened efforts by parents to make certain their children go to school, and increased supervision in school to ensure that students attend class.

By distilling the theories and explanations from youngsters and scholars alike for why students disengage and drop out of school, we can discern the rough contours of a new kind of educational entity devoted to the academic and social development of youngsters who are struggling mightily in school and in life. The novel yet demonstrably indispensable ingredient would be the addition of social-emotional development as a core operating ingredient that stands on equal footing with academic development.

4

Social-Emotional Skills Matter

FOR DECADES, social service agencies, educators, foundations, policy-makers, and researchers have conducted a determined search for program interventions that effectively address the phenomena that imperil the life prospects of at-risk youth. According to Gordon Berlin, president of MDRC, many interventions for at-risk youth that concentrate largely on education and training have been rigorously evaluated over the years. Lamentably, the results have often been discouraging. This disappointment, he observes, has prompted many scholars, experts, and advocates to argue that, instead of focusing on youngsters' deficits, programs should foster healthy development.[1] Balfanz's heightened emphasis on addressing the social and emotional needs of youngsters who are faltering badly in school reflects this growing trend.

James Comer, the pioneering child psychiatrist who created the School Development Program (SDP), is the leading exponent of addressing children's social and emotional needs. He began pressing this agenda back in the 1960s. Dr. Comer acknowledges that the movement for standards-based education has powerfully influenced education policy and practice. However, he contends that it has done little to address the primary mission of schools, which he sees as the preparation of the young for success in childhood, adolescence, and adult life.[2] "To function adequately across the life span," he argues, "children and youths need formative experiences that aid their growth and development along the physical, social-interactive, social-emotional, moral-ethical, linguistic, and cognitive pathways. Academic learning is not an isolated capacity, but an aspect of development. The two are inextricably linked and mutually facilitative."[3]

Life success in this complex age requires a high level of development. According to Dr. Comer, students who come from families and primary social networks that do not provide them with adequate developmental experiences suffer the most. What's more, he contends, "student, staff, and often parental responses to failure—from acting out to increased control-and-punishment efforts to withdrawal and apathy—produce difficult relationship environments and underachieving schools. In time, this leads to dropping out of school."[4]

Since the phrases "social and emotional skills," "learning," "competence," and "development" will recur throughout this book, let me pause to explain what they mean before proceeding. In a book titled *Promoting Social and Emotional Learning: Guidelines for Educators,* the authors provide a succinct and understandable definition:

> Social and emotional competence is the ability to understand, manage, and express the social and emotional aspects of one's life in ways that enable the successful management of life tasks such as learning, forming relationships, solving everyday problems, and adapting to the complex demands of growth and development. It includes self-awareness, control of impulsivity, working cooperatively, and caring about oneself and others. Social and emotional learning is the process through which children and adults develop the skills, attitudes, and values necessary to acquire social and emotional competence.[5]

Dr. Comer elaborates: "Through the developmental process," he explains, "children must gain the capacities to regulate and control their aggressive energies and emotions, express themselves in constructive ways, manage life tasks, negotiate and solve problems, get along well with others, and more. Students who are developing well overall are more likely to perform well academically. Most students who are underperforming in school are in fact underdeveloped."[6]

At the risk of overkill and to cover every facet of the concept, consider one more formulation, this one by the Collaborative for Academic, Social and Emotional Learning (CASEL). In CASEL's view, "social and emotional learning involves the processes of developing competencies that help students stay focused on learning, engage in pro-social behavior, and relieve stress and anxiety. These skills include self-awareness, self-management, social awareness, relationship skills, and responsible decision-making."[7] Social and emotional learning, CASEL continues, helps children and even adults develop the fundamental relationships and skills that include "recognizing and managing our emotions, developing caring and concern for others, establishing positive relationships, making responsible decisions, and handling challenging situations constructively and ethically. They are the skills that allow children to calm themselves when angry, make friends, resolve conflicts respectfully, and make ethical and safe choices."[8]

SEL and Achievement

Why is it critically important for young people to be socially and emotionally competent? To begin with, it bears directly on children's ability to learn and achieve in school. As the authors of *Promoting Social and Emotional Learning* poignantly ask, "Is it possible to attain true academic and personal success without addressing SEL (social and emotional learning) skills? The accumulating evidence suggests the answer is no. Studies of effective middle schools have shown that the common denominator among different types of schools reporting academic success is that they have a systematic process for promoting children's SEL."[9]

The authors of *Promoting Social and Emotional Learning* invoke emerging scientific evidence to reinforce their point. "The importance of SEL for successful academic learning is further strengthened by new insights from the field of neuropsychology. Many elements of learning are relational (or, based on relationships), and social and emotional skills are essential for the successful development of thinking and learning activities that are traditionally considered cognitive."[10]

Continuing in this vein, the authors observe, "Processes we had considered pure 'thinking' are now seen as phenomena in which the cognitive and emotional aspects work synergistically. Brain studies show, for example, that memory is coded to specific events and linked to social and emotional situations, and that the latter are integral parts of larger units of memory that make up what we learn and retain, including what takes place in the classroom. Under conditions of real or imagined threat or high anxiety, there is a loss of focus on the learning process and a reduction in task focus and flexible problem solving."[11]

Robert Sylwester, emeritus professor of education at the University of Oregon, further illuminates the connection between academic performance and social and emotional competence. He contends that "we know emotion is very important to the educative process because it drives attention, which drives learning and memory. We've never really understood emotion, however, so we don't know how to regulate it in school—beyond defining too much or too little of it as misbehavior and relegating most of it to the arts, PE, recess, and the extracurricular program. . . ."[12] By separating emotion from logic and reason in the classroom, Sylwester comments, "we've simplified school management and evaluation, but we've also then separated two sides of one coin—and lost something important in the process. It's impossible to separate emotion from the other important activities of life. Don't try."[13]

The authors of *Promoting Social and Emotional Learning* build on Sylwester's point by noting that social and emotional issues lie at the heart of the problem behaviors that plague many schools, communities, and families, sapping learning time, educators' energy, and children's hope and opportunities.[14] They argue that effectively promoting social and emotional competence is the key to helping young people become more resistant to the lure of drugs, teen pregnancy, violent games, truancy, and dropping out of school.[15]

A report about California's schoolchildren entitled *Healthy Steps Toward Student Achievement* reinforces the connection. According to the report, research shows that physical, cultural, and emotional health, and the school environment in which teaching and learning are expected to occur, dramatically impact a student's ability to succeed. This is true for all students, and more acutely so for low-income students. As the report suggests, "When a student misses school days or is distracted due to physical or emotional health-related issues such as asthma, hunger, insufficient exercise, bullying, violence, discrimination, or boredom and disconnection from school, that student's likelihood of academic success drops dramatically."[16]

Another California report underscores the link between students' emotional state and their readiness to learn. As that report found, nearly a third of middle and high school students in California have felt so sad or hopeless for two weeks or more in the previous 12 months that it interfered with their regular activities. The authors noted that students who experience high levels of stress or depression tend to do poorly in school. More specifically, as the percentage of California secondary school students who said they felt sad or hopeless increased, gains in reading, language, and mathematics test scores declined.[17]

Recognizing that cognitive and noncognitive skills combine to contribute to student success, the influential National Research Council weighed in on the connection between SEL and life success. It appointed a committee of experts in education, psychology, and economics to formulate a definition of twenty-first-century skills and explain their relationship to achieving positive outcomes in education, work, and other areas of life.[18]

According to Paul R. Sackett, a psychology professor at the University of Minnesota who served on the NRC committee, "research . . . points to five key noncognitive indicators that a student will need to be able to complete college and become successfully employed. . . ."[19] He contends that "the biggest predictor of success is a student's conscientiousness, as measured by such traits as dependability, perseverance through tasks, and work ethic. Agreeableness, including teamwork, and emotional stability were the next-best predictors of college achievement, followed by variations on extroversion and openness to new experiences."

Based on its review of the research, the NRC committee concluded that there are three key domains of competence:

- The cognitive domain, which includes thinking, reasoning, and related skills;

- The intrapersonal domain, which involves self-management, including the ability to regulate one's behavior and emotions to reach goals; and

- The interpersonal domain, which involves expressing information to others, as well as interpreting others' messages and responding appropriately.[20]

The NRC committee added that among intrapersonal and interpersonal competencies, conscientiousness—being organized, responsible, and hardworking—shows the strongest correlation with desirable work and educational outcomes. Antisocial behavior, which has both intrapersonal and interpersonal aspects, is negatively correlated with these outcomes.[21]

SEL and Job Readiness

As the NRC panel concluded, social and emotional competence matters enormously not just in formal education, but also in the world of work that awaits young people after school. Following high school, young people will gravitate to community colleges and four-year colleges, career and technical education, and the labor market. Yet as the authors of a high-profile Harvard study, *Pathways to Prosperity*, observed, many youngsters lack the skills and work ethic needed for many jobs paying middle-class wages.[22] In addition to academic competence, they cite self-management, listening skills, and integrity as characteristics valued in the workplace. These crucial attributes are commonly associated with social and emotional development.

The authors of *Promoting Social and Emotional Learning* addressed the implications for employability by noting that businesses of all sizes realize that productivity depends on a workforce that is socially and emotionally competent. "Workers who are capable of managing their social and emotional interactions with colleagues and customers, as well as their own emotional health, are more effective in improving the bottom line and at making workplaces more efficient. . . ."[23] The authors noted that more focus is being placed on problem solving, reflection, perceptive thinking, self-direction, and motivation for life-long learning."[24]

Promoting Social and Emotional Learning includes a chart, labeled "What Employers Want for Teens: 1980s U.S. Department of Labor, Employment, and Training Administration Research Project," that is as germane today as it was when initially published a generation ago. The chart identified the following desired skills that mirror what we call social and emotional competencies:

- Learning-to-learn skills

- Listening and oral communication

- Adaptability: creative thinking and problem solving, especially in response to barriers/obstacles

- Personal management: self-esteem, goal setting/self-motivation, personal career development/goals, and pride in work accomplished

- Group effectiveness: interpersonal skills, negotiation, and teamwork

- Organizational effectiveness and leadership: making a contribution

- Competence in reading, writing, and computation[25]

Writing in the *Economics of Education Review,* Henry Levin and Carolyn Kelly pressed the connection between workplace success and social and emotional competence even more explicitly.[26] They argued that the effectiveness of education depends on the existence of what they called complementary inputs. In the absence of these inputs, education is not likely to live up to its promise for young people. Unfortunately, the economists noted, the complementary inputs that determine the effectiveness of education are being largely ignored by both policymakers and economists who focus solely on education.[27]

Levin and Kelly contend that there are other characteristics of workers besides sheer academic skills that are important in predicting productivity, provided that workers meet minimal threshold levels of proficiency. By way of example, they cited the hiring practices of Toyota in gauging the expected productivity of job applicants. Of the 26 hours allocated for testing and interviewing applicants, the company devoted fewer than three hours to cognitive testing, just to be sure of their basic skills. By sharp contrast, Toyota spent the vast bulk of the time assessing applicants' "soft," or social and emotional skills, such as work habits and commitment, interpersonal skills, and ability to engage productively in teams.[28] Thus, while special efforts must be made to ensure that at-risk students meet a minimum threshold of academic competence, real-world experiences with employers affirm that noncognitive skills matter when it comes to worker productivity.

Daniel Goleman reinforces this point in his influential book *Emotional Intelligence: Why It Can Matter More Than IQ*. As he points out, "Today companies worldwide routinely look through the lens of EI (emotional intelligence) in hiring, promoting, and developing their employees. For instance, Johnson & Johnson . . . found that in divisions around the world, those identified at midcareer as having high leadership potential were far stronger in EI competencies than were their less-promising peers."[29]

SEL and Socioeconomic Status

Given the academic deficits and difficulties discussed earlier, it regrettably comes as no surprise that low-income and minority children are more likely than their economically advantaged white counterparts to exhibit the academic indifference and behavioral difficulties associated with social and emotional deficits. The National Center for Children in Poverty describes the many ways in which low-income children are more prone to demonstrate behavioral problems that will adversely impact their future development.[30] For example, young children in low-income neighborhoods are more likely to experience behavioral problems than youngsters in moderate-income and affluent communities.

As would be expected, the same is true for children from low-income families. Children between the ages of two and five who are on child welfare assistance, including foster care, have greater emotional-behavioral problems than their peers in the general population. In a preview of coming problems, the center reports that African-American children are three to five times more likely to be expelled from preschool programs.

In 2005, the U.S. Department of Health and Human Services estimated that 14 percent of parents living below the poverty line reported social and emotional difficulties in their children.[31] There is little reason to believe this distressing pattern has improved since then. My former Princeton student Caroline Hanamirian wrote a research paper about social and emotional development. Her review of the literature indicated that the higher the family income, the lower the incidence of moderate to severe social and emotional difficulties among children.[32]

Low-income and minority youngsters in particular face what Robert Pianta and Daniel Walsh call "life hazards" that are known to threaten and undermine healthy development.[33] Life hazards, they explain, are largely out of children's control. These stressors, as they also call them, adversely impact the relationship between children, their families, and schools. The familiar life hazards cited by the authors include poverty, divorce, maltreatment, danger, and neglect.

Exposure to these hazards undermines children's ability and inclination to perform in school. As Pianta and Walsh explain, ". . . it was the number of hazards to which children are exposed, not the type of hazard, that accounted for largest proportion of variance in IQ at age four. Moreover, as the number of hazards increased, there was a concomitant decrease in IQ at each age between four and thirteen."[34] Children raised in poverty and exposed to violence, they observe, live under extreme duress. They often exhibit symptoms of post-traumatic stress disorder, including flashbacks, inability to focus attention due to mental distractions, lack of motivation, apathy and depression, and unpredictable behaviors. "The psychological and emotional distress associated with living under dangerous, stressful, unpredictable conditions," Pianta and Walsh conclude, "are some of the primary reasons why these children have difficulty attending and learning in classroom settings."[35]

The authors cite the organization and structure in children's households as often overlooked hazards that impact their development. They found that neglected youngsters suffered in school as a result. These children were exposed to chronic lack of material resources, and their caregiving environments were unhealthy, unsafe, and lacking in supervision or stimulation.[36] They were rejected and unpopular, showing a mixture of aggression and withdrawal. They lacked the social skills necessary to engage peers competently.

Pianta and Walsh found a direct link between maladjustment and educational troubles. "Toward teachers they responded with a similar lack of skill, displaying a marked maladaptation to academic and pre-academic tasks. They lacked persistence, attentiveness, or motivation, often wandering aimlessly around the room. A striking proportion—80 percent—of these children were referred to special education by the end of first grade."[37]

The Role of Schools

Where does responsibility for cultivating children's social and emotional skills lie? Traditionalists see this as strictly a family responsibility. The authors of *Promoting Social and Emotional Learning* explain the reasoning behind this nostalgic view. The thinking is that "the family should be the place where the child learns to understand, control, and work through emotions; social and emotional issues are essentially private concerns that should be left at the door when a child enters a school to go about the business of acquiring academic knowledge."[38]

Yet as Pianta and Walsh point out, the reality is that, whether due to poverty or parental weaknesses, families may be partly the source of their children's social and emotional needs and shortcomings. As the authors of *Promoting Social and Emotional Learning* note, "Many families can make ends meet only when both parents work outside the home—and sometimes at more than one job. Extended families, which once provided a child-care safety net, have all but disappeared. And close-knit communities, once sources of caring adults who guided children and served as role models, are today neighborhoods of strangers."[39]

According to Jennifer Dubin, Dr. Comer believes schools are central to the healthy development of youngsters, which happens when they form positive relationships with adults. When adults, from educators to parents, create school climates where they relate well to one another, they become emotionally available to bond with students. These relationships, she comments, combine with a strong academic curriculum to motivate children to learn.

As Dubin notes, children from low-income families do not receive the needed nurturing because their parents may hold multiple jobs or lack the knowledge to engage their youngsters. In her view, this is why Dr. Comer regards schools as the only institutions strategically located to work with parents and communities to foster the healthy relationships poor children desperately need.[40]

Dr. Comer decries the standards and accountability movement for shortchanging children's social and emotional development. While conceding that it has had a powerful impact on policy and practice, he despairs over the downside. He frets that ". . . the attention of the entire education enterprise—preparatory institutions, practitioners, students, parents, and policymakers—has been riveted on academic-achievement outcomes, not on developmental issues." Dr. Comer is dismayed that "despite a large body of research showing the connection between development, learning, and desirable behavior, supporting development continues to receive inadequate attention, in the preparation of educators as well as in education practice."[41] According to him, too many teachers emerge from teacher preparation programs and enter the profession without even knowing they can support healthy development. "We do not prepare them to 'read' child behavior, but we expect them to respond to it in ways that can be helpful. We do not do that to other professionals."[42]

In Dr. Comer's view, the emphasis on standards, testing, and accountability has stymied the ability of educators who know better to address the social and emotional needs of their students. "Because of the rigid way the accountability component is being applied in most places, many teachers and administrators who understand the importance of child and youth development to academic achievement believe they do not have the time to do anything other than prepare their students to take tests. As a consequence, most teachers and administrators, pre-service as well as in-service, are not being adequately equipped—or even allowed—to create school cultures that can support student development, effective teaching, and learning."[43]

As a result, he argues, "Failing schools are attributed to inadequate effort or ability among the adults involved, rather than to the fact that most educators are being asked to do what they were not prepared to do. Accountability measures that label, punish, and even reward do not address the challenge of staff and student underdevelopment. Moving underdeveloped students into higher-test-score schools, without adequately preparing the schools' staff to promote development, usually does not help those in greatest need. When large numbers of low-performing students are involved, previously high-performing schools perform less well."[44]

Developing the social and emotional competence of youngsters is both an inescapable obligation and an extraordinary opportunity for public schools. It is an obligation because schools are charged with the task of instilling the knowledge, skills, and habits of mind that young people need to become successful and self-sufficient adults. As the authors of *Promoting Social and Emotional Learning* argue, social and emotional skills "are the fundamentals of human learning, work, creativity, and accomplishment. Social and emotional development and the recognition of the relational nature of learning and change constitute an essential missing piece in our educational system. Until it is given its proper place, we cannot expect to see progress in combating violence, substance abuse, disaffection, intolerance, or the high dropout rate."[45] They continue: "[T]he real challenge of education is no longer whether or not to attend to the social and emotional life of the learner. The real challenge is how to attend to social and emotional issues in education."[46]

Yet for schools, addressing the social and emotional needs of children also represents an opportunity, because so many educators already realize this is a necessity and because there is a growing reservoir of knowledge about how schools can develop the social and emotional competence of young people. In other words, this is far less a matter of discovering the ways and more an issue of mustering the will and, yes, the wherewithal.

Thomas Hanson and his colleagues at WestEd captured the opportunity for schools with their observation that, "While schools on their own may not be able to affect the broader socioeconomic factors underlying the achievement gap, they can affect those well-being factors within the school that contribute to it by fostering a comprehensive system of learning supports. Providing safer, more caring, more academically supportive, and more engaging school environments for schools with high African-American and Hispanic enrollment should be part of a comprehensive approach to closing the achievement gap."[47]

The tide does appear to be turning in the direction of increased attention to social and emotional development. A national survey published by CASEL in 2013 revealed overwhelming support for SEL among schoolteachers.[48] Well over 90 percent of teachers believe that SEL is very or fairly important for the in-school experience, that social and emotional skills are teachable, and that they will benefit students from all backgrounds, rich or poor.[49] Fewer than 20 percent of teachers believe SEL should not be taught in schools or that it should be taught only in high-poverty schools. Furthermore, CASEL reports, more than three-quarters of teachers believe a larger focus on SEL would be a major benefit to students because of the gains in workforce readiness, school attendance and graduation, life success, academic success, and college preparation. Of the teachers who mentioned student behavior as somewhat of a problem, three-quarters noted that SEL is very important. Similar proportions of teachers viewed SEL as a solution to negative school climates.

SEL now occupies a more prominent place on the radar screen of the U.S. Department of Education. In the fall of 2012, the agency announced that school districts vying for federal school improvement grants in the $400 million Race to the Top (RTT) competition would be able to earn up to ten bonus points if their applications included plans to collaborate with public and private partners to help improve the social, emotional, and behavioral needs of students.[50] The weighting of this new ingredient in the application was not trivial, because districts overall could only earn up to 200 points in the other stipulated areas. In addition, the DOE required that they pay at least some attention to students' physical and mental health regardless of whether they sought bonus points.

The 16 districts that ultimately won RTT grants in December 2012 pledged to partner with outside groups to improve students' social and emotional well-being and behavior.[51] For the grant competition in 2013, the DOE signaled it may stipulate that applicant districts must make addressing the behavioral, social, and emotional needs of students and parents part of their core proposals, not simply an add-on to attract bonus points.

State efforts appear to be picking up steam. According to Ryan Reyna, program director in the Education Division of the National Governors Association, states are increasingly focused on dropout prevention and recovery and are investing in so-called wraparound social services that complement the standard education offered in schools.[52] For instance, Georgia has invested $40 million in "graduation" coaches to help youngsters navigate and successfully complete school.

Momentum may be gaining at the local level as well. According to Daniel Goleman, many school districts and even some states mandate social and emotional learning as part of the curriculum.[53] The offerings run the gamut from character education and drug prevention to antibullying, violence prevention, and school discipline. For example, Haut Gap Middle School in Charleston, South Carolina, instituted a schoolwide approach known as "positive behavioral interventions and supports" (PBIS).[54] It includes an obligatory 9-week course that, among other positive behaviors, teaches students how to own up to mistakes, accept feedback, and apologize appropriately. School officials report a sharp decline in suspensions as a result of the improved student behavior and school climate. A study of 16,000 elementary schools in the U.S. using PBIS found significant improvements in students' behavior problems, concentration issues, pro-social behavior, and social-emotional functioning.[55]

Prevention and intervention programs with SEL ingredients that focus on actual or potential dropouts are cropping up across the country. Several cities, including Boston and Milwaukee, have established "reengagement centers" aimed at helping returning students connect with social workers and therapists if needed, find new schools or enroll in online classes, and plan for college and a career.[56] A dropout specialist in the Boston program put it this way: "At first, we kind of push academics to the back. We start at the human level."[57]

As CASEL points out, SEL can also be a framework for school improvement.[58] Teaching SEL skills helps create and maintain safe, caring learning environments. According to CASEL, the most beneficial programs provide sequential and developmentally appropriate instruction in SEL skills. They are implemented in a coordinated manner, schoolwide, from preschool through high school. Lessons are reinforced in the classroom during out-of-school activities, and at home. Educators receive ongoing professional development in SEL. Families and schools collaborate to promote children's social, emotional, and academic success.[59]

SEL interventions in schools can take a variety of forms. Familiar examples include:

• Schoolwide management systems designed to ensure that faculty members and staff are devoted to the social and emotional development of youngsters, attuned to their emotional needs and circumstances, and equipped to intervene if needed.

• Direct assistance from external agencies designed to offer social and emotional services for students that the school personnel do not provide.

• Curricula for teachers to help them understand social and emotional development and manage their classrooms more effectively.

• Instructional programs for students to develop their social and emotional competence.

Promoting Social and Emotional Learning emphasizes three primary attributes of school-based SEL programs:

• Effective, developmentally appropriate, formal and informal instruction in social and emotional skills at every level of schooling, provided by well-trained teachers and other pupil-services personnel.

• A safe and supportive school climate that nurtures the social and emotional development of children while including all the key adults who have a stake in the development of each child.

• Actively engaged educators, parents, and community leaders who create activities and opportunities before, during, and after the regular school day that teach and reinforce attitudes and behaviors of positive family and school life and, ultimately, of responsible, productive citizenship.[60]

True to the local nature of public education, school-based SEL programs vary in structure, staffing, financial resources, and intensity. As Maurice Elias and his colleagues write, "The social and emotional education of children may be provided through a variety of diverse efforts such as classroom instruction, extracurricular activities, a supportive school climate, and involvement in community service. Many schools have entire curriculums devoted to SEL. In classroom-based programs, educators enhance students' social and emotional competence through instruction and structured learning experiences throughout the day."[61]

One of the longest-running SEL interventions is Dr. James Comer's School Development Program (SDP). Since the late 1960s, he has implemented the SDP in more than 1,000 schools in over 50 districts around the country. This highly collaborative, rather complex process requires the creation of three working groups in the school—the School Planning and Management Team, the Parent Team, and the Student and Staff Support Team. The three working groups are coalitions of stakeholders responsible for operating the Comer model. These groups devise and implement a comprehensive school plan, train staff, and make modifications, while marshaling the attention and energy of adults to focus on the academic and emotional well-being of students. The teams operate according to three core principles identified by Dr. Comer. They are no-fault problem solving, consensus decision-making, and inter- and intra-team collaboration.

Turnaround for Children is a more localized SEL initiative in New York City founded by Pamela Cantor, a psychiatrist who specializes in childhood trauma. Writing about Dr. Cantor's efforts, *New York Times* columnist Joe Nocera commented, "If children are under stress, the ways they respond are remarkably similar. They get sad, distracted, aggressive, and tune out. The most disruptive children dominated the schools. Teachers didn't have control of their classrooms—in part because nothing in their training had taught them how to deal with traumatized children. Too many students had no model of what school was supposed to mean."[62]

As Nocera explains, Dr. Cantor created Turnaround to help New York City schools address the social and emotional needs of their pupils. Turnaround goes about this by embedding three-person teams in each school for several years. One of them works with the principal to create a positive, disciplined culture designed to encourage students to believe they can succeed in school. Another team member helps teachers develop classroom management tools to handle disruptions while keeping other students on track. The third team member, a social worker, assists the school-based social workers in addressing the psychological and emotional needs of children in poverty and in identifying the most troubled students. The aim is to avoid suspending or expelling them by enlisting mental health organizations to counsel them.[63]

Parochial schools also recognize the importance of social and emotional development. Writing in *Education Week*, Philip Robey of the National Catholic Educational Association, who is a veteran of both public and parochial schools, observed that Catholic schools impart a well-rounded education that, in addition to academics, stresses whole-child development, behavior, character values and ethics, right versus wrong, and interpersonal relations.[64]

Some private schools get the connection as well. For instance, Nueva School, a pre-K through eighth grade school for gifted and talented children in California, is so convinced of the connection that it conducts a Social and Emotional Learning Teacher Training Institute.[65] According to the school's website, research shows that gifted children have special issues, including perfectionism, fear of failure, and heightened sensitivity to social issues. The goal of the institute is to equip faculty members to strengthen their students' "social-emotional acuity." Nueva expects its students to "demonstrate self-awareness, empathy, effective communication, strong interpersonal skills, leadership, goal-setting, perseverance, optimism, trust, and involvement in the greater community."

Clearly, if youngsters who are struggling in school and in life are to succeed, they need social and emotional skills that many of their parents, to be perfectly realistic, may never provide. We can pine for an era of parental responsibility that no longer exists. That means the social and emotional deficits of these youngsters and the challenges they present will persist, unaddressed, to the detriment of the children, their classmates and schools, and society at large.

Or we can accept reality and devise school-based interventions and, better yet, new kinds of schools geared explicitly to addressing their academic and social-emotional needs. For this to happen, education policy and practice must move beyond the prevailing obsession with testing and accountability that distorts academic and social development and risks losing the very children who are being left farthest behind. As the authors of *Promoting Social and Emotional Learning* observe, "Schools have become the one best place where the concept of surrounding children with meaningful adults and clear behavioral standards can move from faint hope to a distinct possibility—and perhaps even a necessity."[66] The precarious status of such large proportions of young people, generation after generation, demonstrates why we cannot afford to treat children's social and emotional development as a fad, afterthought, or, worse still, discretionary component of their education.

5

Can SEL Be "Taught" in School?

THE CONNECTION BETWEEN youngsters' academic performance and their social and emotional competence is by now beyond dispute. As Joseph Durlak, a professor emeritus of psychology at Loyola University and the lead author of a major meta-analysis of SEL programs, has observed: "Extensive developmental research indicates that effective mastery of social-emotional competencies is associated with greater well-being and better school performance, whereas the failure to achieve competence in these areas can lead to a variety of personal, social, and academic difficulties."[1]

Spurred by the strength and consistency of clinical research, as well as studies of prevention-oriented and youth-development programs, many school-based programs have been designed and implemented specifically to promote youngsters' social and emotional development. These interventions range from bolstering children's social and emotional skills and "teaching" teachers to address their pupils' social and emotional needs to organizing entire schools—including faculty, staff, and parents—to attend to the academic and social development of the children. These programs may operate within the official school day, during extracurricular hours, and even outside the building after school ends. They vary from after-school courses taught by specialists to schoolwide efforts incorporating curriculum, teacher professional development, school activities, and parent training.

Is it possible to "bottle" clinical research and deliver it in effective doses to real schools and schoolchildren? In short, do school-based interventions actually work? Do they demonstrably impact students' academic performance and behavior in school? What is the evidence of effectiveness and what are the implementation challenges? To be clear, my purpose in examining the evidence is not to tout specific approaches or call for their replication, but rather to establish whether it is indeed possible to craft interventions that can make a difference for troubled young people.

The leading source of evidence about the effectiveness of school-based social and emotional learning programs is the meta-analysis conducted by Durlak and his colleagues that was published in the peer-reviewed journal *Child Development*.[2] As the authors explained, the goals of the school-based SEL programs they assessed were to foster the development of five interrelated sets of cognitive, affective, and behavioral competencies: self-awareness, self-management, social awareness, relationship skills, and responsible decision making. These competencies, they suggest, provide a foundation for better adjustment and academic performance, as manifested by more positive social behaviors, fewer conduct problems, less emotional distress, and improved test scores and grades.

The Durlak study was the first large-scale meta-analysis of school-based programs that promote students' social and emotional development. It encompassed more than 200 programs involving roughly 270,000 students from kindergarten through high school. While other reviews have focused on one major outcome, such as substance abuse, this meta-analysis examined the effects of SEL programming across multiple dimensions. What's more, the researchers studied the impacts of interventions aimed at entire student bodies instead of focusing on particular subsets of students who were already displaying behavioral problems.

The meta-analysis scanned the research for evidence of student outcomes in six areas, namely, social and emotional skills, attitudes toward oneself and others, positive social behavior, conduct problems, emotional distress, and, of course, academic performance. The results of the meta-analysis affirmed the benefits of social and emotional development programs situated in schools. What's especially noteworthy in terms of education policy and practice, the researchers reported that the academic performance of students served by SEL programs improved significantly.[3] While based on a small subset of reviewed studies, the 11-percentile gain in academic performance generated by these programs was consequential.[4] According to the authors, that difference was equivalent to moving a student who is in the middle of the class academically up to the top 40 percent of students during the course of the intervention.[5]

As the authors commented, "Results from this review add to a growing body of research indicating that SEL programming enhances students' connection to school, classroom behavior, and academic achievement."[6] Of equal interest and import, the gains on participants' academic achievement tests were comparable to the results of 76 meta-analyses of strictly educational interventions.[7]

On the nonacademic side of the ledger, the reviewers found that SEL programs also make a marked difference. Compared with their non-participating peers, students served by SEL programs improved significantly on five key nonacademic measures. They demonstrated greater social skills, less emotional stress, better attitudes, fewer conduct problems like bullying and suspensions, and more frequent positive behaviors, such as cooperation and helping other students.[8]

The researchers did detect some erosion in impacts over time. Even so, they noted that, "while gains in these areas were reduced in magnitude during follow-up assessments and only a small percentage of studies collected follow-up information, effects nevertheless remained statistically significant for a minimum of six months after the intervention."[9]

In their scan of the studies, the researchers discovered there is broad agreement that SEL programs are likely to be effective if they embrace a set of common practices characterized by the acronym SAFE. In other words, the keys are programs that are:

- Sequenced—provide a coordinated and connected set of activities to achieve objectives;

- Active—utilize active forms of learning to help youngsters learn new skills;

- Focused—devote a least one program component to personal or social skills; and

- Explicit—target specific skills rather than targeting skills or positive development in general.[10]

SEL programs that adhered to these SAFE practices produced significant effects for all six outcomes that were the focus of the meta-analysis. Those that did not produced significant effects in only three.

Beyond these important findings about impacts, the meta-analysis offered other important insights. For instance, the researchers reported that members of the school staff can deliver effective SEL programs. Classroom programs conducted by someone other than school personnel yielded more limited gains, mainly improved social and emotional skills, pro-social attitudes, and fewer conduct problems. Students' academic performance gained significantly only when school personnel conducted the intervention.

Interventions are unlikely to have much practical utility or gain widespread acceptance unless they are effective under real-world conditions by being incorporated into routine educational practice. In other words, it matters whether they can be delivered by existing school staff during the regular school day. As Durlak observed, "We learned this is very practical for schools and doable in schools. There can be a payoff academically for these kids that compares to a lot of straightforward academic interventions, which is really sort of amazing."[11]

The researchers also found that SEL programs can succeed at all educational levels (elementary, middle, and high school) and in urban, suburban, and rural schools. But they added an important caveat about execution. Developing an evidence-based intervention is an essential but insufficient condition for success. Execution matters. Their findings confirmed the negative influence of implementation complications on program outcomes that has been reported in meta-analyses of other youth programs.[12]

As indicated earlier, the meta-analysis conducted by Durlak and his colleagues focused exclusively on so-called universal SEL programs, namely those provided on an undifferentiated basis to the entire student body in a school. The researchers did not limit their analysis to interventions targeting children exhibiting behavioral issues or to schools serving low-income neighborhoods with sizable concentrations of youngsters saddled with social and emotional deficits.

J. David Hawkins and his colleagues at the University of Washington in Seattle undertook a study of SEL interventions specifically designed for these more challenging youngsters and school settings.[13] They focused on public elementary schools serving large numbers of children from poor families living in high-crime areas of Seattle. Since their study did not utilize random assignment, it does not meet the putative gold standard of evaluation. Instead, the authors compared outcomes for program participants versus a nonrandomized control group for six years after the intervention ended. The SEL approach in Seattle consisted of three components—a full intervention comprising five days of in-service training annually for teachers from the first through sixth grades; developmentally appropriate classes for parents of first through third graders as well as fifth and sixth graders; and social competence training for all pupils in grades one through six. There was also a late intervention for youngsters in the fifth and sixth grades.[14]

Here, too, the findings affirmed the value of school-based SEL initiatives, based on self-reporting by the former participants and nonparticipants six years on. The researchers found many upsides, but also some shortfalls. Compared with the control group, fewer students receiving the full intervention had engaged in violent delinquent acts or heavy drinking. They also evidenced more commitment and attachment to school, higher academic achievement, and less misbehavior in school. The researchers rated the self-reported improvements in achievement for participants in the full intervention to be "significant." The gains in reported grade point averages and reductions in the proportion of students who repeated grades were deemed nearly significant. However, the decline in the number who dropped out of school was not considered significant. Nor was there any noteworthy effect on the performance of 17-year-old participants on the California Achievement Test.[15] The levels of school suspension and expulsion did not vary appreciably between participants in the full intervention compared to the control group.

The upshot of the study, Hawkins and his colleagues concluded, is that a package of interventions sustained throughout the elementary school years that "trained parents and teachers to promote children's academic competencies and bonding to school, and that developed children's social competencies and skills to resist health-compromising influences produced greater commitment and attachment to school, less school misbehavior, and better academic achievement six years after intervention."[16] The full intervention was particularly effective in improving the behavior, school attachment, and academic achievement of low-income children. Plus, it reduced the incidence of violent criminal behavior, heavy drinking, sexual intercourse, and pregnancy during the six years following the full intervention.

By comparing the impacts of various SEL approaches employed in the Seattle schools, Hawkins and his colleagues reached another crucial conclusion about the starting point and ultimate effectiveness of sustained interventions. Commencing preventive interventions when children enter elementary school and continuing them through the sixth grade, they found, had greater impact on both educational outcomes and risky behaviors than intervening later in the elementary grades. Early and continued intervention in the elementary grades helps place children on a constructive developmental course that is maintained through high school.[17]

Researchers at the University of Chicago Consortium on Chicago School Research (CCSR) conducted an extensive literature review regarding the role of so-called noncognitive factors in influencing student achievement.[18] By "cognitive factors," they refer to such domains as content knowledge and core academic skills that are customarily gauged via tests. Yet scholastic success, the researchers argue, is also influenced by noncognitive factors. These include the degree to which students "demonstrate an array of academic behaviors, attitudes, and strategies that are critical for success in school and in later life, including study skills, attendance, work habits, time management, help-seeking behaviors, metacognitive strategies, and social and academic problem-solving skills that allow students to successfully manage new environments and meet new academic and social demands."[19] Other student attributes that matter include their attitudes about learning, their self-control and persistence, and the quality of their relationships with peers and adults.

The CCSR researchers set out to assess the state of evidence about the impact of these noncognitive factors on student performance and education practice. More specifically, they focused on the relationship, if any, between student performance and their attributes in five areas— academic behaviors, academic perseverance, academic mind-sets, learning strategies, and social skills. To summarize, the CCSR analysis of the research found that:

• Academic behaviors have a strong and direct effect on grades;

• There is a moderate to modest relationship between perseverance and performance, yet the evidence is not decisive enough to demonstrate a causal relationship;

• There is evidence that students' mind-sets are important and that changing their mind-sets can improve academic performance; and

• Despite limitations, research shows that knowing how and when to use learning strategies is associated with higher overall learning and better academic success.

According to the authors, the evidence was weakest on whether there is a direct relationship between social skills and grades. Most of the demonstrated links were correlational instead of causal. The studies tended to mix social skills with other variables, making it difficult to isolate the effect on academic achievement.[20] Based on their exhaustive literature review, the CCSR researchers concluded that, "By helping students develop the noncognitive skills, strategies, attitudes, and behaviors that are the hallmarks of effective learners, teachers can improve student learning and course performance while also increasing the likelihood that students will be successful in college."[21]

The CCSR researchers then pivoted from a focus on desirable student attributes to the school characteristics that are indispensable for student success. "Academic behaviors and perseverance may need to be thought of as creations of school and classroom contexts," they argue, "rather than as personal qualities that students bring with them to school."[22] They go on: "[T]he research evidence to date suggests that trying to change noncognitive factors at the individual level in isolation from context may not be effective in the long term."[23]

CCSR captured the essence of the challenge facing school systems with large proportions of disengaged, low-performing students. "Teaching adolescents to become learners requires more than improving test scores," the researchers argued. "It means transforming classrooms into places alive with ideas that engage students' natural curiosity and desire to learn in preparation for college, career, and meaningful adult lives."[24] They added that this will require schools to build not only students' skills and knowledge, but also their sense of what is possible for themselves, as they develop the strategies, behaviors, and attitudes that allow them to bring their aspirations to fruition.[25]

Dr. Comer's School Development Program is a mature intervention that was launched in two struggling inner-city schools in New Haven, Connecticut, in 1968. A meta-analysis of 29 widely implemented comprehensive—or whole-school—reform initiatives rated the SDP as one of only three such interventions that demonstrate the strongest evidence of effectiveness.[26] The researchers found that the SDP had generated statistically significant and positive achievement effects.

Many participating "Comer" schools and districts report remarkable academic progress by their students. For example, the student body at Hall Fletcher Elementary School in Asheville, North Carolina, is predominantly African American, and most students receive free or subsidized school lunches. The principal instituted the SDP in 1998 when merely 41 percent and 43 percent of third graders scored proficient in reading and math, respectively, on state tests.[27] Those ratios soared to 94 percent and 97 percent, respectively, by 2004.[28] Fifth graders at Hall Fletcher fared even better. By 2004, 100 percent of the fifth graders in the school achieved proficiency in reading.[29] Impressed by the early progress at Hall Fletcher, the Asheville district implemented the SDP in all of its elementary schools. The fifth-grade black-white achievement gap in reading had closed from 40 percent in 1999 to barely six percentage points by 2004.[30] As the principal of Hall Fletcher proudly notes, her school achieved these strong gains without changing the children.

A rigorous, independent evaluation of SDP in ten of Chicago's worst inner-city schools also reported positive impacts.[31] Compared with ten similar nonparticipating schools, the SDP schools experienced improvements in school climate, student achievement, and behavior.[32] According to Christine Emmons, the director of program evaluation for SDP, District 13 in New York City instituted the SDP in September 1995. From 1999 through 2001, the district registered gains in student performance in mathematics and English that outpaced those of New York City students overall.[33] Strong gains associated with SDP have also been realized in Chicago, New Haven, Charlotte/Mecklenburg (North Carolina), and Westbury (New York).[34] Both internal analyses by SDP staff as well as independent studies indicate that Comer schools have positively impacted student attitudes and behavior.[35] Students in SDP schools demonstrate better anger control, greater disapproval of misbehavior, and less acting out in school and out.[36]

Admittedly, evaluations of interventions like SDP can be clouded or even compromised by several factors. Reported improvements may be attributable to changes in the school that have little to do with the intervention per se. Or, as may have been the case in Chicago, nonparticipating comparison schools could mimic some of the reform methods utilized in the so-called treatment schools.[37] This complicates the task of attributing gains, or the lack thereof, to given interventions.

A core challenge facing all education interventions is the quality and integrity of implementation. Conscientious implementation that adheres faithfully to the intervention model is crucial. Ambivalence and conflicting priorities among school personnel, starting with the principal, can undermine the soundest school-reform concept. According to Dr. Comer, SDP schools that rate highest on implementation generate the highest student achievement in language arts and mathematics.[38] The independent SDP evaluation conducted by Thomas Cook and his colleagues echoed this observation. The implementation index they devised correlated closely with student and staff measures of SDP schools' academic and social climate.[39]

Complex innovations that address challenging human and systemic problems need reasonable time, stable funding, and continuity of leadership at the building and district level to take root, iron out imperfections, and make midcourse corrections before they can fairly be subjected to exacting evaluations. As Caroline Hanamirian noted, school culture matters enormously. Interventions cannot be implemented successfully without enthusiastic, committed, and capable principals and the consistent support of the school district.[40] Emmons underscored the importance of school culture when she observed that schools with a philosophy similar to SDP already in place reported faster implementation and quicker results. "If we have support of the district, support of the school board, and sufficient people attend professional development," Emmons noted, "then the enthusiasm tends to build and the principal and staff make changes almost immediately in the schools."[41]

Recall that Durlak and his colleagues concluded it is feasible for school personnel to implement SEL programs that produce favorable results. Yet experience with the SDP demonstrates the implementation challenges confronted even by a frequently effective intervention that relies for its success on the active involvement of principals, teachers, support personnel, and parents.

Illinois took a markedly different tack in 2003 by becoming the first state to mandate statewide goals and benchmarks for social and emotional learning that districts and individual schools are expected to meet. Only two other states appear to have followed suit.[42] In collaboration with the Illinois Children's Mental Health Partnership, the State Board of Education established a Professional Development Project designed to coordinate SEL training and coaching for teachers.[43] According to Hanamirian, the state promulgated three primary goals: building students' self-awareness and self-management skills, promoting positive relationships, and teaching decision-making skills and responsible behaviors.[44]

Despite the state's authority over local public schools, Hanamirian observed, the top-down decree has not meant entirely smooth sailing.[45] The experience in Illinois reveals the challenges associated with incorporating—or even imposing—SEL in existing public schools that face myriad other pressures and distractions. As an external evaluation by the Center for Prevention Research and Development at the University of Illinois noted, several schools withdrew, one school closed down, and another was consolidated.[46] Some schools changed principals. Many schools operated under fiscal duress.

Arguably the biggest obstacle to giving SEL its due remains the acute pressure on schools to meet federally mandated "Average Yearly Progress" goals, reinforced by states' own accountability regimes and the growing trend of factoring students' test scores into the retention, promotion, and compensation of teachers and principals. This undercuts the willingness of schools to incorporate social and emotional learning into their curricula and schedules.

In the sobering view of Jonathan Zaff, vice president of research and policy development for America's Promise Alliance, public schools are not equipped to do SEL well, nor should they be expected to.[47] Educators, he argues, are not trained in the necessary disciplines; they lack the time; and school hours are too constrained to accommodate it. He sees social and emotional development as a community issue requiring community-based solutions.

Principals and teachers in schools that are under relentless scrutiny year after year to improve academic performance may feel they do not have the "luxury" of implementing SEL programs that could take several years to get traction and show results. In the stringent accountability environment these days, SEL can take a backseat to the schools' traditional academic agenda. After all, recurring failure by schools to register satisfactory academic progress could cost principals and teachers their jobs and result in faltering schools being closed. As might be expected, the risks of these dire sanctions being imposed weigh most heavily on schools with the lowliest academic performance.

Clinical research, evaluations of specific programs, and one major meta-analysis of school-based interventions demonstrate that improving children's social and emotional competence can improve both their academic performance as well as their behavior. Some educators, schools, and districts have opted to introduce SEL of their own volition and have done so with authentic commitment and enthusiasm. One state has even mandated SEL. Yet the obstacles to persuading schools to embrace and conscientiously implement SEL training for teachers and instruction for students remain steep among educators who, understandably, are obliged to focus narrowly on students' academic performance since their livelihoods literally depend on it.

6

Needed: A New Paradigm

SOME EDUCATORS VIEW SEL as peripheral. Others clearly see the value but are unable to allocate the time or muster the energy to address it because of the unrelenting pressure to improve students' test scores. The cruel irony, of course, is that the challenges facing educators in the lowest-performing schools are compounded by high concentrations of youngsters whose social and emotional shortcomings impede their inclination and ability to learn.

As Balfanz has observed, in schools with steep dropout rates, only one in five youngsters can be described as typical students whom high schools were designed to educate, who attend school regularly, who are not assigned to special education, and whose reading and math skills are grade level or better. "Four out of five students need substantial and sustained supports in order to succeed at all, let alone in a high-standards, high-stakes testing environment," he notes based on experience.[1]

The picture in high-poverty middle schools is much the same. According to Balfanz, "Here you can have 25 sixth graders with attendance problems, a different 25 with behavior problems, and an additional 50 students failing either math or English, with each group needing different levels of different interventions."[2] In some schools, he notes, more than 80 percent of students are either repeating for the second or third time, in special education, two or more years below grade level, or have missed a month or more. Given the interrelated academic, social, and emotional needs, and difficult circumstances of sizable segments of their student bodies, Balfanz argues, these schools unquestionably are overchallenged and under-resourced.

Anthony Bryk and his colleagues who examined the Chicago school reform initiative reached virtually the same conclusion.[3] They cited the high concentration of youngsters, as many as 25 percent, in truly disadvantaged schools who were victims of abuse or neglect or living under other excruciatingly difficult circumstances. They found evidence that the density of students living under extraordinary conditions affects the likelihood of improvement. "Less than 20 percent of the schools showed improvements on either attendance or student learning in reading and mathematics where the prevalence of abused or neglected children was high, as compared with 30 percent or more when these problems were less prevalent."[4]

Bryk reported that an endemic concern for urban schoolteachers is students with acute personal and social needs. He and his colleagues noted that many urban children live under unstable home and community circumstances, including homelessness, domestic violence, abuse, and neglect. Their lives are devoid of the most basic need for healthy child development—stable, dependable relationships with caring adults. Children reared in these circumstances often make extraordinary demands on teachers. As the authors cautioned:

> "The natural inclination for school staff is to respond as fully humanly as possible to these heartfelt personal needs; but if the number of students presenting substantial needs is too large, even extraordinary teachers can be quickly overwhelmed."[5]

The Chicago evaluators found a clear connection between the youngsters' troubled circumstances and their academic troubles. They reported that "high crime and prevalent child abuse and neglect were powerfully linked to school stagnation in reading, mathematics, and attendance. Schools located in such communities were three to four times more likely to stagnate than were schools in safer, less-violent communities with fewer social problems. Approximately 40 percent of the schools in communities with prevalent crime and child abuse or neglect remained 'dead in the water.'"[6]

These low-income communities suffer from a lack of what Bryk and his colleagues call social capital, which they characterize as exceptional leadership with strong links with organizations both inside and outside the community, relational trust among school community members, a

coherent program of improvement, and an unrelenting focus on gar-
nering community resources to respond to the extraordinary needs in
the school. In their view, "Community social capital is a critical re-
source for advancing school improvement. The presence of such social
capital helps to explain why the essential supports took root in some
schools and not others. Similarly, we have documented that the density
of children living under extraordinary circumstances within a school
community can create a significant barrier for improvement. Virtually
none of the schools with high concentrations of such students managed
to achieve broad-based organizational change during the seven-year
period of our study. Taken together, a weakness in community social
capital combined with a high density of student needs marks the social
context of truly disadvantaged schools."[7]

Many schools in poor neighborhoods must cope with intense concentrations of students with emotional, social, and academic needs.
According to Balfanz, "most students who drop out do so for a combination of academic and social-emotional reasons. . . . [E]ven the best
instruction in the world will have limited impact if students do not attend school on a regular basis, try to succeed, and behave."[8] Educators
and policymakers underestimate the intensity and scale of educational
challenges in high-poverty schools, especially the developmental and
cognitive challenges many youngsters—and their teachers—face. In
addition, there are an insufficient number of skilled and intransient
adults in schools and neighborhoods committed to children's development. The other ruinous environment for children, Balfanz notes, is
schools that seem orderly but where everything moves at a languid pace
and where local expectations prevail.[9]

Based on their study of school reform in Chicago, Bryk and his colleagues observed that, "At both the classroom and school level, the
good efforts of even the best of educators are likely to be seriously
taxed when confronted with a high density of students who are in foster care, homeless, neglected, abused, and so on. Classroom activity
can understandably get diverted toward responding to these manifest
personal needs. Similarly, it can be difficult at the school level to maintain collective attention on instructional improvement when the social
needs of children continue to cry out for adult attention. It is easy to
see how the core work of instruction and its improvement can quickly

become a secondary priority."[10]

Hawkins argues that starting preventive SEL inventions at the outset of elementary school and sustaining them to sixth grade produces better educational and behavioral outcomes for children that persist at least through high school.[11] I certainly concur that early development of social and emotional skills is optimal. Even so, many children will enter preadolescence underdeveloped because their elementary schools never instituted SEL programs or else did so inadequately. Other schools might have wanted to, but could not due to financial constraints. As a result, promoting social and emotional competence must remain a priority for preadolescent and adolescent youngsters during the middle school and high school years.

By now it should be clear that conventional schools are ill-suited to cope with the needs of many youngsters who have completely tuned out of the education offered there. This is evidenced by the patterns of chronic academic failure, disengagement, grade retention, behavioral and disciplinary problems, and, ultimately, dropping out. This stark reality in Chicago prompted Bryk and his colleagues to reach a striking conclusion that should provide the impetus for fresh thinking:

> In communities where there are few viable institutions, where crime, drug abuse, and gang activity are prevalent, and where palpable human needs walk through the school doors virtually every day, a much more powerful model of school development is needed—one that melds systemic efforts at strengthening instruction with the social resources of a comprehensive community schools initiative.[12]

In a recommendation that mirrors the central thesis of this book, Bryk and his colleagues imagine an alternative approach that would entail transforming schooling through a "comprehensive and integrated set of community, school, and related social program initiatives":

> This strategy is anchored in efforts to cultivate local leadership and more productive working relationships among school staff, parents, and local neighborhood services and officials. Building on this human and social resource development is an expansion of

student learning opportunities through increased instructional time, coupled with sustained programmatic activities in all the essential support areas so that this expanded learning time is more productive. Also included is a strong programmatic focus on the myriad of social, emotional, and physical health needs that impede the learning of many children.[13]

Actually, Bryk and his colleagues called and raised themselves by envisioning an even more radical model. "Might new designs for exceptionally strong schools be needed?" they wondered. "Perhaps we should be aiming toward something more akin to a total institution that creates an island of safety and order, established social routing, and new norms for academic effort in order to counter the external forces pushing students in very different directions."[14]

Interestingly enough, this idea roughly echoes the view of Eddy Bayardelle, the erstwhile head of the Merrill Lynch Foundation and a former teacher and principal in the New York City school system, who says schools are filled with youngsters who have tuned out of school.[15] He contends that school systems do not know what to do with them, traditional schools do not reach them, and the youngsters do not particularly care that they don't. They simply aren't "into" the education that's being offered.

Based on his experience with these academically disengaged young people, Bayardelle advocates an entirely new approach to learning.[16] Ideally, these youngsters need to be enveloped in an all-encompassing environment, akin to the military, that helps insulate them from negative forces in school, at home, in the community, and among peers. They need curriculum and instruction that connects them to the real world that they see and touch. Otherwise, they do not get the point of education. Also, these children have energy to burn. Bayardelle argues that to reach these adolescents, schools need to consume some of that energy through physical education, hands-on learning, and the arts. No one expects adults to sit still for six hours or more per day, he notes, yet that's what we expect of youngsters, which makes no sense.

Thus, social and emotional development emerges as a core, indeed coequal, purpose of schools that are custom-designed to address the needs of youngsters who are struggling academically and in life. As

Larry McClure of the Create Stem Success Initiative at the University of California, San Diego, put it, "Limited structural changes are likely to be insufficient to increase student learning, engagement, and achievement. The cultural and social component of schooling must be explicitly addressed as well, and personalization and connectedness must be woven throughout the school community. Ultimately, personalization approaches must move into the core of schooling and instruction. Schools need to integrate strategies of caring into their daily work and overall school climate, as opposed to simply annexing it within an advisory period."[17]

The authors of *Promoting Social and Emotional Learning* make the case even more insistently. They contend that schools have become the best place where the idea of surrounding children with meaningful adults and clear behavioral standards can move from faint hope to a distinct possibility—and perhaps even a necessity.[18] Accordingly, they call for:

- Developmentally appropriate, formal and informal instruction in social and emotional skills at every level of schooling, provided by well-trained teachers and other pupil-services personnel.

- Supportive and safe school climates that nurture the social and emotional development of children while including all the key adults who have a stake in the development of each child.

- Actively engaged educators, parents, and community leaders who create activities and opportunities before, during, and after the regular school day that teach and reinforce the attitudes, values, and behaviors of positive family and school life and, ultimately, of responsible, productive citizenship.[19]

Balfanz even invokes the imagery of public health when imagining the way schools for disengaged middle-school youngsters should be designed and operated to keep them on track for graduation.[20] He contends that the combination of smart organization, effective instructional programs, and teacher quality, along with a public-health prevention model, will generate substantial achievement gains for low-income students.[21] To begin with, he believes that creating smaller, more personalized schools helps, but by itself is not enough. This should be buttressed by interdisciplinary teams of teachers, research-based instructional programs that are challenging and engaging, and high-caliber teachers supported by solid induction programs and high-quality professional development.

These academic components must be augmented and reinforced, Balfanz argues, by a public-health prevention strategy. For this he envisions a tiered system of supports. First, he proposes schoolwide measures designed to prevent poor attendance and behavior and course failure. In the case of students for whom this is not enough, he calls for targeted small group interventions and supports. Finally, he anticipates that some youngsters will need intensive one-on-one attention and problem-solving support.[22]

Stitching together these threads of research and real-world experience, I am convinced that the futility of the prevailing approaches to "educating" disengaged youngsters cries out for fresh thinking and strategies. Tweaking customary methods that repeatedly fall short will result in the continued "miseducation" of youngsters who clearly have dialed out of traditional schooling. Accordingly, I call for an entirely new paradigm, namely public academies devoted explicitly and unequivocally to the academic and social development of youngsters who clearly are struggling in school and in life.

In the next two chapters I will segue to an improbable source of insights, lessons, and models. I refer to the U.S. military, which for decades has embraced the mantra of the "whole person" in its approach to education and training. As is evident from a demonstrably successful quasi-military intervention for high school dropouts known as the National Guard Youth ChalleNGe Program, the military knows how to develop academic and social skills as coequal and mutually reinforcing objectives. Reiterating my request in the prologue, I entreat my readers to look beyond labels that might be off-putting for some people. Join me now in imagining how these military-like education and training methods might be adapted for—and embraced by—public education.

7

Military Engagement in Public Education

IF YOU WERE ASKED which American institutions are deeply committed to the academic and social development of young people, the U.S. military might be one of the least likely to come to mind. Yet the military is actually a promising place to look for insights and ideas about how to develop "difficult" adolescents. It enjoys a well-deserved reputation for reaching, teaching, and training young people from hardscrabble backgrounds who are rudderless and drifting through life.

Writing in the *American Sociological Review*, Robert Sampson and John Laub observed that "military service in the World War II era provided American men from economically disadvantaged backgrounds with an unprecedented opportunity to better their lives through on-the-job training and further education."[1] The authors especially cited the beneficial impacts of in-service training, overseas duty, and the G.I. Bill on soldiers' subsequent occupational status, job stability, and economic well-being.

As Dirk Johnson wrote in *Newsweek*, "For many children growing up without a cohesive family, the military model seems to offer a bedrock of stability—a world of clear-cut rules and unmistakable authority figures."[2] Elizabeth Heneghan Ondaatje of RAND goes further: "The Army's primary contribution to youth development consists of educating and training its own enlistees, many of whom are from disadvantaged backgrounds. The Army's success in this regard is well documented and well recognized."[3]

The military's strengths include proven competence in such areas as training, building teams, organizing small units, ramping up quickly, operating at scale, and transforming aimless recruits and, in earlier years, draftees into focused and productive individuals.[4] The military sets the pace among American institutions in advancing minorities. As the late military sociologist Charles Moskos observed, the Army in particular has achieved credibility among young minorities and their parents, in large part because it is the rare institution not dominated at top levels by whites. "The Army is the only place in American society where whites are routinely bossed around by blacks."[5]

Moskos and John Sibley Butler, coauthors of *All That We Can Be: Black Leadership and Racial Integration the Army Way*, contend that black achievement in the armed forces is more pronounced than anywhere else in American society. As of 1998, African Americans made up 29 percent of all enlisted personnel, 37 percent of senior non-commissioned officers, and 12 percent of all officers.[6] The reason for the Army's success, they argue, is that instead of lowering standards to accommodate black recruits, it invests heavily in ensuring that they have the opportunity to meet the standards.

According to Moskos and Butler, the Army operates one of the largest continuing education programs in the world. Of the 50,000 soldiers in the program known as Functional Academic Skills Training (FAST) in 1998, 60 percent were black, representing a high percentage of black noncommissioned officers. "A level playing field is not enough," they note. "The Army's success in producing black leaders occurs because it recognizes that compensatory action may be needed to help members of disadvantaged groups meet the standards of competition."[7]

Some research suggests that military service enhances employability. For example, a 1990 survey of 600 employers conducted by the Army Research Institute found that "employers believed Army veterans have more of the characteristics they desire than job applicants in general."[8] As Beth Asch of RAND wrote of this study, "Among the characteristics considered the most important by employers for success in entry-level positions were dependability, listening to instructions, caring for company property, seeking clarification, efficiency, enthusiasm, respecting others, punctuality, showing good judgment, working as a team member, sticking with a task, and self-discipline."[9]

The protracted and, for many, exasperating quest to improve public schools and to boost the achievement levels, employability, and life prospects of struggling youngsters has prompted educators, policy-makers, and parents to peer outside the box and consider unconventional approaches that hold promise. Hence the growing curiosity about and receptivity toward military-style interventions.

Its core mission notwithstanding, the U.S. military has a long and productive history of involvement in public education at the secondary school level and in extracurricular youth development programming. In addition to operating their own schools for children of military families, the various branches have both run and collaborated with public schools in operating alternative schools, schools within schools, extracurricular programs, and a youth corps for dropouts.

JROTC

The most venerable collaboration between the military and public schools is the Junior Reserve Officers Training Corps (JROTC), which Congress authorized back in 1916 as a vehicle for promoting good citizenship and responsibility among young people.[10] For decades JROTC operated mostly in public high schools in southern states.[11] That changed after General Colin Powell, then chairman of the Joint Chiefs of Staff, visited South Central Los Angeles following the riots there in 1992. Declaring that inner-city youth needed the discipline and structure offered by the military, he decided to expand JROTC.[12]

All four services sponsor JROTC programs. These days, as many as 3,500 schools and half a million cadets nationwide participate in JROTC in every state and territory of the United States.[13] It operates as an elective course that combines classroom instruction with extracurricular activities and is taught by retired military officers and noncommissioned officers. The Army JROTC, for example, pursues an ambitious set of objectives, including promoting citizenship, developing leadership, helping participants learn to work as team members, enhancing communication skills, strengthening self-esteem, providing the incentive to live drug-free, improving physical fitness, promoting high school graduation, and, not surprisingly, encouraging an appreciation of the military services and their accomplishments.[14]

The JROTC curriculum covers an array of topics, among them:

citizenship via instruction in history and government, career and education planning, health and wellness, geography, financial planning, and drug awareness. The curriculum, which incorporates technology-based instruction, also includes a strong leadership component that teaches students motivational principles, individual and group management, and decision-making skills.[15] Although JROTC is ostensibly not intended as a military recruitment vehicle, and while cadets incur no obligation to serve once they graduate from high school, surveys indicate that approximately 42 percent of JROTC graduates expect to establish some connection with one of the military services and that they are five times more likely than their peers to join the military.[16]

Assessments that admittedly fall short of rigorous evaluations suggest that JROTC adds value to the participating students and schools. According to an analysis conducted by William Taylor of the Center for Strategic and International Studies (CSIS), Army JROTC cadets are more self-disciplined, attend class more frequently, are less likely to drop out of school, and (in the case of high school seniors) more likely to graduate.[17] They performed better than the overall school population in every area that is routinely measured by educators, including academic achievement, grade point average, and SAT and ACT exam scores.

In Chicago, CSIS reports, sustained membership in JROTC over several years paid off. Although many of the enrollees were considered at-risk youth, classroom performance and behavioral indicators equaled or exceeded the average in individual schools.[18] In 2004, 71 percent of the graduating JROTC cadets in Chicago continued on to postsecondary education.[19] Studies conducted by the Army found that their JROTC cadets have fewer disciplinary infractions than the overall student population, higher attendance and graduation rates, and stronger grade point averages and SAT scores.[20]

As with so many interventions for young people, the research sends mixed messages about the impact of JROTC. One study found that JROTC participants have poorer academic outcomes than other students, although a large portion of these effects can be explained by their at-risk status. On the bright side, though, the program appears to have beneficial effects for some demographic groups. The authors particularly cited African-American cadets, who had lower dropout rates than other JROTC participants.[21]

Many educators express enthusiasm and support for JROTC. According to one counselor, "Many JROTC kids have no family ties [and are] wards of the state, with no male role model; JROTC is their family."[22] Another counselor from a school with a high incidence of pregnancies commented that fewer female students who participate in JROTC become pregnant. Other counselors cited "amazing turnarounds, increased confidence, and great enthusiasm." Some educators who were surveyed mentioned that going through JROTC inspections motivates cadets to take more pride in their appearance and in their schoolwork. As one educator told CSIS, students who are enrolled in JROTC for at least one year are rarely seen by the assistant principal.[23] JROTC instructors added that the program provides a base for values, integrity, self-esteem, and teamwork that will affect them all their lives. Younger cadets tend to make more positive decisions, while older students tend to assume leadership roles.[24]

Critics of JROTC and other military-style offerings in public schools worry, understandably, that these programs may become recruitment vehicles for military service, inculcate military history and values, stifle individualism, and encourage unblinking acceptance of hierarchy and authority. In its report, CSIS countered, "Such a perspective on military values, and by extension the values JROTC attempts to inculcate, is far too narrow. Although adherence to chains of command and respect for authority are essential in a profession whose activities can be lethal, the military does not need or want blind submission to authority."[25] Nevertheless, anxieties about the effects of military-style programs on young people persist and must be overcome in any discussion of adapting military education and training methods for use with civilian youngsters and public schools.

March2Success

Another example of the military's engagement with schools is March2Success, a free online service operated by the Army that aims to improve students' performance on standardized tests, such as the SAT, ACT, state exit exams, and the Army's own qualifying test known as ASVAB (Armed Services Vocational Aptitude Battery).[26] Students register online and then take baseline tests in each subject area. Using the test results, March2Success builds a customized curriculum for each student. Those who score below 80 percent receive lesson plans and study materials designed to help improve their competency. The online tutorial content is provided by industry leaders in standardized testing and college preparation.

March2Success demonstrates how the military employs technology to help boost the academic performance of secondary school students. In 2009, the Army conducted a March2Success pilot program for 163 students in Broward County, Florida, using a high school prep mathematics module to improve their scores on state-mandated tests.[27] Following an initial assessment of test results in two math-related subject areas, the students received a customized lesson plan based on their individual scores. The plan entailed roughly 15 hours of training and preparation over a six-week period.

As reported in *Army Education News & Updates*, after completing their course work, the students retook the test, with the following results: 83.6 percent of the Broward students increased their math/general purpose test scores, and 74.8 percent increased their math/problem-solving test scores.[28] Average math/general purpose test scores climbed by 31 percent and average math/problem-solving test scores jumped by 29 percent. Of special significance, students with lower initial test scores showed the most improvement.

Public Military Schools

An all-encompassing yet smaller-scale innovation is public military academies (PMA). A number of school districts have created full-fledged schools roughly in the image of JROTC. Some 20 such schools exist nationwide. A half dozen or so operate as charter schools; the rest are small public schools. Their enrollment typically ranges from 400 to 600 students. Chicago alone operates six academies in partnership with the Army, Navy, Marine Corps, and Air Force. Many PMAs function as schools-within-schools, situated inside existing buildings along with other schools.

Demand for the academies can be robust. For instance, 1,300 youngsters applied to one of the Chicago military schools just to fill 140 openings, and 2,000 applicants vied for 250 slots in Philadelphia.[29] Since the interest in PMAs far exceeds the available slots, they typically utilize application and screening procedures to winnow the pool of applicants. Students are not compelled to attend, nor are they ever obliged to join the military.

Most PMAs operate in inner-city areas, and their student bodies tend to be heavily low-income and minority, with approximately 10 percent classified as special education students. For example, of the nearly 600 students in grades six through 12 at the Oakland Military Institute College Preparatory Academy, roughly 37 percent are Latino, 33 percent are African American, and 22 percent are Asian. Interestingly enough, while girls comprise one-quarter of the entering class in the sixth grade, they display greater staying power and constitute half of the graduating senior class.[30]

It is worth noting, however, that the youngsters chosen for these academies tend not to teeter on the precipice of academic failure. According to Oliver Sloman, my former research associate at the Brookings Institution, public military academies typically are so-called "choice" schools, with competitive admission processes in contrast to regular, nonselective public schools.[31] Applicants may be obliged to write an essay, collect recommendations, sit for an interview, perform at least on grade level in major subject areas, and have no serious discipline infractions on their record. While exceptions may be made, particularly in the case of applicants whose strong interviews offset weak academic or disciplinary records, PMAs usually are not schools of last resort. They tend to target the solid students within struggling school districts who yearn for a safe, serious school environment.

In the words of Russell Gallagher, director of Philadelphia's JROTC programs and an architect of the Philadelphia military academies, "We're looking for well-rounded kids, not geniuses."[32] Army Lieutenant Colonel Rick Mills, who oversees Chicago's military academies and JROTC programs, comments that the academies are for students who perform in the middle range academically.[33] So these schools tend to steer clear of the most troubled youngsters. As Brigadier General Frank Bacon, who headed the Chicago Military Academy–Bronzeville, noted, "They can have been in trouble and still come here. They just can't stay in trouble and stay here."[34]

Public military academies proudly depict themselves as college preparatory schools. They adhere to the academic standards of their states and host school districts. Since most academies are full-fledged public schools, Sloman notes, they face many of the same strictures regarding curriculum, hiring, and spending as other schools.[35] PMAs often attract staff who previously served in the military. That said, the vast majority of their teachers are regular educators certified through traditional channels.

Public military academies pursue a markedly different approach to education than large, comprehensive schools. All cadets wear common attire, take the JROTC course, and follow certain military rituals such as saluting and standing at attention. Other distinctive attributes of PMAs include mandatory leadership and teamwork courses, student chains of command, frequent rewards and recognition, an orderly and safe environment, positive peer pressure, and unique staffing features such as full-time JROTC instructors and a commandant in charge of student well-being.[36] The academies focus on the "whole child" by emphasizing the importance of social and emotional development to achieving academic success.

According to Bridget Bartlett, my former Princeton student who wrote her senior thesis about PMAs, three pillars of the Oakland Military Institute (OMI) typify the philosophy of these academies around the country.[37] OMI's goals are to promote academic excellence, develop leaders of character, and inculcate habits of lifelong physical fitness.[38] As Bartlett observes, "Through placing a premium on the rigorous academic program, the vision of the school clearly demonstrates how the military learning environment bolsters the college preparatory objective of the school. . . . The demanding academic program includes language arts, math, science, and history as well as world languages, leadership, and physical fitness training."[39]

What explains the interest in public military academies? As Robert Cervantes, the military liaison between California's Department of Education and the active armed forces, explains: "Districts are desperately looking for something that works. Traditional schools aren't working. Students aren't getting the attention they need."[40] Cervantes adds that school districts are drawn to public military schools because there are clearer expectations for students' conduct, attendance, and performance. Also, uniforms and military instructors in the classroom foster a more structured learning atmosphere. According to Bartlett, "As school districts have turned increasingly to innovative approaches, many inner cities have embraced the public military academy as an antidote to the disorder within and outside the school walls."[41]

Do public military academies work? Reaching conclusions is tricky because of the small number of these schools as well as their relative youth. Plus, there is a risk of selection bias since these are schools of choice. Students who opt to attend the PMAs may be more motivated to succeed than those in large, nonselective schools. Although the evidence of whether and to what extent these military academies work hardly meets the gold standard for evaluation, the sketchy data available paints an encouraging picture of what these kinds of schools can potentially accomplish.

Based on her overview of the evidence, Kim Harrell, director of JROTC for the Chicago public schools, reports that public military academies have posted some of the largest district gains in virtually every area of student academic achievement. They outscore their host districts on such key metrics as average ACT scores, reading and math performance, freshmen on track, one-year dropout rates, attendance, suspensions, and expulsions.[42]

Bartlett found other signs of positive impact.[43] For instance, the academy in Franklin, Massachusetts, has exceeded the district's pass rate on state exams in English and math every year since 2004. Founded in 2005, the Philadelphia Military Academy-Elverson significantly outperformed its peers in the district. Seventy percent of Elverson's juniors scored at the basic level or better on the state math exam in 2008 compared with the districtwide average of 41 percent. In reading, 88 percent of them met or exceeded state standards, compared with 58 percent districtwide. Just one year after Forestville High School in Prince Georges County, Maryland, was transformed into a military academy, it boosted a higher percentage of students up to proficient levels in English and math compared with the district average. The Phoenix Military Academy made substantial progress as well, registering a 38 percent pass rate on state achievement tests for the 2008–09 academic year, up from a dismal 5 percent the year before.

Other performance measures matter as well. In Philadelphia, the academies' average daily attendance rate of 93 percent outshines the districtwide average of 81 percent. What's more, the teacher absentee rate at the PMAs of less than 1 percent far surpasses the districtwide rate of 8 percent and appears to attest to the teachers' desire to work in this unique environment.

Admittedly, not all comparisons of individual academies with districtwide or state averages are favorable, and academic gaps still separate some military academies from their district and state averages. Yet as Bartlett observes, despite the varied test results, PMAs consistently outperform their district averages in terms of attendance, graduation, and college-going rates, as well as in the incidence of truancy and school violence.[44] These variables—from graduation rates to minimal violence—are meaningful barometers of student engagement and a more positive school culture.

While testimonials by children and parents hardly qualify as rigorous evidence, they do provide a granular and, in my view, credible indication of whether and why interventions make a difference. The compelling stories culled from interviews and newspaper accounts convey the profound difference that this unconventional approach to educating and developing young people can make. Consider these excerpts:

• A cadet at the California Military Institute said: "At my last school, nobody cared if I failed a test, nobody even noticed if I skipped classes, and so I did. I was invisible. But when I decided to come here [to CMI], I knew I'd like that my teachers would know my name, but I was scared that discipline meant everyone would yell and punish me for everything. But it's not like that at all. Discipline here is really just people caring about me, telling me what I did wrong, how I could do it better next time, and they actually tell me what I've done right even more, even when I didn't think anyone would notice. No one's ever cared that much about what I do at school, and now I actually care."[45]

• Marcia Colbert is the single mother of Tatrell Sims and three other children. The Oakland Military Institute represents her last hope of ensuring that Tatrell gets an adequate education.

Earlier in the year, he was causing disruptions and was often asked to leave the classroom because he couldn't settle down.

Tatrell and his mother meet regularly with his teachers to discuss his behavior, devise plans, and set daily academic goals for him to succeed. She says: "Right now he is on an academic point system. I'm trying out everything. When he was in public schools, I wasn't consistent about making him go to bed at the right time and do all his homework. But the school is keeping me strong and it is helping me be consistent." If Tatrell does well in each class, he receives a number of points for which he is rewarded at the end of the week.

According to Tatrell, "At my other school, I use [sic] to be a follower, but now I'm a leader. I used to believe that if other kids could do bad stuff, I could do it too. But I'm a squad leader now. And I feel good because I never did anything like this before."

Marcia Colbert poignantly sums up the difference OMI has made in her son's life: "So far, the school is working well for Tatrell. They are working with him. This is the only school that has gone the extra mile for my kid. They aren't trying to kick him out. They are trying to build up a sense of tolerance in his life. The teachers are trying to work with him, but it is up to him. If he makes it through this first year, hopefully, next year he'll do better."[46]

• Christopher Woody originally insisted that Forestville Military Academy hadn't done him any good, that he shouldn't have to put up with teachers who scream at him like he's a soldier, that his mother was raising him just fine without the military's help. He spent the early months in the academy fighting change with the fierce determination that the school wanted him to apply to his conduct and his studies.

The Christopher who first roamed the halls wearing baggy jeans and shoulder-length cornrows was not the same 14-year-old who four months later knew how to march, dress for school in a uniform, and respond to teachers in Army speak. According to his mother, Linda Woody, "I was getting desperate. I felt like, I know this child is bright, I know he's creative. He's not dull. We can expect more of him."

The changes in his behavior have been quite noticeable. Last year, Christopher came home scuffed and bruised and bloodied from the many fights he got into at Andrew Jackson High School. This year, his mother hasn't noticed a scratch. His grade point average, which had sunk to 0.5 out of a possible 4.0 during part of eighth grade, stood at 1.29 for the first report card at Forest-ville. His highest grade was C and he had earned four of them. Even so, Christopher claimed that the Forestville environment was too controlling. "I don't want a father figure. . . . The military is not for everyone. It's not for me."[47]

A year later, there are times when Christopher Woody sur-prises even himself. He's now the one who inspects his classmates to make sure every shoe is polished and every shirt is tucked. At lunchtime he stands at attention until his instructors grant permission to talk. After strongly resisting the rigor and rituals imposed on cadets, the transformation in Christopher has not gone unnoticed by his instructors. They gave him the "Most Improved Cadet" award at the end of the school year. He agreed reluctantly to be a cadet corporal, the highest rank given to sophomores. His GPA is still not stellar, at just over 2.0 out of 4.0, but it's an improvement over his 1.29 at the end of last year's first quarter and the 0.5 he got for a while in middle school.

His mother summed up her gratitude for Forestville: "They seem to have something invested in Christopher."[48]

As is evident from these examples, the military has engaged quite productively with public schools for generations. While "difficult" youngsters may not constitute the bulk of the PMA student bodies, these academies clearly have taken on academically and socially trou-bled youngsters, affirming that the military understands the challenges facing adolescents and their schools. And thus, the military's construc-tive track record of involvement with public schools demonstrates why its methods for reengaging disaffected young people are well worth un-derstanding and applying in public school settings.

8

ChalleNGe: A Successful Case in Point

HOWEVER WELL INTENTIONED educators may be, schools typically address social and emotional development as a peripheral activity at best. They offer it as a course for students and/or teachers or as an extracurricular activity after regular school hours. Some schools, notably those embracing the SDP, view it as an all-encompassing strategy that fundamentally shapes the way schools are organized and operated as well as how the adults, from principals to parents, relate to one another.

Under all these scenarios, SEL must compete for precious time and resources with other priorities considered more urgent and imperative for educational or political reasons. In other words, SEL is seldom perceived, respected, or embedded as an essential, indispensable, nonnegotiable feature of the educational enterprise. For youngsters who are disengaged and dialing out of school, in substantial part because of weak social and emotional skills, this marginalized treatment of SEL helps seal their fate as students destined to fail in school and, oftentimes, in life.

The National Guard Youth ChalleNGe Program, a quasi-military intervention for school dropouts, represents an entirely different paradigm. It treats academic and social development as coequal objectives, and deeply and seamlessly embeds SEL into every facet of the program. The program draws on the Army's authentic commitment to developing the "whole person" that dates back to the 1980s. To paraphrase an adage familiar when I was a child, educators and policymakers could learn a thing or two from ChalleNGe.

Launched in 1993 and operating in more than half of U.S. states, ChalleNGe is an intensive residential program aimed at getting high school dropouts back on track by making basic lifestyle changes through a rigorous program of education, training, and service to the community. The straightforward mission of ChalleNGe is to "intervene in the life of at-risk youth and produce a program graduate with the values, skills, education, and self-discipline necessary to succeed as a positive and productive adult."[1]

Origins

ChalleNGe owes its existence to an unusual confluence of circumstances. In the mid-1970s, I was a partner in an urban affairs consulting firm in New Haven, Connecticut. Around that time, the Taconic Foundation, a small foundation headed by Yale Law School professor John Simon, awarded our firm a grant to examine the nagging issue of why so many black teenagers, particularly males, languished outside the labor market with scant hope of ever getting ahead. And more importantly, to see if we could come up with a creative and potentially effective programmatic response. I served as project leader for the study.

The problem of chronically high unemployment among young black males leaped out from all the data. The theories behind why this was the case ran the gamut from lousy education and stunted social skills to outright discrimination by employers and structural flaws in the labor market. Some economists even spoke of a "dual" labor market. Abstract theories are fine. Reliable statistics that substantiate the scope of a problem are indispensable. Yet for me, the pivotal question, always, is whether there are program interventions that could work and make a big enough difference to attract the attention of policymakers and justify a sizable enough public investment to make a dent in the problem.

As my colleagues and I casted about for ideas about what to propose, I recalled growing up in Washington, D.C. When I was a teenager in the mid to late 1950s, some of my male classmates could have cared less about school. Try as the teachers might, they just could not turn these fellows on to learning. Some were cutups and truants. A few of the boys were what in those days we quaintly called roughnecks, knuckleheads, and thugs who barely avoided reform school. Perhaps they possessed some of those nonacademic "intelligences" that Howard Gardner of

Harvard Graduate School of Education has identified and that made school an unbearable bore.

As soon as they could, these aimless adolescent boys would drop out of school and out of sight. I remember encountering several of them a few years later. Somehow they had managed to enlist in the military, or else they had been drafted. Either way, they strutted about ramrod straight in their crisp uniforms, full of pride and purpose. Since I never served in the military, I was clueless about what had happened to them or how they had been transformed. The radical change in these young people's mind-sets and deportment intrigued and mystified me.

When my colleagues at the consulting firm and I examined the presumed benefits of military service for rudderless boys, we started imagining a contemporary equivalent of the Army experience and came up with the concept of a quasi-military domestic youth corps for dropouts. Essentially, our idea was that youngsters would enroll voluntarily and be assigned to military bases, where they would receive intensive academic training, perform community service, and develop self-discipline.

We were excited by what we thought was a breakthrough idea. I sent a draft description to my mentor at the Ford Foundation, a vice president named Mike Sviridoff, to see if it piqued his interest as well. He replied affirmatively and offered to convene a group of eminent labor economists to hear our case and critique the concept. We trekked to Ford's imposing headquarters in New York City, confident we could persuade these renowned experts that we had discovered the antipoverty equivalent of nuclear fusion.

The economists assembled by Sviridoff listened politely, perhaps even indulgently, as we laid out our concept of the quasi-military youth corps. Then they opened fire from every direction. I do not recall a favorable comment the entire time, although I may have been so shell-shocked that I have repressed virtually all memory of this meeting. None of our responses to their pointed questions satisfied the naysayers.

How to explain the debacle? No doubt there were flaws in our idea and operational issues we had not thought through. But the experts displayed so little curiosity that I remain persuaded to this day that a big reason for the chilly reception was dreadful timing. With the nation emerging in the mid-1970s from the politically fractious Vietnam War, policymakers, government officials, and foundation executives simply were in no mood to embrace a military-like or military-lite solution to a domestic problem, especially one involving young people. Many liberals, presumably like some of the economists in the room, recoiled at the idea of anything that smacked of military. When the meeting ended, we sheepishly zipped up our briefcases, tucked tail, and headed home to New Haven.

By nature I am persistent and patient when convinced the cause is right. So when I joined New Haven City government a couple of years later as Human Resources Administrator, I saw a chance to rekindle the quasi-military corps idea. HRA ran or funded an array of after-school, senior citizen, preschool, and antipoverty programs. A colleague from the consulting firm joined me as the agency's director of strategic planning. Soon after taking office, we approached the head of the local public housing authority, which coped with idle teenagers on a daily basis.

Together we devised a variant of the quasi-military youth corps that would operate within the New Haven Housing Authority. Participants would be assigned to various units in the agency, from the central office and property management to maintenance and landscaping. They would be supervised and mentored by full-time personnel. They would receive training and could climb the ladder of responsibility if they performed well. Those who succeeded might actually land permanent jobs with the agency.

We needed external funding to implement this version of the corps. I intended to use a combination of CETA (the federal public service employment program authorized by the Comprehensive Employment and Training Act) and other federal demonstration grants. However, my funding scheme came a cropper because the CETA funds were deployed, understandably enough, to help curb unemployment during the recession at that time by hiring jobless workers and averting municipal layoffs. Thus this second attempt at launching the quasi-military youth corps proved again to be a nonstarter.

Fast-forward, two careers and a decade later, to the Rockefeller Foundation. In the fall of 1988, I joined the foundation as vice president with responsibility for school reform and equal opportunity. A month after arriving, I attended a school reform conference at Stanford University School of Education. Groggy from jet lag as I sat in the audience, I perked up when one of the speakers—Edmund Gordon, a mentor, distinguished Yale psychologist, and avowed pacifist—ventured the provocative opinion that the conditions in which inner-city teens were being reared were so detrimental that it might be time to consider conscripting them for their own good.

I sat bolt upright and muttered to myself: "Have I got a program idea for you!" Could we, I wondered anew, get one of the branches of the military to create a domestic youth corps for school dropouts? It would operate on military bases, with all of the structure and training of the military, except that kids would perform community service instead of learning to wage war. One of the many privileges of serving as vice president of a proactive foundation like Rockefeller was that I could make modest grants to seed innovative ideas. I decided on the spot to pull the quasi-military corps out of hibernation and try yet again to make it happen. Perhaps the third time would indeed be a charm.

As a check against getting too carried away with the idea, further due diligence was the first order of business. The idea needed once more to run the gauntlet of seasoned experts who would spare no criticism. Eddie Williams, a friend who headed the think tank known as the Joint Center for Political and Economic Studies, put me in touch with a colleague there named Ed Dorn, a former undersecretary of defense who subsequently became dean of the Lyndon Baines Johnson School of Public Administration at the University of Texas in Austin. Dorn in turn convened a cross-section of experts and advocates to vet this idea anew.

I emerged from the spirited exchange at the Joint Center encouraged that, while some still questioned the quasi-military approach, others felt it had considerable merit. Interestingly enough, the doubters tended to be child advocates who typically fret the loudest about the plight of black teenagers. Most valuable of all, that meeting brought me into contact with key players in the defense establishment, including the noted military sociologist Charles Moskos and former assistant secretary of defense Larry Korb.

By then I had become convinced that if the idea was to get anywhere this time, it had to be championed, indeed "owned," by an entity closely associated with and perhaps even embedded within the national defense establishment. I reasoned that an ostensibly liberal foundation like Rockefeller could not carry the water on this one because military officials and experts might dismiss it almost in a reflex action.

Therefore, in my exploratory conversations, I trolled for someone or some entity in the military sphere that would catch the vision and run with it. Pride of authorship took a backseat to propelling the idea. If some strategically situated organization that could aggressively drive the idea wanted to assume ownership, I considered that an institutional and personal sacrifice well worth making.

Aided by Dorn and Korb, I obtained two introductions that, in football parlance, finally helped move the idea downfield. First, I met with William Taylor of the Center for Strategic and International Studies (CSIS), a prominent defense policy think tank in Washington, D.C. He liked the idea immediately and proposed creating a high-profile task force of leading policymakers and military experts to study the feasibility of the concept. Since CSIS had scant experience working with urban youth, I introduced them to friends at Public/Private Ventures, a highly regarded outfit that operated and evaluated youth development programs for at-risk youngsters. My thinking was that the complementary expertise and credibility of these two groups would be immensely useful during the feasibility analysis and once it came to marketing the idea, assuming we got that far.

Invoking the discretion I enjoyed as vice president of the foundation, I authorized grants to CSIS and P/PV to collaborate in conducting the feasibility analysis. The combined grants to these groups over two years totaled a rather modest $372,000. The investment was well worth it. I felt that a "good housekeeping seal of approval" by an esteemed and politically wired think tank like CSIS was crucial to the credibility of the idea inside Pentagon and congressional circles. Working with P/PV, CSIS then established a study group known as the National Community Service for Out-of-School Youth Project, which was cochaired by Senator John McCain and Congressman Dave McCurdy.

The other introduction orchestrated by Larry Korb turned out to be even more of a game changer. In the spring of 1989, I secured an appointment at the Pentagon with General Herbert Temple, the national commander of the National Guard. He was joined by Dan Donohue, the Guard's director of public information. To my utter astonishment, both of them embraced the idea with great enthusiasm and minimal persuasion on my part. I almost could not believe my ears. General Temple surprised me further when he commented that military people basically are youth workers at heart who happen to train their charges to make war, but who can train youngsters to do and be anything.

Without downplaying the CSIS-P/PV effort, General Temple and Dan Donohue said feasibility studies were fine. However, they intended to forge ahead with mobilizing the National Guard to launch the quasi-military corps for dropouts, including rounding up funds from Congress for pilot sites. Little did I realize when I first met him that Donohue is one of those unheralded organizational geniuses inside mammoth institutions who know how to move complex bureaucracies forward and make things happen. In a further stroke of good fortune and fortuitous timing, he had wanted for years to develop an intervention akin to this quasi-military idea, and he was now authorized by his boss to proceed. With General Temple's enthusiastic backing, Donohue focused intently on designing the intervention and persuading Congress to appropriate funds for pilot sites. The CSIS report helped smooth the way in the upper echelons of the Pentagon and the political establishment.

This collective effort spawned what came to be known as the National Guard Youth ChalleNGe Corps (subsequently rebranded the ChalleNGe Program). In 1993, ten pilot sites opened in ten states, including Camp Ella Grasso, in Connecticut. The program design called for participants, all of whom must be school dropouts, to spend five months on a military base. The nation's first contingent of ChalleNGe cadets graduated from Camp Grasso later on in 1993. The U.S. Coast Guard in nearby New London hosted the ceremony, which was covered by CNN. Young people who six months earlier had been written off as borderline worthless strode down the aisle proudly decked out in caps and gowns. An audience of nearly 1,000 parents, grandparents, children, and other well-wishers cheered them on. Some grizzled American Legion veterans bestowed the Legion's traditional "top student" honor on one of the graduates. A chorus made up of participants who first met at the camp sang several tunes, and surprisingly well at that.

I continued proselytizing for the program. Dan Donohue and I even appeared on the nationally syndicated *Montel Williams* television show with a small contingent of ChalleNGe cadets who were spiffily dressed in their uniforms. As a Navy veteran, Williams loved the program. The appearance was a hoot, especially when he staged those corny reunions on camera, like the one between a fellow who had joined ChalleNGe and his father, who never thought he'd amount to "nuthin."

Program Design

Proud as I am of my role in planting the seed for the quasi-military youth corps concept, Dan Donohue is justly recognized as the founder and architect of ChalleNGe. The model he came up with drew on his long-standing commitment to and experience with the "whole person core component model" that he developed in the mid-1980s.[2] During the design phase, he consulted widely with educators, sociologists, behaviorists, law enforcement officials, business leaders, youth program directors, and hundreds of young dropouts. As a result, he decided to focus on young people at greatest risk who had the highest potential for reversal. Donohue envisioned ChalleNGe as "an intervention, rather than a remedial program. We would deal with the symptoms and underlying causes in a construct that fully embraced a 'whole person' change and readied the students for the postprogram environment. We would arm them with the skills and experiences necessary to succeed, and we would ensure there was 'a way back' to mainstream society."[3]

Donohue and his design team further concluded that "an eclectic, whole person intervention was necessary. Our reasoning was that a single-track focus on education, behavior, or discipline alone would not succeed. Our student cohort had deficits well beyond 'just academics.' There were behavior, motivation, attitude, and environmental issues that had to be addressed as part of the greater whole."[4] They made academic excellence the central theme. However, they defined it broadly to encompass obtaining at least a high school diploma or GED certificate, as well attaining functional literacy so that the graduates would be employable and productive.

The ChalleNGe model assumed that four factors primarily influence youngsters' growth, development, and maturation. These pivotal influences are families, schools, peers, and communities. Ideally these influences should impact youngsters favorably and foster healthy growth. Yet as Donohue realized, these forces can be counterproductive for many youngsters and result in dysfunctional behaviors, unhelpful relationships and affiliations, and inappropriate or self-defeating coping mechanisms.[5]

In 1993, the National Guard Youth ChalleNGe Program began operation with pilot sites in ten states. Donohue's design called for participants to spend 22 weeks on a military base. They would be immersed in an experience approximating the kind of vigorous, highly structured regimen expected of a military operation. The curriculum, drawn from years of Pentagon research and experience, aimed to improve their life-coping skills and employment potential.

These days the ChalleNGe Program operates 34 sites in 27 states, Puerto Rico, and the District of Columbia. The number of sites vacillates slightly depending on the fiscal condition of participating states. The program serves upwards of 5,000 young people annually. Since its inception in 1993, more than 115,000 former dropouts have graduated from ChalleNGe. Participating states operate under a Master Cooperative Agreement with the National Guard Bureau. Most states run a single 100-bed program serving 200 youngsters in two cycles. A few states operate multiple sites. The funding level—about $14,000 per participant—is basically unchanged since the program's inception. For most of ChalleNGe's existence, the Defense Department paid 60 percent of the cost, while states covered 40 percent, with some supplemental funding from other federal agencies, like Justice and Labor, as well as a few corporations. In recent years, Congress boosted the federal share to 75 percent, presumably to help ChalleNGe weather the economic crisis by reducing the state share.

Over the years, the ChalleNGe program became a favorite of politicians whose constituents needed somewhere to send youngsters they could not handle or who were adrift. I once introduced myself to President Bill Clinton and Senate Majority Leader Trent Lott at a gala dinner in Washington, D.C., in the mid-1990s. When I mentioned in the next breath my association with ChalleNGe, broad grins crossed their faces as they told me how much they liked the program. As further indication of the program's popularity, the Youth ChalleNGe Foundation, a nonprofit support organization, stages an annual fundraising gala in Washington, D.C., that draws several thousand paying patrons plus members of Congress, Pentagon brass, governors, "first spouses," and entertainment celebrities.

The program serves 16- to 18-year-olds who have dropped out or been expelled from school. They can be unemployed or underemployed, but they must be drug-free, never convicted of a felony, and not on parole, probation, or under indictment.[6] In a survey conducted by MDRC, participants described themselves as 88 percent male, 42 percent white, 34 percent African American, and the remainder primarily Latino.[7] Some came from inner-city neighborhoods saddled with violence, drugs, and poverty. Others hailed from middle-class and even upper-class homes, with parents who were professionally employed. The participants also varied in terms of educational preparedness (from elementary school level to beyond high school) and performance within the program. Some were second-chance participants, having been dismissed previously.

The survey helps fill out the picture of who joins the program.[8] According to MDRC, "As expected, the participants . . . had not done well in school before leaving. About half reported that their grades had been mostly Ds and Fs, and more than 80 percent reported that they had been suspended from school at least once. Nearly one-third reported that they had an Individual Education Plan, which indicates special education status."[9] Roughly one-third admitted they had used drugs or alcohol, a pattern that MDRC believes may have been understated.

Supplemental interviews conducted by MDRC illuminated the cadets' lives prior to joining ChalleNGe. There were common themes that tend to explain why young people enroll in rigorous programs like this one. These include: "disengagement from school (truancy, disruptive behavior, disrespect for teachers and school authority, a sense that teachers did not care about them, victimization by bullies), conflict with parents (disrespectful behavior, family disintegration or dysfunction, parental substance abuse, physical abuse), negative social environments (gangs, violence, drug sales and use, poverty), a history of substance abuse, and a desire to have a GED or a diploma even though they were far behind in school."[10]

The ChalleNGe experience consists of a 22-week residential phase, typically on an underutilized military base, followed by a one-year postresidential mentoring phase. Participation begins with a two-week pre-ChalleNGe orientation period, also on the military base, where they are preliminarily exposed to the experience that awaits them and screened for suitability and readiness for the rigors ahead. Those who clear this hurdle then segue to the heart of the program, namely the 20-week residential phase.

According to Dan Bloom, the pre-ChalleNGe phase serves as an adjustment period for young people whose lives were unstructured. They may have been disengaged from school, defiant of parental authority, using drugs or alcohol, unemployed, and unencumbered by any schedule or responsibilities. In the program, they are expected to live completely structured lives. The transition can be a rude awakening for some adolescents. This orientation phase is dominated by physical instruction. As Bloom notes, "Candidates . . . go through a process of detoxification from their former lifestyle during these early weeks of the program."[11] They do so under the constant scrutiny of the so-called cadre, the military veterans on staff who supervise and monitor them around the clock. In a preview of rituals to come, candidates who successfully complete pre-ChalleNGe are promoted to cadet status in a culminating ceremony. Roughly 18 percent of enlistees wash out in the grueling early going, which is aimed at determining who has the ability and gumption to persevere.[12]

The heart of ChalleNGe is the 20-week residential phase that follows. It focuses on generating basic lifestyle changes through a rigorous regimen of education, training, and service to the community.[13] As might be expected, cadets wear uniforms and their hair is cut short. They live in barracks and belong to platoons and squads. They are subjected to military-style discipline and closely supervised by the cadre on staff. The tight structure is designed to minimize some potentially negative effects of placing many at-risk young people together in a setting where they would otherwise be exposed to negative peer influences or peer contagion.[14] As a result, cadets have scant unstructured time. Their days are chock-full of purposeful activity built around eight core program components summarized below. As the residential phase continues, the instructional approach evolves from "teach" to "coach." The cadets start assuming more leadership responsibility and disciplining themselves and one another, under close supervision of the cadre and other staff. They rotate through roles of leading their squads, platoon, and, in some cases, even entire company.[15]

The third and final facet of ChalleNGe commences midway through the residential phase. That is when the cadets are paired with volunteer mentors from their communities, often of their own choosing, who stick with them for one year after they graduate. These mentors work with the graduates to help sustain the positive new outlook and lifestyle engendered by ChalleNGe. They also aid the young people in coping with problems that may arise, encourage them to complete their educations, and assist with landing jobs and applying to college or training programs.

Key Components

What distinguishes ChalleNGe from some other interventions focused on youngsters who have disengaged from school or dropped out is the totality of its approach to turning around their lives and life prospects. Drawing on years of Pentagon research and experience, the program design aims to improve participants' academic proficiency, life-coping skills, and employment potential. The eight core components described below reflect the National Guard's authentic commitment to the academic and social development of whole adolescents.

Academic Excellence—This component entails a dramatic shift in the cadets' routines. Having previously dropped out of school, they resume attending classes and face demanding instructors on a daily basis. There they prepare for the high school diploma, GED (General Education Development) certificate, or, failing those credentials, improved reading and math proficiency. Most cadets pursue the GED. At the other end of the continuum, some sites actually offer courses with college credits.

Leadership/Followership—As MDRC describes this unique component, "cadets begin to learn followership from day one, as they learn to heed the instructions of cadre, teachers, and other adults. They also begin to learn to follow one another as the cycle goes on, as opportunities arise for individual cadets to lead."[16] In keeping with the chain of command, they all get the opportunity to lead their own squad at least once, and based on their performance, some will lead larger contingents of cadets.[17]

Responsible Citizenship—In this component, cadets study what Donohue calls the critical dimensions of life in American democracy, including the rights and obligations of citizens, the voting process, the responsibilities of various levels of government, and the U.S. legal system. In addition to course work, cadets gain practical experience by participating in student government, developing and enforcing standards of conduct, meeting with elected officials, and assisting at state legislative functions.

Service to the Community—Cadets devote at least 40 hours to community service projects that enhance their awareness of community needs while providing opportunities for career exploration. Illustrative service projects include tutoring in schools and after-school programs, visiting the elderly, assisting with roadway cleanup and disaster preparedness, and, in the case of Hurricane Katrina, helping with post-storm cleanup. As Donohue explains, these activities also provide opportunities for experiential and applied learning since the cadets must design and organize their projects, estimate the supplies needed, and execute the plan.[18]

Life-Coping Skills—Through a combination of classroom instruction and discussion along with the structured living environment, cadets develop skills and strategies for dealing with anger, stress, and frustration. The life skills that are cultivated include managing peer pressure, making choices, interpersonal relations, parenting, household management, and use and abuse of drugs and alcohol. Cadets also learn to manage personal finances, sometimes through classes given by local banks and credit unions.[19]

Physical Fitness—Physical fitness is a core component used to build team spirit and improve conditioning, especially for youngsters who enter the program woefully out of shape. The fitness program is based on the President's Challenge, a battery of tests using data collected from several sources, including the President's Council on Physical Fitness and the Amateur Athletic Union Physical Fitness Program. Cadets participate in the Marine-sponsored nationwide high school physical fitness competitions. For young people accustomed to failure, physical fitness provides a tangible means of demonstrating improvement and developing self-esteem.[20]

Health and Hygiene—When they enter the program, most cadets have unhealthy eating habits and many have been sexually active.[21] Through classroom instruction and group discussions, they examine the benefits of proper nutrition and hygiene, as well as the effects of substance abuse and sexually transmitted diseases. Not surprisingly, junk food is banned except on special occasions.

Job Skills—Consistent with Donohue's design, this component uses a mix of academic instruction, mentoring, and applied learning.[22] Although the content and methods vary somewhat, the sites typically focus on exploring career options, developing résumés, filling out job applications, and preparing, dressing, and sitting for job interviews. Some sites offer job-specific training. According to Donohue, the goal is to help cadets determine their career interests and options, develop a plan for attaining their goals, and create experiences that enhance their ability to meet them. This often entails establishing mentoring relationships with employers and unions.

Academic Environment

Each core component features its own curriculum and criteria for gauging the cadets' knowledge and competency. The courses of instruction for each component are derived from national and state standards. To graduate from ChalleNGe, cadets must demonstrate at least 80 percent proficiency on the competency measures for each component.[23] In a notable departure from the fixation on tests in traditional schools, the ChalleNGe assessments are based on a combination of written tests, oral examinations, and observed progress.

For most students, MDRC noted, the academic component of ChalleNGe is quite different from what they experienced in their high schools. Teachers at local ChalleNGe sites exercise some discretion in developing their syllabi and organizing instruction as they see fit. As a result, ChalleNGe instructors believe the program delivers more education in less time than traditional high schools. Instructors typically utilize computer-assisted learning programs geared to specific cadet needs in concert with classroom instruction and individual tutoring.[24] In this respect, ChalleNGe is well ahead of most public schools, which are just beginning to introduce so-called blended learning that mixes traditional teaching with computer-assisted instruction. Like their peers in traditional schools, many teachers use lectures, labs, and workbooks.

The distinctive approach to instruction in ChalleNGe makes a difference to the cadets and staff alike. MDRC commented, "In all cases . . . the instruction appears to be interactive: Students are able to receive high levels of personal attention. The relatively small classroom size and the commitment of the instructors facilitate this individualized approach."[25] Cadets notice and appreciate the personalized instruction and attention as well. "Many cadets described high school classrooms that were overcrowded, taught by indifferent teachers, and somewhat chaotic and lacking discipline."[26] MDRC continues, "Cadets welcomed the small class size, tailored instruction, and self-paced approach, and most of those interviewed were responding well. . . . Even the students who reported that they were still struggling somewhat with their classes reported positive academic experiences in ChalleNGe."

Staff members appreciate the instructional climate in ChalleNGe. In contrast to typical high schools, those who have daily contact with cadets pointed to the "distraction-free environment" in ChalleNGe and the emphasis on teaching young people about choices as a key to the program's success. They see the cadets as individuals and work to build their self-esteem. "It's not about tearing these kids down," staff members told the researchers. "You need to build them up."[27]

The differences between traditional schools and ChalleNGe do not end there, according to MDRC. "Both the classroom environment and the cadets' behavior are different in ChalleNGe. This is largely due to the foundation of discipline throughout the program. The program prepares cadets for the classroom experience by training them on proper conduct, including proper dress, addressing others with respect, and following instructions without arguing—and by meting out consequences for failure to follow these rules. Many cadets noted that not talking back, in particular, was difficult for them to do before they came to ChalleNGe."[28]

The military mentors, or cadre, establish a ubiquitous presence in

ChalleNGe, with about one cadre member for every four students. "To reinforce standards of behavior," MDRC observed, "the cadre remain with the cadets in the classroom (or just outside the door). Their presence tends to quell any latent tendencies to fall back into patterns of insubordination. Cadets who act out in the classroom are removed immediately by the cadre and counseled. Thus, instruction can continue for the other cadets, and the cadre can seek a solution to the problem of the individual cadet."[29] Teachers in ChalleNGe commented that the removal of the discipline function from their duties increases their ability to focus on instruction, meet students' needs, and accomplish curricular program goals.[30]

As Donohue explains, the educators, behaviorists, and cadre work as a team to craft individual learning plans for each youngster. In addition, they help the cadets develop plans for life after ChalleNGe. Together they map out a customized plan with realistic short, intermediate, and long-term goals coupled with a delineation of the resources needed to realize them. The goal is to enable cadets to achieve the highest level of performance and competency possible.[31]

Staffing Configuration

The staffing patterns at ChalleNGe sites differ markedly from traditional schools. According to Donohue, "We recognized that no one career field was capable of meeting the varied needs and objectives, so we developed a triad of broad specialties. While ChalleNGe is built on a quasi-military model, it is not a military program. The staff is comprised of a team of state-certified educators, state-certified social, career, and psychological counselors, and a state-selected cadre of full-time personnel, most of whom are military veterans, military retirees, or members of the Guard and reserves working . . . as civilian employees. No one field is more important than the other—they carry equal weight and importance—the legs of a three-legged stool, if you will."[32]

The program director and deputy director oversee all program elements. The director focuses on external matters—marketing, fundraising, policy, state and federal relations, and community relations, while the deputy director concentrates on internal responsibilities.[33] Next, the commandant is responsible for ensuring the safety of cadets, training the cadre, and monitoring and training cadets by maintaining the daily schedule, including what they do throughout the day. The commandant may also be responsible for the community service component.

The cadre members constitute the staff unit that is truly unique to ChalleNGe. They report to the commandant. They are considered the heart of the program since they have the most direct and frequent contact with the cadets. They are the adults that cadets turn to for guidance and support. Cadre members come from a variety of backgrounds. Most have military experience. Many attended a leadership school during the course of their military careers, where they learned specific techniques that bear directly on their work as members of the ChalleNGe cadre.

Cadre members manage and monitor the cadets' activities around the clock, with two shifts during the cadets' waking hours and one night shift. Most of their job involves listening to and counseling the cadets.[34] Cadre members directly supervise the cadets and correct behavior on the spot. They see to it that cadets attend to personal hygiene and dress appropriately. They even sit in classrooms and patrol the area around classrooms. They conduct physical training activities as well as drill and ceremony exercises. They also monitor cadets' homework activities in the evening. Overall, their job is to keep cadets on task throughout the day.

As for the remaining staff, local sites typically employ six full-time instructors and most have more. Some hire their instructors directly. Others draw them from the local school district and community colleges. Instructors teach the academic courses, whether geared to high school diplomas or GED. These courses include math, science, writing and language arts, and computer skills. In addition to academic courses, the instructors may teach portions of other core components, such as responsible citizenship and job skills. They often handle some extra-curricular activities.

The counselors on staff typically hold bachelor or master's degrees in psychology, social work, mental health, alcohol and drug counseling, or school counseling. In some programs, they focus mainly on placement matters and refer cadets out for therapeutic counseling if needed. At other sites, counselors provide both placement and psychological counseling.[35] While counselors have no supervisory responsibilities, cadets confide in them about problems that their parents or other staff may not be aware of.

The staff divvies up responsibility for the nonacademic core components, with the division of labor varying by site. Cadre members typically run the leadership, followership, and physical fitness components. Counselors often handle life coping and job skills, as well as health and hygiene. As would be expected, teachers take the lead with the academic and citizenship components. Some commandants manage the community service component.

As is evident by now, the mission and structure of ChalleNGe differ strikingly from traditional schools, particularly in ChalleNGe's unabashed commitment to advancing students' academic and social development. The core components, curriculum, and staff composition reflect the duality of its mission. The critical question, to which we turn next, is whether and to what extent this unique intervention succeeds with youngsters who have disengaged from school to the point of dropping out. And if it indeed works, are there lessons we can draw from ChalleNGe that would inform the design of a new educational and developmental paradigm for youngsters who are struggling futilely in school and in life?

9

Impact and Implications of ChalleNGe

Does ChalleNGe indeed make a difference in the lives of young-sters who complete the program? And if so, is it a wise, cost-effective investment for society? For most of the program's existence, the National Guard kept statistics on cadets' high school graduation rates, GED completion rates, and other indicators of how the youngsters fared once they were finished. Yet this method of assessment was less than scientifically rigorous since it did not randomly assign youngsters to the program and to a control group and then compare results.

This evidentiary weakness ended in 2005 when MDRC, one of the premier evaluation outfits, embarked on a random assignment evaluation of ChalleNGe. Applicants, all of whom met the criteria for admission, were alternately assigned to the program and to a control group. In 2005–2006, some 3,000 applicants for ChalleNGe entered the study at ten sites and were randomly assigned to groups of program participants or nonparticipating controls.[1] MDRC surveyed the participants and nonparticipants three times over the course of three years. The first time was nine months after they entered the study and not long after the cadets finished the residential phase.[2] The second happened roughly 21 months after entry.[3] The third survey occurred three years after participants entered the program.[4]

The fact that the findings stem from a random assignment evaluation conducted by one of the leading firms in the field lends important credence to the impacts and implications presented in the report. What's more, the MDRC evaluation provided the evidentiary foundation for a companion assessment that is rather rare among social programs. The RAND Corporation conducted a rigorous cost-benefit analysis that shed important light on whether and to what extent ChalleNGe is a valuable and thus convincing investment for society.

The impacts reported by MDRC, roughly three years after cadets entered and more than a year after the postresidential phase ended, were mostly positive and significant, although some results were equivocal. On the favorable side of the ledger:

- Cadets in ChalleNGe were much more likely than controls to have obtained high school diplomas or GED certificates. The proportions were 72 percent vs. 55 percent, respectively.

- Participants were more likely than nonparticipants to have received vocational training, earned college credits, or enrolled in college. For instance, 40 percent of cadets received vocational training compared to 33 percent of nonparticipants. Cadets were twice as likely to have completed at least one college course for credit. While fewer than a quarter of former cadets were furthering their education or taking training courses, a higher percentage of cadets compared with controls were enrolled in college courses.

- Program graduates were significantly more likely to be employed. The relative proportions here were 58 percent vs. 51 percent, respectively.

- Moreover, participants on average earned 20 percent, or $2,266, more per year than the control group. The former averaged $240 in earnings per week compared with $210 for the latter.

- Overall, during the year prior to the MDRC survey, participants were employed for 8 out of the 12 months in contrast to 7 out of 12 for controls.

- On the family front, ChalleNGe graduates were less likely than controls to be living with their parents. One-quarter of former cadets were living in their own home as opposed to one-fifth of controls. Similar proportions of both groups were reported to be married or living with a partner. Just over a quarter of former cadets either indicated they had at least one child or, in the case of females, said they were pregnant.[5]

Other impacts were unimpressive, perhaps surprisingly so. Some advantages enjoyed by participants as of MDRC's first report on early results weakened by the third and final one. By then, there were no consistent differences between the former cadets and the control group when it came to criminal activity or civic engagement.[6] Military enlistment rates were similar. There was little distinction between them when it came to personal health, patterns of sexual activity, or incidence of substance abuse. Interestingly enough, graduates were also more likely to be overweight and less likely to use birth control.

Despite the equivocal findings about pregnancy, there are intriguing indications from some sites that ChalleNGe can potentially help curb teenage pregnancy. According to Andrea Kane of the National Campaign to Prevent Teen and Unplanned Pregnancy, the ChalleNGe programs in Louisiana and Georgia have begun using an evidence-based pregnancy curriculum. Georgia tailors one curriculum for girls and another for boys.[7] Kane reports that the early indications from both sites are encouraging, although it is too early for either to have been subjected to rigorous evaluation. This experience suggests that ChalleNGe programs that use carefully designed, evidence-based approaches might become more effective vehicles for improving health and lifestyle outcomes for participants.

MDRC found no clear explanation for the ambiguous results, although it did note that the program appeared to yield more positive effects on older participants. ChalleNGe staff reported that younger participants were more difficult to work with because they generally were less focused and mature. The results may also have been impacted by the reality that the younger 16- and 17-year-old cadets have fewer placement options once they graduate.

The MDRC findings stand out among studies of interventions for disadvantaged young people. In particular, the evaluators cited the staying power of some of the positive impacts of ChalleNGe, while acknowledging that the advantages weakened but did not disappear over time.[8] During the last three decades, MDRC commented, various programs focused on disadvantaged youth have undergone rigorous evaluations.[9] The results of many so-called second-chance programs are mixed. None of the studies that followed participants for more than a couple of years found lasting improvements in economic outcomes.

In some cases, early gains in earnings faded over time.

ChalleNGe stands out by comparison. As MDRC noted, the main goals of its residential phase are to help participants obtain a secondary school credential and develop attitudes and behavior patterns that will help them succeed in the future as students, workers, and citizens. The evaluation's qualitative and quantitative data indicate that the program succeeds in this respect for many participants.

Yet the data also suggest that it is difficult for many young people to maintain momentum after completing the program in a society and labor market with constricted opportunities for young people who have limited family support and do not follow a linear trajectory through high school and on to college. MDRC found that several of the program's key impacts diminished in size over time. The in-depth interviews revealed that some program graduates appeared, like many people their age, to have difficulty gaining a firm foothold in college or the labor market.[10]

One can only speculate how much brighter the outcomes might have been for the cadets—as well as for the controls—had they graduated into a more normal economy instead of one ravaged by the most horrific recession since the Great Depression. Would the opportunities customarily available in a reasonably tight labor market have provided ample encouragement and incentive for even more of the cadets to build on the ChalleNGe experience by forging ahead with their educations and careers? In a healthier labor market, these young people would face far less competition for entry-level jobs from more mature applicants with stronger credentials. In a "normal" job market, would the sizable initial advantage that the cadets enjoyed over the controls have narrowed as much or perhaps even have widened due to the leg up provided by ChalleNGe?

Since the MDRC evaluation has run its course, we will never know whether the demonstrated advantages gained by investing in the cadets' academic and social development will resume growing as the youngsters mature and as the economy gradually recovers. The delayed, long-term benefits of interventions like career academies and high-quality child care offer reason for encouragement that the differential between cadets and controls may widen over time.

The cost-benefit analysis conducted by RAND concluded that ChalleNGe pays significant dividends to society.[11] RAND based its projections on MDRC's finding that the principal benefit of the program consists of the increases in educational attainment, employment, and earnings. When the program effects were measured three years following randomization, the cadets averaged only 20 years of age. Research suggests that the benefits of obtaining higher levels of education accrue over an entire lifetime. Therefore, according to RAND, estimating the full benefits requires first calculating how education affects lifetime earnings.[12] Drawing on published research, RAND calculated that the effects of receiving a high school diploma and attending a year or more of college would be substantial. However, earning a GED does not generate a statistically significant increase in earnings.

Table 2 summarizes RAND's estimated benefits and costs per cadet. Since I lack the technical expertise to critique RAND's cost-benefit methodology, I must rely on its reputation for caution and integrity. To be fair, the researchers acknowledged some uncertainty with their methodology.[13] Let me recapitulate RAND's rendition of how it arrived at its findings. After establishing the operating cost per cadet, RAND set about estimating the benefits and costs of the youngsters' involvement in the program. The most obvious effect of educational attainment and vocational training is on labor market outcomes such as employment and earnings. Moreover, RAND contends that to estimate the full benefits of a program, it is necessary to project how education affects lifetime earnings.

RAND further observed that educational attainment is correlated with many other outcomes that have private and social value, including reduced social welfare dependency, lower criminal activity, improved health, greater happiness, more active civic engagement, and improved economic growth. Since the causal relationship between education and these nonfinancial outcomes is much less well established, RAND opted to focus its cost-benefit analysis on labor market outcomes, notably lifetime earnings. Social welfare dependency was not directly measured by the MDRC evaluation. Therefore, RAND calculated the potential benefit by estimating the effect of educational attainment at age 20 on subsequent social welfare dependency.

Other ambiguous or even negative findings from the MDRC evaluation complicated RAND's calculations. RAND factored in savings from

Table 2 Baseline Cost-Benefit Comparison [14]

COSTS	
Operating costs	-11,633
Opportunity costs	-2,058
Deadweight loss of taxation	-1,745
Total costs	-15,436
BENEFITS	
Lifetime earnings	43,514
Cost of education	-4,860
Social welfare dependency	249
Criminal activity	662
Service to community	423
Deadweight loss of taxation	997
Total benefits	40,985
COST-BENEFIT COMPARISON	
Net benefits	25,549
Benefit-cost ratio	2.66
RETURN ON INVESTMENT	
Internal rate of return	6.4%

early reductions in criminal activity even though they did not hold up as of 36 months. At the time of the initial nine-month survey, participants were less likely than controls to have been arrested or convicted of crime and less likely than controls to have been incarcerated over the previous 9 to 12 months. At the time of the 21-month survey, the participants were still less likely to have been convicted of crime. They also reported being involved in fewer violent incidents and property crimes. Yet none of these effects were evident as of the 36-month survey.

The MDRC evaluation revealed no consistent or statistically significant differences in various life skills or civic engagement. In terms of their health, participants were more likely to report being in good or excellent health and less likely to be obese as of the nine-month survey. But these gains dissipated by the time of the 21-month and 36-month surveys. Interestingly enough, MDRC even found that former cadets were more likely than controls to have used illegal drugs, less likely to always use birth control, and more likely to have had a child.

These inconsistencies in reported impacts notwithstanding, RAND arrived at a bottom-line estimate of the effects of participation in ChalleNGe:

> Subtracting the estimated present discounted value of costs from benefits, we find that, for each admitted cadet, the program generates net benefits of $25,549. Total benefits of $40,985 are 2.66 times total costs, implying that the ChalleNGe program generates $2.66 in benefits for every dollar spent on the program. The estimated return on investment (net benefits divided by costs) in the ChalleNGe program is 166 percent.[15]

Actually, RAND believes that the net benefits could be even greater. As it stated: "Because higher educational attainment yields benefits to individuals and society that are not fully captured in the outcomes considered here, it is likely that, all else being equal, these benefit estimates understate the social return on investment in the ChalleNGe program, although to what extent is unknown."[16] The bottom line of RAND's cost-benefit analysis is clear: the costlier investment in the academic and social development of dropouts pays impressive dividends for the young people and for society.

There are caveats, however.[17] As RAND cautioned, the participants in ChalleNGe do not constitute a representative sample of all high school dropouts. In fact, one can readily imagine a more problematic cohort, all of whom come from poor families, tough neighborhoods, and dysfunctional peer groups, and who lack the motivation to volunteer for an emotionally and physically taxing program like ChalleNGe. After all, cadets must meet certain eligibility criteria. Local ChalleNGe programs exercise discretion over how to target their recruitment efforts to achieve particular racial balance and to select eligible cadets who they believe are likely to succeed in the program. Lastly, participation is voluntary. The decision to enroll may be a result of important personal characteristics, such as motivation and self-discipline, that set them apart from the most difficult and unreachable segment of the dropout population.

Dan Donohue, the architect of ChalleNGe, sees other limitations in the cost-benefit analysis.[18] He worries that it does not do adequate justice to the intervention. He argues that it fails to reflect the program's holistic analysis or take full account of the whole-person intervention model as reflected in the eight core components. RAND focused on education and its impacts, while the seven other core components received less attention. Donohue acknowledges that he may have created a model that, at least thus far, defies comprehensive quantification using available assessment protocols. To date, he contends, no one has successfully designed and validated a model attuned to a holistic intervention like ChalleNGe.

Donohue argues further that a cost-benefit analysis is not the same as a cost-avoidance analysis. In fact, the tools for the latter probably are imperfect or may not even exist. Another shortcoming of both studies is that the time horizons for capturing and analyzing the impacts of interventions are often so short-term that crucial longer-range impacts may never be detected. Were it not for the longer-term horizon, for instance, we would never know about the significant yet latent economic and noneconomic benefits captured by evaluations of career academies and high-quality preschool education.

An illuminating, albeit unscientific, method of assessing ChalleNGe can be gleaned from the comments of cadets and their parents. MDRC conducted three surveys of participants. By the final one, most of them were 20 years old.[19] MDRC did in-depth telephone interviews with two dozen of these ChalleNGe alumni who, in fairness, were not a representative sample even of the cadet population but who were considered motivated.

As MDRC observed in its final report, "the young people who were interviewed spoke fondly of the ChalleNGe program and described how their participation had resulted in profound, positive changes in their attitudes, expectations, and self-confidence." Nearly all the interviewees described a striking transformation in their attitudes and self-confidence as a result of their participation in ChalleNGe. The respondents indicated that the program made them aware of their own potential and cultivated a sense of worthiness and agency. While high school had not been working for them, and although many did not like ChalleNGe at first, they all appreciated the combination of the strict regimen and individualized support they experienced.[20]

The evaluators noted that many of the interviewees expressed particular appreciation for the program's structure and discipline. Ironically, while not all of them had positive feelings about it right away, many strongly emphasized that this aspect of ChalleNGe was what they ended up liking the most.[21] According to the interviews, the structure of the residential period offered something of a clean slate. Many of them struggled to maintain the attitudes and behaviors they had learned in the program. Yet they acknowledged that ChalleNGe enabled them to break bad habits, understand the consequences of actions they might have taken impulsively in the past, and focus their attention on what they needed to do to succeed in the future.

Several of the interviewees explicitly pointed to the heightened sense of responsibility they gained in ChalleNGe. As one graduate who was training to become a firefighter put it, "To achieve a goal, you have to put your mind to it. ChalleNGe taught me how to really do that, how to see that you really have to achieve a lot of small stuff to get to the big stuff, so that [when you get out] you can actually have a thought process about what you need to do to deal with the situation."[22]

MDRC added that those who felt they had made the greatest progress after ChalleNGe repeatedly described to the interviewers how they had made a conscious effort to avoid the kinds of social interactions that had gotten them into trouble before, such as "hanging out on the street," and drinking. MDRC continued: "Those interviewees who did associate with their old friends conveyed a sense that they were maintaining stronger boundaries in their social interactions, that they knew how to 'do their own thing' and would not get pulled back into the behavior that had gotten them into trouble before."[23]

One young man who had gotten into repeated trouble for fighting in school described the way the program continued to influence his thinking. "When I'm in a [potentially violent] situation now," he commented, "I put myself back where I was three years ago . . . and I can apply what I learned there. For the first time, I haven't lashed out at anyone. I've learned how to keep a clear head and mind." Another graduate said, "It was an experience that I needed—I needed someone to push me. ChalleNGe pushed me to my limit. I never really had anyone that said: 'You can do this.' That's what they did. I also got a lot of common sense out of the program. I learned how to think for myself instead of following everyone else."[24]

Nevertheless, MDRC found that overall, most respondents agreed they were not as far along as they would have liked in meeting their education and employment goals and fulfilling their desire to live on their own. In spite of this inconsistent progress, most did not report lapsing back to extremes, such as drinking and doing excessive drugs, getting arrested, or hanging out with the wrong people.[25]

Regrettably, both the survey and the in-depth telephone interviews with ChalleNGe graduates indicate that many of them struggled to maintain momentum after leaving the residential program and returning home, where they had relatively few supports and also faced the brutal job market of the Great Recession and the sluggish recovery following its supposed end. Their travails should come as no surprise. As MDRC noted, "Various studies have shown that young adults and low-skilled workers have been among the hardest hit by the economic recession. The fact that most of the ChalleNGe graduates had, at best, obtained either a high school diploma or a GED meant that they were still at a disadvantage compared with those who had more employment experience or educational credentials."[26]

By the time of the interviews, most of the cadets had earned their GEDs in the program. Few of them had made much additional educational progress. Several started college but had difficulty gaining traction. Most had held two or more low-skilled, low-wage jobs. Thus the labor market experiences were mixed, especially as time wore on. Every interviewee had found work relatively quickly upon returning home, usually in fast-food chains or retail stores, or in manual labor. These jobs are consistent with what one would expect a 19- or 20-year-old with little work experience to find. Yet many interviewees did not hold on to their jobs for long and expressed a desire to get a better, higher-paying job or to pursue an educational goal.

The cadets' experiences are not unusual for young people in their early 20s.[27] They commonly start and stop their education due to conflicting pressures, particularly for those who must pay for their own education.[28] MDRC's own research on community college students suggests that many want to earn a degree, but are hindered by competing demands of work, family, and school. In addition, their progress may be impeded by poorly tailored instruction, insufficient financial aid, or inadequate student services.

The stalled momentum and labor market difficulties notwithstanding, MDRC was struck by the impact of ChalleNGe on the emotional and coping skills of the cadets they surveyed. While the reported results showed no significant impacts on leadership and life-coping measures, "the graduates who were interviewed repeatedly spoke about these themes without being prompted." In MDRC's view, "The program appeared to have a real effect on these graduates' belief in their own ability to succeed with enough work. It is possible that the program exposed them to a heightened sense of possibility, which could make goals such as college and skilled employment seem more real than they otherwise would have."[29]

The interviews suggest that the relatively short duration of the program, coupled with weaknesses in the postresidential mentoring phase, may have stunted the graduates' progress, especially given the dicey labor market. As MDRC noted, "The program was a transformative experience in their understanding of themselves and their capabilities. However, the abrupt end of services and inconsistent mentoring left them largely reliant on the supports that already existed in their lives. For some, this meant very little support." Given their youth and the problems they had before they entered ChalleNGe, MDRC commented, the interviewees' struggles to gain a foothold in the labor market and make strides in their education are not inconsistent with those of many of their peers. "Low-wage jobs and inconsistent engagement in post-secondary education are common experiences among young people, particularly those with fewer supports and resources."[30]

As MDRC summed up its takeaways from this informal assessment of ChalleNGe, "What was most salient from the interviews were the graduates' descriptions of their attitudinal development and self-esteem. Many attributed an enhanced sense of leadership and potential to the support that they received at ChalleNGe—a novel experience for many of them. Several described the combination of structure and encouragement as integral aspects of the program."[31] MDRC continues: "Even two years after completing the program's Residential Phase, the graduates who were interviewed pointed to the experience as a turning point in their understanding of what steps they would need to take to move toward their goals. In spite of continuing difficulties many of them faced, they spoke with an understanding that they were responsible for their own progress and that they would have to take initiative to move in a positive direction."[32]

The perspectives of parents help fill out the picture of the program's benefits. Here, too, the comments that follow are anecdotal. But they convey the potential of ChalleNGe to turn around the lives of deeply troubled teenagers.

> "Our son, Devin . . . was on the path of self-destruction. . . . The constant skipping of school (which reflected on his report card straight Ds, Fs), lying, being disrespectful to authority, sneaking out of the house at all hours of the night, experimenting with alcohol . . . was getting him nowhere except in a lot of trouble and he knew it. Devin enrolled in the ChalleNGe Corps, the National Guard program for dropouts. When he came home to visit . . . we witnessed a young man with respect, dignity, and a positive outlook on life. . . . Devin is now in the top five percentile of his class. . . ."[33]
>
> —Devin's mother

> "I gave YC [Youth ChalleNGe program] an angry, confused, unhappy child, and you returned to me a not so confused, a happier, and somewhat not so angry young man. You gave me a young man with a purpose, a goal, and foundation to be a man. Also, just as important, I received back a young man who still managed to keep his uniqueness and his weird sense of humor (which I love)."[34]
>
> — Deborah Hughes of Georgia

> "My son lost interest in school (ADD), because he didn't understand, therefore he was retained to ninth grade for the third time. He was hanging around the wrong crowd, smoking and drinking, and had a very bad anger toward me, his mother. Being a single mom, I had to work and lost control over him. My son started Youth ChalleNGe in Fort Stewart, Georgia, in January 2004.

When I picked him up on his pass for the weekend, I couldn't believe that I picked up the same child that I had dropped off. He was courteous, seemed so grown-up, even told me, 'Mom, I realize I'm becoming a man.' And the biggest difference, he was a gentleman toward me and a very helpful big brother."[35]

— Angel of Georgia

ChalleNGe profoundly affected the attitudes of these former dropouts about themselves and their progression toward adulthood. "When asked to reflect on the program's enduring effect on their outlook, the interviewees consistently described a maturation that one would not expect from a five-month period. Of course, as has been noted, those who were interviewed were not representative of all program participants. . . . But nonetheless, it is noteworthy that their descriptions of ChalleNGe's effect on their self-understanding and outlooks tended to cluster around a small group of themes: confidence and responsibility, feeling of self-control, and sense of leadership and potential."[36]

Many issues and implications flow from the evaluation and cost-benefit analysis of the Youth ChalleNGe Program. In my view, two sets of enduring impacts suggest that the model may hold insights and lessons for the design of a new generation of educational and developmental entities devoted to youngsters who patently have disengaged from traditional schools. The first set of impacts clusters around the encouraging educational, employment, and earnings gains of the graduates. The second set reflects the evident progress in social and emotional maturity registered by the graduates. Taken together, these gains validate the potential power of educational enterprises devoted explicitly to the academic and social development of adolescents who are saddled with deficits in both aspects of their lives. Therefore the salient questions posed by what we now know about ChalleNGe—and other quasi-military approaches—are these:

• Is it possible to design an educational entity that is unequivocally devoted to the academic and social development of its students, as reflected in the mission statement, curriculum and instruction, testing and assessment modalities, staffing patterns, and schedule?

- Is it feasible to design an educational entity that draws significantly on the lessons from ChalleNGe and that would serve a more problematic cohort of low-income and minority youngsters who have disengaged from school but not yet dropped out?

- Would a model that starts earlier and sticks with them longer, namely all the way through high school and that perhaps even begins as early as middle school, generate even better and longer-lasting outcomes for the youngsters and for society?

- Could a curriculum and extracurricular menu be devised with a greatly fortified career component and strong employer linkages to enhance students' educational and employment options upon graduation?

- Which elements, approaches, and attributes of ChalleNGe should be adapted to public education?

- What attributes of ChalleNGe should we make certain not to import so that it is crystal clear we are creating civilian, not military, academies?

- If a variation of ChalleNGe is adapted for public education, how should the overall design and core components be refined to produce even stronger and more durable gains for young people?

- How should such an entity be staffed in light of its dual mission?

- Is such a model affordable in an age of acute fiscal austerity for governments at every level?

- What role might instructional technology play in accelerating learning and managing costs?

This is merely a sampling of the questions generated by ChalleNGe. It is to these questions that we now turn in the hope of contributing fresh perspectives and ideas to the debate over how to address the needs of young people who are chronically disengaged from school.

10

Attributes Worth Emulating

BEYOND THE DISTINCTIVE PROGRAM ELEMENTS found in ChalleNGe, JROTC, and public military academies, military education and training programs feature many core values and generic attributes that contribute to young people's success. These could be incorporated in a new approach to educating and developing youngsters who are falling way behind academically or are basically disengaged from school. Each attribute has merit in its own right. In combination, they represent a compelling vision on how to design and operate educational entities whose mission is to boost the chances of troubled adolescents for success. By the way, these characteristics are not exclusive to military programs. They are found to varying degrees in YouthBuild, Job Corps, youth conservation corps, as well as some charter schools, small schools, and effective traditional schools.

Educating and Developing the Whole Adolescent

Interestingly enough, the most compelling core value of a program like ChalleNGe is the very one that the terms "military" and "quasi-military" are least likely to bring to mind. I refer to the overriding commitment to the education and development of "whole" adolescents. Remember that the eight components of ChalleNGe are: academic excellence, leadership/followership, job skills, responsible citizenship, service to the community, life-coping skills, physical fitness, and health and hygiene.

As Edmund Gordon, the eminent clinical psychologist and avowed pacifist, once remarked at a Brookings Institution policy forum:

One of the things that we can learn from what they do in those [quasi-military] schools, and it is reflected in the ChalleNGe program, is that they appear to be taking an almost public health approach to education. They recognize that the isolation of educational problems in the school doesn't make sense when there are so many things outside of schooling that influence both healthy development and learning how to think.[1]

The ChalleNGe program probably "gets" the whole-child philosophy more so than most public schools. After all, its mission statement proclaims that the purpose of the program is to "Intervene in the life of at-risk youth and produce a program graduate with the values, skills, education, and self-discipline necessary to succeed as a positive and productive adult."[2]

What is most distinctive about ChalleNGe is not its academic curriculum and instructional methods per se, but rather the breadth of its approach to turning these youngsters around. The key is the alignment of the eight core components of ChalleNGe with its commitment to educating and developing whole adolescents.

Valuing and Believing Every Youngster Can Succeed

Many young people who struggle inside of school and out yearn for adults who genuinely value them and believe they can be successful. Claude Steele, a social psychologist who is dean of the Stanford University School of Education, finds that this problem is especially acute among black children. He refers to this phenomenon as:

[A] culprit that can undermine black achievement as effectively as a lock on a schoolhouse door. The culprit I see is stigma, the endemic devaluation many blacks face in our society and schools. This status is its own condition of life, different from class, money, culture. . . . [I]ts connection to school achievement among black Americans has been vastly underappreciated.[3]

Devaluation is not limited to black children. Other low-income and minority youngsters, children with attention-deficit disorder, and students prone to placement in special education probably are susceptible to being underappreciated by their teachers. "Doing well in school requires a belief that school achievement can be a promising basis for self-esteem," Steele argues, "and that belief needs constant reaffirmation even for advantaged students."[4]

In his view, children who are devalued academically may "disidentify" with doing well in school. "Here psychology is everything: remediation defeats, challenge strengthens—affirming their potential, crediting them with their achievements, inspiring them." The key, he argues, is ensuring that youngsters who are vulnerable on so many counts get treated essentially like middle-class students, with conviction about their value and promise. As this happens, Steele continues, vulnerability diminishes, and with it the companion defense of disidentification and misconduct. "Where students are valued and challenged, they generally succeed."[5]

The military excels at valuing and challenging young people, and at believing in the potential of every recruit and cadet. For instance, the determination of Lavin Curry's commandant and instructors at the Chicago Military Academy to pull him back from the abyss of academic failure exemplifies this philosophy in action. Or as Shelly Garza recalls, when her daughter, Kazandra, who attends the Oakland Military Institute, landed on probation, the OMI staff started "doing double time" to help her catch up. "Her grades dropped because she spent the first two weeks lollygagging, but that tells you in itself something is working, because she used to do the same thing in public school and no one ever noticed."[6]

Cherry Campbell's story mirrors Shelly Garza's. In a newspaper interview, she fought back tears while describing how OMI changed her son's attitude toward learning, as well as his habit of cursing and the "challenging" behavior that resulted in many trips to the principal's office at his former school. "Every other school [he's] been at, he's been an outcast," she recalled. "Now, since the educator has a lot more control of the classroom, he's much more focused."[7]

Experiential Learning

As my former Brookings colleague Oliver Sloman has observed, another intriguing facet of programs like ChalleNGe is their departure from traditional pedagogy, which clearly has not worked with youngsters who chronically lag behind academically and lose interest in school.[8] These military-like programs emphasize learning by doing, variously referred to as experiential learning or, in the case of the Army, "Functional Context Education" (FCE). True to the military's predilection for fast-track training, FCE is designed to generate swift gains in reading and math skills by teaching academics "in the context" of learning and actually performing a given task. Military researchers have found that, compared with general literacy instruction, this kind of learning-to-do instruction generates rapid and robust gains in job-related literacy that endure over time.[9]

The Youth ChalleNGe program combines general and job-related literacy instruction akin to FCE. As Donohue explained at a Brookings forum, youngsters in ChalleNGe receive classroom instruction that incorporates technology-assisted learning, all provided by a certified teacher. This is augmented by experiential or applied learning.

For example, as part of their community service requirement, cadets may be required to build a winding, quarter-mile path for disabled children in a park. First, they must define the project in writing. This requires the application of logic and judgment, coupled with a determination of the key elements of the project. Then the cadets must utilize their math skills to measure the surface of the winding path, the depth of the gravel bed that must be dug, and, therefore, calculate how many cubic yards of gravel will be needed. They also determine the flow of the job and the other supplies that will be needed. The youngsters then go to the hardware store, select the materials, read the labels and estimate coverage per can or package, and determine the number of containers and total cost of the materials they will need to complete the job. Since the cadets cannot build the quarter-mile path by themselves, the community service assignment also hones their teamwork, organizational, and leadership skills. Thus the youngsters actually apply and practice much of what they have learned from many of the core components.[10]

Technology and Training

The military pioneered in the use of technology and other fast-track learning methods to mobilize as quickly as possible and maximize the efficiency of its mammoth investment in manpower. As Saul Lavisky of the Human Resources Research Office (HumRRO) at George Washington University pointed out decades ago, "An organization with such a heavy involvement in training, one for which procuring and training manpower is a major mission, must be—and is—very much interested in the benefits to be derived from training research and from a technology of training."[11] By World War II, he notes, military researchers began to make routine and thorough use of the behavioral sciences and advances in the technology of training to improve military operations.

According to Lavisky, the Defense Department views training research as having three principal objectives: (1) bring the proficiency of the training course graduate up to the level required for him to function effectively in a system; (2) reduce the time needed to bring a trainee up to a specified proficiency level; and (3) reduce the cost of training. Clearly technology is no substitute for the human interaction needed to help troubled youngsters cope with their social and emotional issues and grow into whole adolescents. Yet the military may well have mastered the use of custom-tailored, technology-based instruction to help close gaps in young people's basic academic proficiency and, arguably, to do so more expeditiously and cost-effectively than traditional modes of classroom instruction. This might especially be true of tech-savvy youngsters who have tuned out of school. At least this is a premise and a promise worth examining in any new approach to educating dropout-prone young people.

Curriculum and Instruction

The military programs described earlier gear their curriculum and instruction to the academic circumstances of the youngsters they serve. As the NAEP results indicated, large proportions of adolescents perform Below Basic. The threshold goal of ChalleNGe is to lift cadets to the level of functional literacy that equips them to fill out a job application and read—as well as comprehend—an instructional manual that enables them to navigate the job market and life.[12]

Bella Rosenberg, a former senior advisor to the president of the American Federation of Teachers, observes that the military has experience promoting literacy on a large scale. During World War II, the Army and Navy taught its poor readers to read using the "Private Pete" and "Seaman Sam" texts.[13] More to the point, she believes that the military approach to cultivating functional literacy is germane to contemporary students who read poorly. By focusing literacy training on the content and learning demands of relevant tasks, she notes, it is possible in a relatively short amount of time to develop reading competence not only in the tasks at hand, but also in general reading.[14]

To make up for lost time, fast-track approaches to instruction should be a staple of educational programs aimed at youngsters who are far behind academically. Given the sharp rise in reading skills registered by ChalleNGe cadets in a matter of merely five months, the program evidently utilizes an instructional method for rapidly closing the most fundamental of achievement gaps.

Functional literacy is not the endgame for young people served by quasi-military programs, any more than it should be for students in regular schools. Given the convergence of academic skills required for college and the workplace, these programs should strive for this minimal level of proficiency in every young person they serve.

Belonging

Researchers cite a wide array of reasons for why teenagers belong to street gangs. These include low self-esteem, hunger for respect, limited economic opportunity, peer pressure, need for physical protection, alienation from parents, financial incentives, communal honor and loyalty, and fellowship.[15] The most memorable and insightful explanation I have ever come across was offered by Tee Rogers, a Los Angeles gang leader who would know. According to Rogers, "What I think is formulating here is that human nature wants to be accepted. A human being gives less of a damn what he is accepted into. At that age—11 to 17—all kids want to belong. They are unpeople."[16]

Norman Johnson, a retired Army colonel who helped found and then ran the Integrated Design and Electronics Academy Public Charter School in the nation's capital, explains the appeal of military models.[17] "In order to get the attention of the inner-city youth, you must first relate to them in some way. The military structure has (been) successful in relating to them because the military has a belonging atmosphere in which inner-city youth feel they can relate." Inner-city youth understand the "gang structure" and the sense of belonging, he adds, so they can easily adapt to this type of structure at the eighth-through twelfth-grade levels.

Early adolescence is the age of highest "influenceability," according to Carol Goodenow of Tufts University. The student-teacher relationship frequently deteriorates just at the stage in their development when many teenagers begin to look to adults outside of the family as potential role models or sources of support.[18] Goodenow argues that heightened self-consciousness, increased significance of friendships and peer relations, and decreased personal contact with teachers combine to make the middle or junior high school classroom a social context in which students' sense of belonging, personal acceptance, and social-emotional support are both crucial and problematic.[19] She goes on: "Although expectancy of success was the primary predictor of academic effort and grades, the subjective sense of belonging and support was also significantly associated with these outcomes. . . ."[20]

While the evidence often consists of self-reporting, surveys suggest that belonging to positive youth groups may boost participants' self-confidence and curb risky behaviors. As school psychologist Steven Rosenberg observes, outcasts need to feel that they belong to a socially acceptable group. Research and common sense tell us, he says, that many problems in schools derive from the desire of young people to belong to a group—a group where they matter, where they are depended upon, where their presence or absence is noticed.[21] Rosenberg adds that success with fringe students begins by giving them a reason to behave appropriately—by giving them, first, the experience of belonging and contributing to a positive peer group dedicated to a mutually agreed-upon project and, second, the experience of both positive and negative consequences of the peer group's actions.[22]

Given their sheer size and anonymity, traditional schools typically are the antithesis of belonging. Schools and other youth programs patterned after the military hold so much promise because, among many other reasons, they epitomize belonging. As Goodman comments, many students who gravitate to the Chicago Military Academy seem to find it a place of belonging. JROTC classrooms, she says, often have the feel of a clubhouse, and like any popular club, they offer alluring perks: the field trips, dances, drill competitions, and community service projects build camaraderie and self-esteem.[23]

Belonging to the right kind of "gang" can transform the attitude of youngsters like Robert Shores, a student at Chicago Military Academy. His mother was a drug addict and his father a disappearing act. He got into lots of fights. Yet the academy managed to reach him. As the young man remarked, "If you feel like nobody cares about you, then you feel like a nobody. But there's a lot of people here who really like me. They'll pull me aside and tell me what I did wrong. And they tell me what I've done right."[24]

Teamwork and Interdependence

Basic training in the Army, which lasts between six and eight weeks, introduces enlistees to the rigors and expectations of military service. General Colin Powell, the former U.S. secretary of state and chairman of the Joint Chiefs of Staff, once gave me a brief primer on the purpose of basic training.[25] As he explained, basic training is about many things. One goal is tending to the recruits' health and improving their physical fitness to prepare their bodies for whatever military assignment awaits them. Basic training also aims to erase any effects of bad upbringing and parenting. It seeks to remove negative habits by making it clear there are immediate consequences for inappropriate behavior. The message transmitted throughout basic training is simple, Powell noted. If you want to be here, you must perform. If you don't want to be here, then go home, as do 25 to 30 percent of recruits.

Drill instructors do lots of shouting at slackers to make them look foolish. The point, General Powell commented, is to teach recruits that they are part of a team and that everybody pays a price if even one individual fails to perform. The team only succeeds if its members do what they are supposed to do. Close-order drill creates group consciousness and behavior. Eventually those who initially do not perform well begin to get the hang of it and feel proud that they have. This instills an ethos of discipline, accountability, and achievement very early on.

Basic training breeds a sense of collectivism. Instructors utilize the buddy system and embed deeply in recruits' minds and behavior the indispensable military values of taking care of oneself while also being responsible for—and to—someone else. Discipline, accountability, and faithfulness to the task at hand breed pride in the organization as well as pride in being part of the organization.[26]

Young people who "belong" become part of teams. As CSIS noted in its report about military culture, "Cohesion and esprit de corps are the fourth foundation of U.S. military culture. Cohesion is the shared sense of sacrifice and identity that binds service members to their comrades in arms. Esprit de corps is pride in the larger unit and service as a whole. Morale, a close relative, represents the level of enthusiasm and satisfaction felt by individuals in a unit."[27]

In his description of basic training, General Powell emphasized the importance of teaching young people to function as team members upon whom others can rely, rather than Lone Rangers answerable to no one. In the real world, mutual reliance and interdependence are commonplace since workers routinely function in units with supervisors, peers, and subordinates. Success hinges on how efficiently and harmoniously the unit or team performs. By the same token, team members learn that everyone—from their companies and colleagues to their family members and friends—could suffer if they fail to perform or behave responsibly. Absorbing this lesson is one of the keys to growing up and getting ahead in civilian life. And it's an essential attribute of the military approach to educating and developing young people.

Motivation and Self-Discipline

Many researchers have identified persuasive linkages between lack of motivation and low achievement.[28] Interestingly enough, a survey reported in *Education Week* found that high school dropouts themselves were far more likely to say they left school because they were unmotivated, not challenged enough, or overwhelmed by troubles outside of school than because they were failing academically.[29]

This worrisome motivation deficit appears especially among low-income and minority youngsters. The explanations for these counterproductive attitudes run the gamut from the chilling effects of socioeconomic disadvantage to the related inability to see a connection between academic achievement and opportunity for success in life, and to an embrace of so-called oppositional cultures that reject academic achievement. As Roslyn Mickelson has observed, working-class and minority youths have parents, older siblings, and neighbors whose real-world experiences deviate from the myth that education equals opportunity for all.[30]

The strict discipline long associated with military training helps instill the motivation that may be in short supply among some young people. As CSIS stated, "Those who train military recruits, however, along with any experienced parents, will attest that discipline is part of what young people need most. It appears in many forms, whether it makes an athlete rise at dawn to train, drives a writer to spend personal time finishing a chapter, or motivates a military recruit to follow a squad leader's instructions. . . . Self-discipline, a significant factor of maturity, is what allows parents, tired from a day's work, to still care for a home and children, and it is what makes them go to work in the first place."[31]

In the blunt words of Phyllis Goodson, former principal of the Chicago Military Academy, "Military is the culture we follow; we say 'Yes, sir' and 'No, ma'am.' But we're not seeking outward control or manipulation of our students. We're taking dependent children and teaching them self-discipline, self-control, and confidence."[32] She adds: "When they come in, they're looking down. As they begin training, they begin to walk straight, they hold their heads up. I'm watching them grow. I'm watching them change. A lot is possible. You just have to give them the right possibilities."[33]

Structure and Routine

For many youngsters who have disengaged from school or dropped out, the antidote for deeply ingrained behavioral problems and dysfunctional parenting is heavy doses of structure and regimentation, which the military is renowned for. As Goodson says of the Chicago Military

Academy, "In urban societies, negativity is encouraged. You have to come across as not smart to fit into the organized, structured world of gangs. Here, we have a structure, but we move in a positive way, by giving students responsibilities and allowing them opportunities to achieve."[34] Goodson adds that "putting on a uniform is a focusing device. . . . They know there are certain things they can't do when they're in uniform. Similarly, having them march is part of a military context that has a specific purpose: it makes them walk tall. The discipline that we impose on them provides a structure for them to build on. They leave here more independent. They become contributors."[35]

As one illustration of the structure and regimentation in these programs, cadets at the Oakland Military Institute wear uniforms and participate in early morning marching and flag-raising drills.[36] Members of the National Guard monitor classrooms to support the teachers and help keep the cadets in line.

Students like Lavin Curry have responded favorably to the strict military-like atmosphere. When Lavin arrived at the Chicago Military Academy as a freshman in 1999, he was brash. He was wild. As Frank C. Bacon, then the academy's superintendent and a retired Army brigadier general, said of Lavin, "He was a bad little sucker, always into something, always thought he was right."

Lavin couldn't live with his mother and he never met his father. He was raised by his cousin. By the time he got to high school, he was drinking, smoking, and ignoring everyone. "I just didn't care about the rules of the school," Lavin recalls. "I didn't think about the consequences of my actions."

One day he got drunk before first period and passed out in the school bathroom. He was almost kicked out of school. Instead, his instructors and the commandant prodded him to change his behavior and salvage his academic career. Lavin was allowed to stay after he promised to attend a weekend counseling program.

A traffic accident in which his cousin was injured proved to be a turning point. Lavin came to realize that his teachers had simply been trying to give him what he needed: some order in his life. The marching, the saluting, the obeying of rules were all part of turning him into someone who deserved respect.

As Lavin acknowledges, "They changed my life. They fought for me to stay in school. They really cared about me."

Now, at 17, he has stopped drinking and smoking. He has bumped his grades up to As and Bs and begun talking about college, maybe even law school. He's also a running back on the football team, sketches Japanese animation characters, and holds a part-time job at a Loews Cineplex.

In the halls of the military academy, Lavin Curry feels safe. "I don't have to worry about somebody jumping me in the hallways or someone messing with me." But outside is different. He knows not to look directly at some teenagers in the neighborhood, especially when wearing his uniform.

"I feel proud when I go out in my uniform," Lavin says. "There's something about wearing it. You carry yourself differently."[37]

Mentoring and Monitoring

ChalleNGe and programs like it pay close attention to how participants are faring personally and academically. While this level of attentiveness to students' overall development obviously requires more intensive staffing than traditional schools, young people evidently appreciate and profit from the heightened attention.

The mentoring and monitoring extend to personal matters. As Heath Seacrest, a senior JROTC cadet at Mattoon High School in Mattoon, Illinois, told National Public Radio, "Down here, you can talk to them about anything; personal problems. They're like your parents, your counselors; they're like everybody to you. You can come down here and just say, 'I'm having a bad day,' and they'll sit down and talk to you."[38]

Rewards and Recognition

In education, the prevailing practice is to recognize and reward the top achievers in any given category, whether for exemplary scholastic accomplishments or community service. This is perfectly understandable. The trouble is that students who are struggling academically or disenchanted with school may perceive these traditional forms of recognition as hopelessly out of reach. Thus these methods do little to stoke the motivation of these students.

The military is particularly adept at demonstrating to the broad swath of their charges that their contributions and accomplishments are genuinely valued. It long ago mastered the art of frequent recognition for virtually any contribution of value. As Donohue puts it, in the military soldiers wear their importance on their shoulders and their worth on their chests.

Ceremonies and rituals affirm that society values the contributions and accomplishments, be they impressive or modest, of those who are celebrated. The military ritualistically metes out frequent doses of recognition at ceremonies and rites of passage. This approach seems to work in high schools as well. As the supervisor of the JROTC program at Lackey High School in Charles County, Maryland, says of the students who are honored, "It gives many of them an opportunity to do things and be recognized where they might not otherwise receive recognition. The top scholars and top athletes get recognition. This is a place where they're recognized within their own."[39] At the Oakland Military Institute, a public high school started by then mayor Jerry Brown over much local opposition, awards assemblies are held twice a week.

Young people appreciate and profit from the kinds of rewards and recognition bestowed by these programs. As Heath Seacrest told NPR, in the beginning other students mocked his JROTC uniform and called him "green bean." Seacrest weathered the hazing and now says: "The uniform's awesome. Started in July—wearing the uniform—got promoted—got rank and I love my uniform now. I'm like a Christmas tree."[40] Travis White recounted the time he and other cadets from DuVal High School's JROTC program wore their uniforms on a field trip to the Air and Space Museum in Washington, D.C. He recalls with wonderment and pride how tourists mistakenly took them for officers from the Pentagon and asked to pose with them for pictures.[41]

Accountability and Consequences

One staple of military-style programs is immediate accountability and predictable consequences for misbehaving. This applies to those who foul up, of course, but may also extend to members of their unit, even to those who were not involved in the misdeed. As Nancy Trejos, a *Washington Post* reporter who writes about public military academies, once observed, the military is not known for forgiveness, whereas forgiveness is bestowed almost daily in public high schools. Striking the right balance has been a challenge in some public military academies. Eric Lyles, principal of Forestville Military Academy, comments: "My military instructors are not used to giving and receiving excuses. I'm working with them to remember they're dealing with adolescents."[42]

Military programs take accountability and sanctions so seriously because they want to establish an orderly climate where faculty can focus on teaching and where students need not fear for their safety. The threat of sanctions also transmits a clear message that students are expected to learn or else there will be unwelcome consequences.

Penalties at public military academies come in many forms. A cadet caught with his hands in his pockets may be told to drop to the floor and do push-ups. At one school, cadets who disobeyed orders were required to count the bricks in a wall. Failure to complete homework assignments can result in punishment, like cleaning scuff marks off the gym floor, even in demotion, suspension, or, if the recalcitrance persists, expulsion from school. If a student acts out in class or sasses a teacher, parents will be called and told about their child's misbehavior. Students who do not attend mandatory tutoring are banned from taking free time in the gym. In some instances, teachers or military monitors mete out the punishment. At Chicago Military Academy, demotion as well as promotion is often determined by peers.

The point is not punishment for its own sake. In Oakland, cadets with behavior problems are assigned to a separate platoon of 16 youngsters. There they receive more attention for the purpose of improving their attitude and enabling them to rejoin their peers in regular classes. OMI students on academic probation must attend Saturday school, an evening tutoring session four times a week, and classes during holiday breaks.[43]

To reinforce the military philosophy of collective responsibility for the conduct of team members, onlookers may even pay for the misdeeds of perpetrators. One day at the Chicago Military Academy in Bronzeville, several students hurled raisins in the cafeteria during lunch period. Afterward, all 70 students in the cafeteria at the time had to clean up the mess and then write essays about proper lunchroom conduct and get their parents to sign off.[44] The next day, students in all of the lunch periods were required to sit in silence. Not surprisingly, some students thought the universal punishment was unfair. But James Phillips, a freshman, got the point: "It was a message sent out to let you know the school wasn't playing any games. I bet no one will ever throw raisins again. . . . It's a lesson not to do it, even if you didn't do it. It's like saying, We can't let one of us do bad because the rest of us will be punished. We have to activate as a group. We have to work together."[45]

Safety and Security

Since the chaos and violence of urban neighborhoods often spills onto school grounds and even inside the classroom, military-like programs and academies stress safety and security. Military reservists and retirees roam the corridors and classrooms to keep a tight lid on acting out and gang activity. This enables educators to teach and cadets to learn without fear of disruption or danger.

Although some academies struggle on this front in the early going, most eventually succeed in establishing and maintaining order. Students affirm that they feel safer in quasi-military settings where the gangs they encounter in their neighborhoods and at other public high schools are not tolerated.[46] For example, when La'Camii Ross was a sixth grader at Roosevelt Middle School in Oakland, weapons and violence were all too familiar realities of campus life.[47] Some Roosevelt students, she recalls, were out of control, stole play equipment, and made learning nearly impossible. At La'Camii's new school, the Oakland Military Institute, the strict codes of behavior and discipline appear to have kept it free of many problems affecting other schools in the city.

Seventh graders sporting military-like dress uniforms assemble just after sunrise every day on the former parking lot at the Oakland Army Base. This orderly morning ceremony sets the tone for the entire day.[48] Louis Adams, a savvy 14-year-old at the Philadelphia Military Academy, echoed why safety matters. "Most people take a look at today's political situation—Iraq and all—and don't want to come," he commented. "They don't know this isn't a boot camp but a controlled environment where you don't worry about the kid next to you pulling a knife on you."[49]

Demanding Schedule

The quasi-military programs described here impose stiffer physical and time demands on young people than regular schools. Of course, ChalleNGe is a residential program that houses participants on military bases around the clock for five months. Even public military academies operate longer hours. It is commonplace for cadets to line up in formation by about 7:30 in the morning. At the Chicago Military Academy, cadets convene for the band and drill team at 6:30 each morning.[50] Extracurricular activities often run late into the afternoon, while extra help is offered on Saturdays. In addition, CMA students must complete 40 hours of community service prior to graduation. The school year may stretch out as well. OMI operates 220 days per year, in contrast to 180 days at other public schools.[51]

Devotion to Mission

Arguably one of the most distinctive and indispensable attributes of quasi-military programs like ChalleNGe, JROTC, and public military academies may actually be the one least susceptible to replication in a nonmilitary entity or environment. I refer to the zeal inculcated in military personnel to pursue and successfully complete whatever mission they undertake. With the possible exception of firefighters, police officers, and ardent participants in various social movements, this determination, bred of a profound sense of camaraderie and of duty, is seldom matched by civilian agencies and bureaucracies. Deeply committed to accountability and results, the military sets measurable goals and definite timetables for accomplishing whatever it sets out to do.

This sense of mission matters enormously to the effectiveness of the programs discussed here. Any new education paradigms derived from these approaches that ignore this level of personal commitment risk underestimating or misconstruing the distinctive way that the military works. Put another way, any civilian counterpart that aspires to adapt these military attributes and approaches must endeavor to instill this sense of mission throughout. Otherwise, the enterprise could gradually degenerate into business as usual, crippled by operational distractions and indifference, competition and collective ignorance, and, worst of all, debilitating skepticism about young people's ability and potential.

11

Issues and Limitations

DESPITE MY CONVICTION THAT some military methods can be adapted to help struggling students and schools, I understand and respect the misgivings of those who fret about the very idea. Patterning the education of civilian youngsters after the military does raise legitimate anxieties and worrisome issues. The military approach should not simply be mimicked because the purpose of its training is markedly different from that of public education. The key is to embrace and customize those attributes that strengthen the education and development of children who have disengaged from school, while avoiding the characteristics and techniques that do not belong in a civilian enterprise like public education.

Constraints on Individuality

Military service differs from civilian entities in significant ways, including the tension between cohesion and individuality. As CSIS acknowledged in its report on military culture, "Although civil and military cultures share many values in a democracy, there must be significant differences between the cultures. For example, while our civil culture appropriately emphasizes liberty and individuality, military culture downplays them and emphasizes values such as discipline and self-sacrifice that stem from the imperative of military effectiveness on the battlefield."[1]

CSIS elaborated on the distinction between military and civilian entities. Since the driving imperative behind U.S. military culture is the unique responsibility to fight and win the nation's wars, CSIS observed, basic individual freedoms in the military are often curtailed for the sake of good order and discipline. The armed forces reserve the right to dictate strict rules of behavior that would be clearly inappropriate for a civilian employer.[2]

Educational programs that emulate the military must be mindful not to stifle the individuality and creativity that civilians have every right to enjoy and that especially ought to be nurtured in young people. In designing interventions for youngsters who have disengaged from traditional schools, striking the right balance between military-inspired structure and cohesion, on the one hand, and opportunities for self-expression and discovery, on the other, will be challenging but unavoidable. This tension should be weighed and resolved at the very outset, and monitored continuously.

On several visits to public military academies, I was struck by the refreshingly kid-friendly atmosphere, with plenty of easygoing banter between the cadets. Faculty and students interacted effortlessly yet respectfully. At the Philadelphia Military Academy/Leeds, for instance, the JROTC instructors served as counselors and mentors for the youngsters, who have their cell phone numbers. The principal, whose leadership style was supportive but insistent, always kept his door open, and I saw youngsters streaming in throughout the day to chat with him. While my impressions hardly qualify as rigorous evidence, the atmosphere in the school buildings and classrooms that I visited was decidedly not oppressive or anti-individualistic.

Inappropriate Discipline, Tone, or Fit

Military-style educational programs geared to adolescents mete out punishment and sanctions, but obviously there is a line of physical and psychological intimidation they ought not to cross. After all, these youngsters are not Army recruits enrolled in basic training. Not surprisingly, some students who join quasi-military programs become alienated by the structure, pressure, and threat of sanctions. One father felt the JROTC instructors yelled at the teenagers too much and suspended them too frequently.

Typically, military-style programs try to screen out youngsters who are not likely to handle the discipline and thrive in the atmosphere. Some youngsters transfer to other schools. Still others may be expelled if they act out too egregiously and repeatedly. Yet the strong demand for these programs affirms that there are youngsters who summon the inner strength to overcome their initial wariness and end up prospering in the quasi-military setting.

As Brian Mockenhaupt noted several years ago in an illuminating article, the military's view of harsh discipline has oscillated over the years. As far back as 1879, he wrote, Army Major General John Schofield told West Point cadets that ill treatment breeds not respect and compliance, but resentment. "The discipline which makes the Soldiers of a free country reliable in battle is not to be gained by harsh or tyrannical treatment," Schofield warned. "It is possible to impart instruction and to give commands in such a manner and such a tone of voice as to inspire in the Soldier no feeling but an intense desire to obey, while the opposite manner and tone of voice cannot fail to excite strong resentment and a desire to disobey."[3]

The military's philosophy is evolving with the times. As Mockenhaupt observed, the Army has shifted the culture of basic training away from the demeaning treatment and harsh indoctrination that have always characterized standing armies. Drill sergeants act more as coaches and mentors than as feared disciplinarians. They yell less, while swearing and abusive language are no longer tolerated.[4] Mockenhaupt quotes Colonel Kevin Shwedo, director of operations for the Army's Accessions Command within the Training and Doctrine Command: "We don't have to break a person down to make him a great soldier. As a matter of fact, you are going to find that tyrannical treatment is absolutely the wrong way to go. The most effective teams don't focus on breaking you down; they focus on building your skills up and developing your self-esteem and ego."[5]

Mockenhaupt notes that today's drill sergeants are trained to "insist and assist." Their role is to explain the military's performance standards and then help recruits meet them. This is consistent, he suggests, with the Army's drive for drill sergeants to be coaches and mentors who are respected rather than feared.

Value of the GED

The MDRC evaluation of ChalleNGe reported appreciable gains in GED (General Educational Development) attainment for cadets compared with nonparticipants. This finding begs the question, though, of the actual educational and economic value of the GED certificate.

In a literature review conducted for the U.S. Office of Educational Research and Improvement, Bettina Lankard Brown summarized the limitations and benefits of the GED certificate.[6] She found that those who earn GEDs earn substantially less than high school graduates over the long term. It is worth noting, she added, that graduates spend four times as much time in classes, while GED students experienced problems related to their attitudes, values, and behavior that led to dropping out.

Yet the GED certificate did generate discernible benefits. Brown reported that GED recipients achieved more than dropouts and that the certificate was a passport to continued education and training.[7] What's more, compared with dropouts, they had higher self-esteem and satisfaction with their lives, as well as greater likelihood to encourage their own children to complete high school.[8] These upsides of the GED certainly are not trivial.

As with many other aspects of education, the expectations and tests are getting tougher. The emerging common core standards adopted by most states provide a case in point of new, more rigorous national academic standards eclipsing less onerous state-by-state standards.

The GED exam is undergoing an upgrade as well.[9] In keeping with the stiffer educational qualifications for many jobs, the American Council on Education, which has administered the GED for 70 years, decided to up the ante by aligning it with the tougher new common core standards for most high schools. While most GED test-takers claim they plan on pursuing postsecondary education, the council is concerned that only 35 percent actually enroll within seven years, and only 12 percent earn any higher education credential. The revised exam is designed to gauge, among other things, whether students have the skills to get through the first year of college with remedial courses. Test takers will receive separate scores related to their college readiness and career readiness.

Since the upgraded exam is so new, the jury is out regarding its impact on various segments of test takers when it comes to pass rates, affirmation of readiness for good jobs or higher education, and value of the credential in successfully pursuing either. Clearly the new exam, like the common core standards, raises the performance bar for programs designed to serve those who have faltered in traditional schools.

Male Orientation

One of the earliest qualms expressed about ChalleNGe was that it would be too oriented toward boys and ill-suited for adolescent girls who are also prone to dropping out of school and who might want to join the program. With the benefit of hindsight, I confess that in my enthusiasm for the idea of ChalleNGe, I was not sufficiently attuned to this potential issue.

Concerns over the severe difficulties facing minority young people in particular are so acute these days that innovative programmers have dared to establish schools specifically geared to African-American boys, as well as programs aimed at black fathers. At the risk of appearing chauvinistic, I confess that I believe significant progress trumps no progress, even if it means gearing some initiatives to one gender or the other. By the same token, an intervention that uniquely works for young women would be a welcome victory over the palpable adversity and bleak outlooks facing far too many adolescent girls.

In any event, it took a provocative term paper by one of my Princeton students, Danielle Vildostegui, to awaken me to the shortcomings of ChalleNGe vis-à-vis young women and to the possible strategies for modifying such interventions to improve outcomes for them.[10] In her paper, Vildostegui argued that boys are twice as likely as girls to attribute dropping out to behavioral factors. Girls are more likely to mention such personal reasons as pregnancy, marriage, or family problems as the primary reason for dropping out. Also, the overwhelming majority of female dropouts who had previously been retained in grade cite that as a major reason, suggesting that their diminished self-esteem contributed to their disengagement.[11]

In designing ChalleNGe, Donohue focused on creating an intervention for the types of dropouts who tended to land in prison because of gang involvement or possession and use of guns. As Vildostegui noted, those types of behavioral and disciplinary issues are far less prevalent among female dropouts.[12] That seems to explain the stark enrollment disparity along gender lines. For instance, at the time of random assignment, the sample of ChalleNGe participants covered by the MDRC evaluation was 88 percent male and merely 12 percent female.[13] The research sample underrepresented females, who typically compose about 20 percent of program graduates nationwide.[14] Vildostegui also argued that the emphasis in ChalleNGe on platoon structures, where cadets face physical challenges akin to diluted basic training, is not responsive or appealing to the needs of many girls who have disengaged from school.

Interestingly enough, JROTC programs in high schools enjoy far better success in attracting female cadets. In some schools, they even involve more females than males. Nationwide, 40 percent of JROTC cadets are female vs. only 21 percent of ChalleNGe participants.[15] According to Vildostegui, girls are especially attracted by the respect they gain through JROTC that may not otherwise be available in their schools. One female cadet at PMA-Elverson mentioned that the JROTC uniform was a symbol of pride and courage that makes her feel like she can stand on top of the world.[16] By wearing a cadet uniform, female students feel trusted and respected not only by their peers and commanding officers, but also by the school and community at large. As one JROTC colonel commented, "I think ladies come out [to JROTC] because they know that they'll be treated with respect in JROTC. They see they can advance well, and that everyone here is equal."[17]

Girls routinely ascend to the top rungs of JROTC, with a majority of those positions occupied by women.[18] The significant presence of young women in top leadership roles may contribute to the gains in self-esteem realized by female compared with male cadets. Research indicates that female JROTC participants exit the program with higher self-esteem than both male cadets and females who did not participate.

According to Vildostegui, participation in JROTC's extracurricular programs may offer Latino girls in particular a degree of freedom and autonomy that would otherwise be unavailable because culturally they are expected to be in the home. She also noted that JROTC's regimented emphasis on organization and leadership and the variety of extracurricular activities are more aligned with female learning techniques than the ChalleNGe program's method of instruction. Her research suggests that females learn best when working with peers, incorporating others' ideas, and associating with a team. In a program like ChalleNGe that emphasizes physical prowess and military-like basic training, males are more likely to thrive due to the fact that "boys are more competitive, work to contribute their ideas independently of one another, and define themselves through differences from their peers."[19]

The upshot of Vildostegui's analysis is that interventions aimed at rescuing youngsters from the precipice of disengagement and dropping out should be attuned to the distinctive motivations, needs, and learning styles of adolescent girls and boys. Some elements and attributes may coincide, while others may need to be custom-tailored according to gender.

Travails of Implementation

Despite the military's deserved reputation for execution, the quasi-military programs it runs or partners in operating face many of the same start-up and ongoing implementation struggles confronted by other innovative programs in public education. Reservists and veterans who are recruited for these programs must be screened carefully and then trained to work effectively with youngsters who have serious academic shortcomings and personal issues. Educational and military personnel working alongside one another need to establish a sensible division of labor and reconcile the civilian and military cultures, lest they conflict and foment confusion in the school building and the minds of students.

Leadership turnover at the top levels of school districts can impede operations in the schools. Superintendents come and go with destabilizing frequency. They may view their predecessors' priorities and initiatives with skepticism, determined to implement their own, thereby undermining the continuity of solid programs already in place.

The RAND Corporation studied the rollout of JROTC career academies and found that they encountered many of the same problems that have bedeviled other efforts to launch new small schools. For instance, these innovative schools may have gotten off the ground, but they often proved less successful in changing their curricula and instructional focus. The host school district may lack sufficient funding for common planning time for teachers, and the state-mandated curricular guidelines may limit the flexibility they need to devote to the occupational focus of the academy.[20]

As with any innovation, quasi-military programs can be works in progress during their formative years. Colonel Charles Fleming, then principal of the Chicago Military Academy, counsels realism, patience, and persistence. "It's going to be more expensive right up front than your everyday high school. Give it time to let it work—at least five to seven years—then the dividends will pay down the road."[21] Or as Brigadier General Ralph Marinaro, OMI's superintendent at the time, put it wryly: "This isn't instant pudding; you can't just add water and get a college-bound student."[22]

Nonissues

Over the years, I have encountered other concerns about applying military-like approaches to education and training in public schools. These reservations generally fall into three categories:

- Military content in the school curriculum;

- Use of programs as vehicles for military recruitment; and

- Unstable reliance on military participation due to other demands.

The issue of male orientation discussed previously raises a not-unrelated concern, namely the risk of sexual abuse or assault. In recent years, the U.S. military has been roiled with accusations, actual convictions, and charges of cover-ups and lax oversight. Yet with only one exception gleaned from a search on Google, ChalleNGe has not suffered any such scandals. Obviously I hope this remains a nonissue and never besmirches the concept I am advancing.

While I appreciate these various concerns in the context of avowedly quasi-military programs like ChalleNGe, JROTC, and public military academies, they actually are not germane to the idea I am advancing in this book. What I have in mind is a strictly civilian enterprise that is informed by military methods, but would not incorporate any military ingredients per se. There would be no military content in the school curriculum or extracurricular activities whatsoever. There would no more military recruitment on premises than school districts permit in their other buildings. And all personnel would be employed as civilians and no more vulnerable to active duty call-ups than any reservists or National Guard members.

Evoking the military in conjunction with educating children can cause heartburn for some parents, educators, and child advocates. How their understandable concerns are addressed obviously will have significant implications for whether and to what extent these approaches should be adapted for use in public education. Educators and parents understandably need assurance that these qualms have been eliminated in any civilian application of quasi-military education and training models. Indeed, the optimal course of action is to devise a new recipe, borrowing those ingredients deemed appropriate and bypassing those ill-suited to a strictly civilian intervention designed for children.

12

Public Academies for
Disengaged Adolescents

TRADITIONAL SCHOOLS ARE ILL-SUITED to the needs of youngsters who have tuned out the kind of education offered there. This is evidenced by the chronic patterns of academic failure, disengagement, grade retention, behavioral and disciplinary problems, and, ultimately, dropping out. As discussed earlier, this stark reality in Chicago prompted Anthony Bryk and his colleagues to conclude that no districtwide systemic reforms can cope with these extraordinary conditions.[1] As they argued and as I completely agree, "in communities where there are few viable institutions, where crime, drug abuse, and gang activity are prevalent, and where palpable human needs walk through the school doors virtually every day, a much more powerful model of school development is needed—one that melds systemic efforts at strengthening instruction with the social resources of a comprehensive community schools initiative."[2]

In Bryk's view, that powerful model would entail expanding "student learning opportunities through increased instructional time, coupled with sustained programmatic activities in all the essential support areas so that this expanded learning time is more productive. Also included is a strong programmatic focus on the myriad of social, emotional, and physical health needs that impede the learning of many children."[3] He imagines exceptionally strong schools "akin to a total institution that creates an island of safety and order, established social routine, and new norms for academic effort in order to counter the external forces pushing students in very different directions."[4]

Persuaded by this research and by the lessons from ChalleNGe, I call for a new paradigm, namely the creation of public academies devoted explicitly and unequivocally to the academic and social development of youngsters who clearly are disengaged from school. The aim of the public academies I envision is not simply to prepare students to pass high-stakes tests. Rather, the mission must be to advance both the academic and social development of these problematic young people so that they are better equipped for success in school and then in the real world that awaits them. This dual mission would drive the structure, curriculum, staffing, schedule, and funding for this enterprise. If any of these core aspects of these academies get short shrift, the students will suffer.

Target Groups

Who should these public academies serve and how should they be selected? One option is to open them to all comers, perhaps even to youngsters who are relatively problem-free, engaged in school, and performing well. But doing so would undercut the very purpose of creating the academies in the first place. At the other end of the spectrum, the entire student body could consist of youngsters who are troubled and troublesome, performing poorly, drifting through school, disengaged, frequently disciplined, and repeating grades. Under any scenario, an appropriate cohort of special education students should be included in the mix.

While the academies should do their best to prepare their students for college, these should not be perceived as college prep schools per se. The youngsters these academies primarily are intended to serve will start out way behind the eight ball academically. At a minimum the goal should be to ensure that they acquire the requisite academic and social skills needed to earn a high school diploma or, as a fallback, GED certificate and then qualify for good jobs. Wherever possible, the academies should aim even higher—reputable career schools, community colleges, and four-year universities—for those students who are up to it academically. As the principal of a public military academy put it succinctly: "The selection of the students should be based on where do we want [them] to be at the end of this program. . . . The focus should be on education, on what they are going to do post–high school graduation."[5]

I lean toward concentrating, primarily if not exclusively, on the risk-iest, most challenging mix of students for two reasons. First, these youngsters desperately need to be placed in academic and developmental settings that are uniquely attuned to their needs. Second, inducing or, if need be, requiring them to transfer from traditional schools will enhance the ability of teachers in their former schools to succeed in educating the more academically oriented students who remain enrolled and engaged. Filling academies with youngsters who may be difficult to handle and teach will present formidable obstacles for the staff. But as the experience and results from ChalleNGe indicate, a robust intervention focused on developing whole adolescents can prevail over seemingly steep odds.

Even within this target population, it is possible to achieve some diversity among students. While at Brookings I commissioned Dan Donohue to write a working paper on the concept of nonresidential schools in the image of ChalleNGe.[6] Based on his analysis, Donohue spotlights two subgroups of weak achievers. One is youngsters who basically have good attitudes and behaviors, but who experience learning difficulties so dispiriting that they disengage. These academies could offer them a remedial course of study that might even enable them to return to regular schools. The other cohort, in Donohue's view, might be students who have significant behavioral and attitudinal problems that are not solely rooted in or the result of academic frustrations. They especially need the behavioral as well as academic components of the academies that would be tailored to their needs.[7]

What age group(s) should the academies serve? The most obvious target is high school students. If the academies succeed, they could re-engage these youngsters, rescue them, and turn around their lives and life prospects before it is too late. As we learned from RAND's cost-benefit analysis of ChalleNGe, investing in youngsters who are adrift in the high school years can pay significant dividends for them and for society. Therefore, focusing on ninth through twelfth graders goes without saying.

We also know from research by Balfanz and others that earlier interventions can make a positive difference. I certainly do not advocate creating these kinds of academies for preschoolers or elementary school students. However, I can readily imagine academies for middle-school students in the sixth through eighth grades who are struggling mightily in school and already exhibiting worrisome signs of deep disengagement. Some public military academies, such as the Oakland Military Institute in California and the Military Magnet Academy in South Carolina, start at the sixth-grade level. As Sloman observes, the emphasis in the academies I envision on belonging and peer leadership may have a particularly profound impact on middle-school-aged students.[8] Of course, the curriculum, social and emotional program components, and other attributes would have to be calibrated with care to ensure that they are age-appropriate. Similar care must be taken in selecting staff who are trained and attuned to working with young adolescents.

One of the toughest design considerations is whether attendance should be voluntary or mandatory. Juvenile court judges, police departments, social service agencies, officials at other schools, and family members are likely to refer youngsters to the academies. In weighing the merits of mandatory attendance, Donohue acknowledges that it could be counterproductive to require youngsters to attend schools that are stigmatized as serving those who are intellectually slow and/or troublemakers.[9] Preferably, the academies would be perceived so favorably that youngsters will want to attend.

The risk, as Donohue notes, is that catering solely to volunteers may not generate a student body comprising youngsters with the most pressing need for concerted academic and social development. If school systems cannot require deeply disengaged students destined for failure in regular schools to attend these academies, then what other avenues are available? Should the schools just wait it out until these youngsters finally drop out? Should they expel them or shunt them off to other alternative programs? What greater good is served by those outcomes? Should school systems instead pray that an inspiring teacher will finally reach them and transform their attitudes toward school along with their academic performance? How much more damage will the presence of profoundly disenchanted youngsters do to the education of their more motivated peers if the schools muddle along, unable to find a formula for turning them on to learning? I have no illusions that these are easy choices. As always, the key consideration is what serves the best interests of the achievers and the disenchanted?

Since middle-school youngsters are required to attend school, districts have more leverage in telling them where. Besides, Donohue argues, a decisive intervention would be more effective at that age.[10] Insisting that 16- to 18-year-olds attend an academy would be more difficult because they have the right to refuse and drop out entirely once they turn 16.

Whatever the criteria for inclusion, the related issue is how youngsters are selected for the schools. Slots could be filled on a first-come-first-served basis. Alternatively, assuming there are more applicants or referrals than positions, pools of eligible prescreened students could be created, with the slots then allocated by lottery. This method may be preferable to first-come-first-served because it enables school officials to consider the youngsters' attributes, needs, and interests to create a diverse and balanced student body. But administrators should avoid using prescreening to cream the applicant pool by selecting the least-challenging students because that would defeat the point of creating the academies in the first place. It is also important to ferret out youngsters who are so hostile and/or immersed in gang culture that their very presence could undermine the entire enterprise. Since cohesion and consistency are crucial to the academies I envision, school officials should also focus on creating a class that starts the academic year as a unit and hopefully stays together throughout.

The key is for administrators in charge of the academies to establish and adhere to a transparent selection process. During the academic year, some youngsters may leave involuntarily or of their own volition. However, students should not be permitted to transfer in once the academic year begins because that would disrupt the flow of the academic and social development components of the program. Suffice it to say, the selection criteria and process must be crafted with care because the ability of the academy to fulfill its mission will hinge to a substantial degree on how incoming classes are composed and chosen.

Size and Site

Whether focused on middle and/or high school grades, the academies should be small, between 300 and 500 students. Small public schools, charter schools, and public military schools count on students and adults forming meaningful relationships and knowing one another by name. According to Sloman, small school size facilitates student-centeredness, mentoring and close monitoring of students, rewarding and recognizing them, and emphasizing order and discipline.[11]

In a comment that applies to all small schools, a senior administrator said of his public military academy: "My program only has 350 kids. That way I know every kid . . . when the parents call, they know me—we have no problem, they walk in anytime. When you're talking about hitting 1,000 [students in a high school]. . . the kids easily get lost between the cracks [and] you don't see a lot of things. The kids in today's school, because of the surroundings of their home environment . . . don't get enough attention. And in reality, if you make it so much bigger, then the connection and the nourishing that they need is not provided."[12]

A teacher at the same academy explained from personal experience why small schools make a difference. "Kids want to be personal. . . . I know everything about [my] kids; I know the parents. I've watched them as they grow from the ninth grade to the twelfth grade. I know where they're going to have a hard time and where they're going to really excel. They're going to come back to you, if they had you in ninth grade, and they're seniors—they're going to come back and talk to you about things from the past and the way they're looking at the future. They still have you as that guide. They don't get lost."[13]

Many small public schools and charter schools are situated in larger school buildings where they share space with other small schools, some of which are unconventional like them, but others may be truncated versions of traditional schools. Donohue argues passionately and persuasively that this school-within-a-school approach would be a grave mistake for the kind of academy that focuses equally on academics and development.[14]

He believes instead that the schools should operate in free-standing buildings. A stand-alone building reinforces the fact that this intervention is fundamentally different compared with traditional schools. The school culture and roles of staff and students are unique. The academies would demand different behaviors of students when it comes to respect, decorum, common attire, and standards of peer discipline. The staff would have greater authority and commensurate responsibility than their counterparts at traditional schools. A separate physical plant would provide leverage in implementing all the core components and attributes of the academy.

A shared facility, while a minimally acceptable option if need be, would be significantly less desirable because it compromises the ability to establish and sustain a focus on developing the whole adolescent. As Sloman noted, shared arrangements can be inconvenient and at times disruptive.[15] Scheduling problems with shared spaces such as gyms and auditoriums arise, and student safety can be an issue with different disciplinary standards operating in different parts of the building and potentially conflicting in common areas.

More fundamentally, the academies I envision would create a distinctive school culture that is reinforced by specific behavioral codes, regulations, and standards. Sharing space with unaffiliated students can undermine this environment. As a student at a public military academy remarked about sharing space: "I mean, it is really distracting sharing a school with another school, because while we're just beginning class, the other kids are going to another class, screaming in the hallways, talking. We always have to shut our doors, and you know, we don't have air-conditioning right now, [so] it's really uncomfortable."[16]

Finding separate buildings for these academies may be feasible. There may be vacant, closed, or underutilized public schools that could be converted to academies. In addition, Catholic archdioceses are closing parochial schools all over the country. These decommissioned school buildings may be available and well suited for conversion to academies.

Academic Approach

At the high school level, the academies would award traditional diplomas to all who can earn them. For youngsters who are not up to that but who want to burnish their academic credentials and achieve some degree of closure with their secondary education, the academies should also provide GED prep courses and award GED certificates.

As for the curriculum, the academies would offer the courses typically mandated by the state and host school district. If the state concurs, the academies might provide a variation on the traditional curriculum by configuring the rigorous civic responsibility component as a civics course incorporating experiential learning. Perhaps the health and hygiene component, which includes sex education, could be designed to satisfy the customary science requirement. The physical fitness component should easily meet any physical education requirements.

Other core components of ChalleNGe could be fashioned as courses that qualify as credible electives and extracurricular activities. With the active participation of local businesses, the job skills component could cultivate specific competencies and attitudes that are aligned with actual job opportunities, pair youngsters with mentors and summer internships, and steer them to actual jobs upon graduation. The life-coping-skills component, which runs the gamut from behavioral ingredients to personal financial planning, could be adapted to a civilian program. Community service incorporating experiential learning would fit right into the curriculum of the academies.

Donohue further suggests that the leadership and followership component could easily be adapted to a civilian program. Students typically are leaderless aggregations, he observes, with no formal student chains of command where they get to learn and practice leadership and followership skills under the tutelage of staff. Based on his experience, Donohue believes that an effective leadership and followership component, taught using a combination of standard instruction and experiential learning, would improve the classroom environment and help students develop a moral compass.

Experiential Learning

For youngsters who are deeply disengaged from school and thus from traditional modes of studying and learning, a starkly different approach to instruction could be another key to turning them around. The familiar terms for what I have in mind are experiential learning, project learning, or, in military parlance, Functional Context Education (FCE). As Sloman notes, the FCE instructional method is derived from years of research and experimentation.[17] Researchers found that generic remedial courses rarely improved soldiers' math and reading skills rapidly enough to meet the military's needs. Instead, they determined that the most effective way to train a soldier who wants to be, say, an auto mechanic but who is not functionally literate is to teach job-related and literacy skills simultaneously.[18]

In practice, this means teaching the recruit how to read using work-related materials, such as an auto mechanic's manual. Postcourse testing showed that soldiers taught using FCE improved their job-related and general reading ability at a faster clip than those in the generic remedial courses.[19] Moreover, these gains lasted longer. Due to a complex mixture of motivational and cognitive effects, these soldiers, while by no means advanced readers, were soon able to perform relatively complex jobs despite their initial literacy deficits.

Some public schools employ so-called project-based learning for youngsters who have tuned out traditional instruction. For instance, the Kennedy School of Sustainability in Cottage Grove, Oregon, is an alternative high school that serves youngsters who had "blown out of the regular school" and needed more real-world, relevant kinds of learning opportunities.[20] Nearly 40 percent of the Kennedy students are homeless; many live in trailer parks in abject poverty; and 14 percent are parents.

As Liana Heitin wrote in *Education Week*, many of the Kennedy students had been demoralized in traditional school.[21] In an approach that mirrors ChalleNGe's combination of community service and experiential learning, the principal of Kennedy got the students to undertake projects that would hopefully earn praise from members of the community and help restore the students' sense of self-worth. Their projects relate to a theme, such as agriculture, energy, forestry, or water. The goal is to have a tangible, positive effect on the community. As the principal commented, "We've flattened the walls of the school."

The students meet with the same teacher for the entire day, giving the teachers complete control over their schedules. The fluid schedules enable teachers to take their students on day trips or even extended trips of up to two weeks. The students spend one day per week doing fieldwork for their thematic projects. According to Heitin, one group may farm tilapia, while another builds Aleutian kayaks and takes them out to monitor water quality.

The Cottage Grove superintendent, Krista Parent, acknowledged the need to combat the perception that academic standards at alternative schools like Kennedy have been diluted. Disputing this criticism, Tom Horn, the principal of Kennedy, describes project-based learning as "working down Bloom's Taxonomy instead of up," referring to the hierarchy of cognitive skills many teachers use. "With project-based learning," he notes, "the students are given a task that requires higher-order thinking skills—often to create something—and they must learn and practice lower-level skills along the way." The academic standards are embedded in the projects and each student has an individualized plan.

Project-based learning has paid dividends for Kennedy's students.[22] The attendance rate has soared from 23 percent in the fall of 2006 to about 90 percent. The dropout rate stands at 12.5 percent, down from 20 percent in 2004–05. Although still below state averages, test scores at Kennedy have improved significantly. In 2011, 52 percent of students passed the state reading assessment for grades 10 and 11. That is appreciably higher than the 2008 passing rate of 9 percent, but still below the state rate of 83 percent. The pass rate for writing fluctuates and fell back to 28 percent in 2012. Even so, experience with ChalleNGe and with schools like Kennedy suggests that experiential learning should be embedded in the curriculum of the academies that serve youngsters turned off by traditional instructional methods.

Career Preparation

Another crucial ingredient of the academies I envision is career exposure and exploration, especially for marginal students who are destined to struggle in the labor market unless interventions like this succeed. As the authors of *Pathways to Prosperity* argued, one of the most fundamental obligations of any society is to prepare adolescents and young adults to lead productive and prosperous lives.[23] This means providing all young people with a solid foundation of literacy, numeracy, and thinking skills.

According to the authors, there is growing evidence that many young adults lack the skills and work ethic needed for jobs that pay middle-class wages. As of 2007, the proportion of workers with a high school education or less had shrunk to 41 percent of the workforce. Nearly two-thirds of the 47 million jobs that the U.S. economy is projected to create through 2018 will require some degree of postsecondary education. Almost half of those jobs will go to people with associate's degrees or occupational licenses or certificates.

The stark reality is that only four in ten Americans obtain either an associate or bachelor degree by their mid-twenties.[24] Fifty-six percent of those who enroll in four-year colleges attain a bachelor degree within six years. Fewer than 30 percent of those who enroll in community college obtain an associate degree within three years. The education shortfalls are even more dismal for young people of color. Merely 30 percent of African Americans and fewer than 20 percent of Latinos in their mid-20s possess an associate degree or higher.

However appealing the rhetoric about "college for all" may be, the authors of *Pathways to Prosperity* argue that the U.S. must focus more attention and resources on career-oriented programs and pathways that do not require bachelor degrees, but do prepare young people for the kinds of middle-skill jobs that provide decent livelihoods.[25] The academies I envision would develop the scholastic as well as social and emotional, or "soft," skills that young people need to succeed in the workplace. According to *Pathways*, too many youngsters cannot see a transparent connection between their program of study and tangible opportunities in the labor market.[26] The authors continue: "Every high school graduate should find viable ways of pursuing both a career and a meaningful postsecondary degree or credential. For too many of our youth, we have treated preparing for college versus preparing [for] career as mutually exclusive options."

The authors noted that students who are bored and at risk of dropping out need to be engaged more effectively. They need to know that there are navigable pathways leading to rewarding careers in the mainstream economy.[27] They acknowledged that it is essential to ensure that all students leave high school with a solid enough foundation of core literacy and numeracy skills to keep on learning. "However, the course-taking requirements for entry into the most demanding four-year colleges should not be imposed on students seeking careers with fewer academic requirements. Indeed, there is evidence that imposing such requirements can be counterproductive. Many of the states that

have sharply raised graduation requirements, including math and science requirements, have experienced a decrease in high school
completion rates."[28]

Pathways to Prosperity calls for cutting-edge career and technical education (CTE) that bears little relationship to the old vocational
education programs that often were little more than dumping grounds
for students who could not handle college prep coursework. Today's best
CTE programs, the authors argue, do a better job of preparing many
students for college and careers than traditional, strictly academic programs.[29] "In the U.S., our goal should be to assist every young adult
beginning at the end of middle school to develop an individualized
pathway plan that would include career objectives; a program of study;
degree and/or certificate objectives; and work-linked experiences. These
pathway plans would hardly be set in concrete, and young adults would
not be forced into tracks. But the merits of this approach are obvious.
Young adults simply can't chart a course if they don't have a goal."[30]

More specifically, the authors laid out a pragmatic agenda for systematic career exposure and exploration that the academies I envision
should emulate. In their view, the goal is that beginning no later than
middle school all students should have access to this system of employer
involvement and assistance. Elaborating on this point, they added: "In
middle school, this would include career counseling, job shadowing,
and opportunities to work on projects or problems designed by industry partners. In high school, it would include programs of study
designed in collaboration with industry leaders, as well as opportunities for more intensive work-based learning such as paid internships."[31]

Virtual Learning

So-called "blended learning" combines traditional, face-to-face classroom instruction with virtual or computer-assisted learning. Out of
curiosity, fiscal necessity, declining enrollments, or some combination
thereof, public school districts around the country are experimenting
with blended learning. The same is true of colleges and universities,
even the most prestigious, which are anxious to develop more
cost-effective approaches to delivering high-quality education.

Undeterred by whether academically weak students can cope with online instruction, the Youth Connection Charter School, a Chicago-based network of 22 charter schools, specializes in serving dropouts and students at great risk of dropping out.[32] Its alternative schools offer online courses for credit recovery and provide teachers in classrooms with students as they take courses online. The Philadelphia school system, one of the nation's largest urban districts, intends to establish the Philadelphia Virtual Academy for sixth through twelfth graders.[33] It will deliver courses exclusively online. The academic schedules will be custom-tailored to students' needs, and they will have access to online tutors and mentors.

Private entrepreneurs view dropout recovery as a promising market for their online and hybrid credit-recovery offerings for young people seeking to catch up academically.[34] As might be expected, the allure outpaces the availability of solid evidence that the approach works with this challenging population. The surge of interest and activity will generate important lessons about the uses and limits of online instruction for students who have struggled mightily with traditional teaching.

Principals of schools that have embraced virtual learning report noticeable savings. For instance, a principal in Broward County, Florida, indicates that the state's online course requirement helped the school maintain the class size requirements while saving $100,000 that would have been spent on teachers. A KIPP Academy in Los Angeles lost state funding equivalent to several teachers' salaries, yet utilized instructional software to prevent student-teacher ratios from getting appreciably worse.[35]

Besides the efficiencies, the academies I envision should push the envelope on virtual instruction because technological literacy is critical to economic self-reliance. Computer-assisted instruction facilitates personalized learning and self-paced learning. Even more important, youngsters today must be technologically literate to survive and thrive in a world in which there is a direct connection between literacy, technology, employability, and economic competitiveness. Electronic devices and thus technological literacy are integral aspects of even the most mundane jobs, where tablets, smartphones, and other handheld wireless devices are indispensable tools of the trade. Without falling for quackery, those who design the curriculum, experiential learning, and other components of the academies should immerse students in virtual learning to the maximum extent practicable and justifiable based on the evidence about effectiveness. On this front as well as others, there is much to learn from the military about how best to harness technology for educational and training purposes.

Intensive Schedule

The academies would consume more of the youngsters' time and energy than do traditional schools. The combination of courses, other components, experiential learning outside of school, extracurricular activities, tutorials and counseling, and career exploration with employers, among other activities, will necessitate a longer school day, week, and year.

In projecting the requirements for a roughly comparable intervention model, Donohue imagines a 13½-hour day, 6½-day week, and 150-day school year.[36] This taxing schedule more than doubles the program immersion time, reduces opportunities for unsavory external distractions, and makes maximum use of waking hours. A 5½- to 6-day schedule would be almost as taxing and perhaps more attainable. Either way, a schedule this dense would test the commitment of the students and their families by crowding out many opportunities for the youngsters to earn money from jobs outside of school. Whether and to what extent that is realistic for the target population requires careful thought and soundings with youngsters and their parents. A lengthy school day may also mean a grueling commute for some students, which would be another test of their commitment.

An intensive intervention like ChalleNGe requires youngsters to participate full-time for five months, in effect serving as a transition back into school, into GED prep, or onward to a career-training program, job, community college, or four-year institution. By contrast, the academies I envision would supplant traditional schools and become the place where youngsters enroll in the sixth or ninth grade and then remain for the equivalent of their middle school or high school years. The entire curriculum and other components would be designed and implemented with this expected longer duration in mind. That means the students' engagement in such components as health and hygiene could taper off as they absorb the lessons. They would then segue to even more traditional courses. Other ingredients and approaches, such as experiential learning, would be sustained throughout. Some students may require varying "doses" of instruction and practice in life-coping skills, while their involvement in job skills and career exploration would intensify as they mature and approach graduation from high school or receipt of a GED certificate.

One critical design question is whether students in these academies will be able and expected to stay enrolled for the duration of their middle school and/or high school years, or whether they would be required to return to a traditional school, presumably once their academic and social skills have improved. I believe the academies should be viewed not as fleeting interventions, but as full-fledged schools that enable students to develop and ripen on the vine, so to speak, over time. After all, the idea is to immerse them in a distinctive environment with intensive mentoring and supports to undo deleterious behavioral patterns and develop stronger academic and social skills.

This developmental process takes time and sustained support. Optimally, youngsters should transition from this experience directly into early adulthood with ample support and minimal risk of interruption in their healthy development. That is why the academies should be construed and structured as full-fledged alternatives to school, not as short-term interventions.

Culture and Climate

In well-run schools, be they traditional, parochial, small, or charter, culture and climate matter enormously. This would especially be true for those serving young people who tend to be disengaged, disrespectful, disruptive, or unruly. There are manageable, nondraconian mechanisms for maintaining order and discipline. The academies I envision could adapt some of the best practices from other institutions. For instance, as Sloman writes, public military academies at their best are places where students are respectful and well behaved, but still relaxed and expressive.[37] These schools use a variety of methods to empower students to take responsibility for their own behavior and that of their peers. They impose rules governing classroom and hallway behavior. To counteract consumerism and gang culture, parochial schools and many public schools require students to wear common attire, sometimes with different outfits on different days.

One public military academy in Philadelphia instructs its students to wear their common attire and maintain the same behavior standards en route to and from school and whenever they represent the school at outside events. The pride they take in their appearance and decorum extends beyond the school to how they comport themselves in the community.[38] The following passage in the PMA-Leeds student handbook articulates this expectation: "[When traveling to and from school], please be mindful and display the courteous attitude of a PMA student. Do not loiter or walk on residents' property, grass, or steps. Do not litter or use profanity on the way home. Also remember to wear the complete uniform (including tucked shirt) until you arrive at your home. Your appearance and behavior during your travel to and from school is a reflection of the Philadelphia Military Academy and yourself."[39]

Ranks and Recognition

Public military academies and JROTC programs utilize a "student chain of command" to help promote esprit and provide students with an incentive to abide by the school's rules. Equally important, the chain of command enables students to excel outside the classroom, rise through the ranks based on their performance, practice leadership and followership, and earn coveted positions of leadership that are respected in school and out. As Sloman points out, it is important to remember that students in military academies do not enforce discipline entirely on their own.[40] Teachers and staff back up student leaders when necessary. Students are taught to view their student leader as the first point of contact for most of their concerns.

Not only does this system teach leadership and self-confidence, it also reduces staff workloads. At PMA-Leeds, the commandant, who one would normally assume concentrates on discipline, focuses more on academic advising and the health and well-being of students and considerably less on enforcing rules. Even JROTC instructors rarely administer discipline directly once the school year gets under way and the student leadership establishes itself.[41] Some public military academies employ student courts to adjudicate honor code violations and appeal disciplinary actions and demotions. The use of these arrangements is an extension of the idea that the students themselves have primary responsibility for meeting and enforcing the behavioral norms.

According to Sloman, students attain higher rank in the chain of command based on meeting a variety of performance measures, which differ from school to school.[42] Not accumulating demerits and more severe sanctions, such as in-school and out-of-school suspensions, are a key to promotion and maintaining one's rank. Candidates for top positions in the chain of command often need the recommendation of their student leaders and at least half of their classroom teachers. Thus the student chain of command creates positive peer pressure to behave. When this system is effective, students do not compete over who is the best-dressed or most socially adept. On the contrary, younger students aspire to leadership positions and model the behavior of their student leaders. One cannot become a leader without being well behaved and exemplifying school standards.

The lesson to be drawn from public military academies is not that there is one way to enforce order and discipline, but that young people benefit from structure, rigorous behavioral standards, and opportunities to belong, lead, and earn respect.[43] Academy discipline is not an infantilizing or disillusioning force. On the contrary, it builds students up while ensuring that teaching and learning can occur in a respectful, orderly setting.

Public military academies employ a variety of mechanisms for monitoring students' progress. They send interim report cards to parents as frequently as once per month. The staff is also more willing to call students' parents about minor infractions, such as wearing inappropriate attire or using a cell phone in school multiple times.[44] The academies lay out their high expectations from the outset. Without intense monitoring from staff and student leaders, these expectations would have less meaning and impact on student behavior.

The academies I envision could emulate the PMAs' approach to mentoring and monitoring students, as well as the critically important and closely related functions of rewarding and recognizing them. As Sloman writes, the heart of the reward structure in PMAs is the student ranks that constitute the chain of command.[45] Ranks are denoted on students' attire, and higher-ranking students may wear special attire several days per week.

The criteria for earning rank vary and are meant to make the promotion process challenging and transparent. To attain the threshold rank of Cadet Seaman Apprentice at the Rickover Academy in Chicago, for instance, cadets must maintain a GPA of 2.0 with no F grades. These requirements are gradually ratcheted up, but only to a high point of a 3.0 GPA and no D or F grades. This ceiling is intentional so that students with less than stellar grades have an opportunity to attain high ranks.

Other criteria include maintaining strong marks in the school's specialty courses; maintaining a 90 percent or higher attendance rate for classes and morning inspection; wearing proper attire; memorizing and reciting numerous pledges and creeds; not accumulating demerits, honor code violations, or other punishments; obtaining recommendations for promotion from teachers, student leaders, and, at higher ranks, senior administrators; passing written and performance-based tests on certain subjects related to the chain of command; satisfactorily completing all tasks assigned by the student chain of command; and being an active member of one or more unit or school activities. At the highest levels, Sloman adds, students must also pass an oral interview with a promotion board, attend extracurricular activities such as Basic Leadership Training, and write a "Statement of Motivation."[46] The promotion system is not rigidly based on seniority. Sophomores can outrank juniors and seniors if they work hard enough.

As in public military schools, the academies I envision could award promotions four or five times per year. This would allow for frequent recognition, along with frequent monitoring. So many factors go into a promotion that this process is a perfect opportunity to monitor students' progress. As a staff member at one military academy commented: "So four times a year we do that and it gives us an opportunity to see who is really struggling, who is not."[47]

Judging from students' responses to the ranking system, it achieves the desired effect. Students do not take the rankings lightly. According to a teacher at a military academy, "When I get the freshmen on the first day of school, they come in with nothing. Not even a name tag. After the first and second quarter, as they start getting things on their uniform, a lot of them start really looking forward to [it] because, you know, they want what the sophomores and the juniors are getting to put on. And some of them, in one of my classes, they're actually going through the cadet handbook and looking at it, like, 'I did this, I did this, I did this,' but when they get it, it's like, 'I got it, all right, now where's the next one? I've got to do the next thing now.' And when they get their rank, you know, as soon as they get it when we do roll call, they like to start sounding off with their new one."[48]

As Sloman notes, this teacher's comments describe a well-functioning ranking system in which students are highly motivated to continue moving up the chain.[49] They model the behavior and aspire to be like the student leaders. When they achieve what they were aiming for, they are clearly proud of the accomplishment—of being able to "sound off" with their new rank—but they already have their eyes trained on the next level. Since so much of the ranking system requires sound academic performance and behavior, students are drawn into success by a combination of rewards, incentives, and competition.

The promotion system helps curb and co-opt disruptive behavior. As one student observed, "The sophomores came in, they went all wild and crazy like 'I don't care, I don't care,' but it's like you give them rank and they turn into a whole different person. . . . And they'll want more. They're crazy and doing bad stuff, but then you give them rank and they're like, 'Oh, I have power, I'm going to make sure my uniform looks nice, I want to shine my shoes today.'"[50]

Consequently, student and adult leaders are not shy about making strategic decisions when recognizing students. While the system must be transparent and fair, certain students are given extra encouragement. As the same student explained: ". . . [T]here's people we target because we feel they're on the verge of being either a leader or a knucklehead. You know, there's some fence that they're straddling, and sometimes you can push them over the fence if you give them one, and you reward them in some way. [Talking to JROTC instructor:] And I don't know if you noticed we rewarded one freshman with three awards this time, and we're really looking for him to really branch over to that side of the fence."[51]

Rankings are far from the only form of recognition students at public military academies are eligible to receive, says Sloman.[52] They also wear ribbons on their uniforms that denote specific accomplishments. These accomplishments run the gamut from perfect attendance to fewest demerits, from participating in service activities to completing leadership training and representing the school in parades. At one military academy, there are both a commandant's list and a superintendent's list for academic success.[53] The superintendent's list recognizes students with all As and no more than two Bs, while the commandant's list denotes students with all Bs. These students receive gift cards from a bookstore, and their names are posted on the hallway bulletin board for the entire semester. The purpose of the less exclusive commandant's list is to make academic honors feel within reach to more students, push B students to believe they can join the superintendent's list, and celebrate strong as well as exceptional performance.

At large traditional schools, opportunities such as these are often rare and out of reach. The top athletes and students receive recognition, but most earn nothing. At the academies, students notice and appreciate the attention. As one student remarked:

> I think we are [rewarded more often] because back when I was in elementary school, it was at the end of the school year, not every quarter. . . . I think that we are . . . rewarded and praised a lot cause I know many occasions when [the superintendent] has talked to us and said, oh, you guys are doing great . . . or you guys are so smart and everything and praise us all the time. So it's like we know we're not stupid, and we know that evidently we're doing something good. So it's not like we're just sitting here like I'm doing my work but nobody cares. Like, all our teachers care.[54]

Taking a cue from PMAs, the strictly civilian academies that I am proposing could establish robust rewards systems that reach and motivate the broadest array of students who have made academic progress or contributed in other valued ways. Of course, it is critically important that the academies promote a culture of achievement so there is no negative stigma attached to scholastic success. As Sloman notes, pageantry unquestionably helps.[55] The purpose of holding awards assemblies, distributing specially designed ribbons, and "sounding off" of ranks is to let students know that their accomplishments are valued and important to faculty, fellow students, parents, and the broader community.

Much of what public military academies do by way of mentoring, monitoring, rewards, and recognition could be adapted and customized—without any military trappings—for civilian academies. As Sloman indicated, the key generic ingredients that are readily transferable include: issuing frequent report cards; contacting parents when appropriate; administering a demerit system; providing tangible incentives to motivate students to achieve; placing ribbons or other markers on students' attire to denote specific accomplishments; creating awards akin to the commandant's list and superintendent's list; and honoring students for scholastic improvement and nonacademic achievements.[56] A civilian equivalent of the student chain of command is also quite conceivable and could be an integral feature of the culture of the academies.

Staffing the Academies

Staffing obviously is another key to the ability of the academies to accomplish their unique mission. The standard academic courses require state-certified teachers. Since virtual learning should be a major component of any course of instruction, it is critically important to hire teachers who enthusiastically embrace and effectively employ the technology instead of resist it. It is also essential to recruit teachers who want to work with "these" youngsters in "this" setting. As we learned from ChalleNGe, authentic devotion to the young people and the program contribute to the success of both. Teachers may relish the opportunity to teach at the academies because, assuming they function as expected, the atmosphere will be orderly, the students will be well behaved and focused, and the mentors and rewards will motivate them to learn.

While educators without military backgrounds clearly can function in the academies, it should be possible to recruit qualified teachers who have served on active duty or else in the reserves or National Guard. For instance, Troops to Teachers, a Department of Defense program, helps military personnel transition into teaching careers. According to Sloman, Troops to Teachers screens candidates extensively and has accumulated a strong track record of successful placements.[57] Tapping this relevant talent pool also increases the prospects for diversity on staff.

There are rather significant advantages to hiring properly vetted teachers with military backgrounds. To begin with, the culture of the academies, albeit nonmilitary, will be familiar to them. The odds are that in their military training, they have utilized and benefited from blended, virtual, and experiential learning approaches that should be an integral feature of instruction in the academies. Moreover, their military training equips them to handle such components as leadership, followership, and responsible citizenship. They will be steeped in the culture of mentoring, recognition, and rewards that is essential to the success of the academy. Thus, hiring teachers with military backgrounds presents many opportunities for staff efficiencies. Needless to say, teaching candidates must be vetted with care to avoid selecting those who may have been so traumatized by active military duty that they do not belong in the classroom or counseling young people.

Given the mission and program components, the academy staff must consist of more than teachers. ChalleNGe, for instance, owes its success to the presence of counselors and so-called cadre. The rationale for having state-certified social, career, and psychological counselors on the team is self-evident. Drawing on the ChalleNGe model, the civilian equivalents of cadre members would handle some nonacademic program components, serve as mentors and advisors to students, help maintain discipline and order, monitor classrooms and corridors, and oversee the student chain of command.

Appropriately screened applicants with military backgrounds are well suited to these roles. When it comes to teaching leadership and followership, for instance, military veterans can draw on past experiences and temperament to bring lesson plans to life.[58] A civilian teacher at a public military academy provided an apt description of what sets that school's JROTC instructors apart:

> I don't necessarily think that nonmilitary people have the experiences or the set of circumstances that you [a JROTC instructor at PMA-Leeds] or people in the military have that would be able to let them teach a class in leadership. I don't think everybody has it.

It's a special thing that you have and other military people have that can model leadership, and the kids pick up on that. If you gave [the JROTC manual] to [regular teachers], it wouldn't come off the same way. I mean, you'd just be reading out of the book. Take conflict resolution—you know it firsthand, from the big scale of war to the smallest scale of dealing with your troops. That's a set of experiences that the average teacher coming in out of college doesn't have.[59]

Recruiting staff with military backgrounds is not tantamount to militarizing the academies that I have in mind. The idea is to tap into skill sets and life experiences that will help groom young people who heretofore have been woefully underdeveloped when it comes to social skills and self-discipline. Military veterans are by no means the only source of talent worth exploring.

People trained as athletic coaches as well as teachers may be another promising source of staff who can both teach courses, mentor youngsters, and handle other components, such as physical fitness, leadership and followership, and community service. The sluggish labor market may lure applicants with broad qualifications to opportunities like these.

To underscore the civilian nature of the academies, I lean toward calling these crucial staff members something like life coaches instead of cadre, which obviously has military connotations. Clearly the portfolio of these life coaches would be broader than a traditional athletic coach. Their basic role in the academies would be to counsel the students and help them acquire the social and navigational skills needed to function successfully in school and in life.

Since the academies must be extremely careful and highly selective, they need to be run with minimal impediments, union or otherwise, to hiring, promoting, or dismissing staff based on the best interests of the students. The academies could be designed as small, themed public schools, provided they have the requisite authority over hiring and are not excessively constrained by union rules. If need be, they could be constituted as charter schools, which enjoy greater discretion over hiring, length of school days and years, and so forth.

Finally, what should these academies be called? Branding helps instill pride among the youngsters who attend and reduces the risk that they will be stigmatized as losers. Therefore an upbeat brand, such as Strivers Academy, or a name associated with a fabled local figure, might create a favorable image that erases any stigma. Ultimately, the most effective counter to any stigma will be the success of the academies and their graduates.

13

Gauging Academy Effectiveness

IN PUBLIC EDUCATION TODAY, assessment serves many purposes—and masters. Politicians insist on holding schools, teachers, and students accountable. High-stakes tests administered by states, school districts, schools, and teachers are the primary tool for gauging whether students are progressing academically, stagnating, or even regressing, whether teachers should be promoted or retained, whether principals should be renewed or fired, and indeed whether schools should continue operating or be closed. The statistics are aggregated into reports released to the public. Beyond serving as the primary mechanism for external accountability, assessment is also a critically important means of helping educators gauge whether their pupils are making suitable progress, whether adjustments in instructional strategies or supports are indicated, and whether parents need to be alerted. Lastly, assessment data provide indispensable material for independent evaluations.

The prevailing methods of appraising the performance of schools, teachers, and pupils that capture the attention of policymakers, politicians, and the public typically concentrate on standardized test results. Yet this measure alone is too narrow to gauge the effectiveness of programs that address students' academic and social development. A recent study by the National Research Council found that the accountability methods employed these days utilize assessment systems that are not attuned to young people whose weak academic performance and behavior patterns are the sources of greatest societal concern.[1]

The Educational Testing Service created the Gordon Commission on the Future of Assessment in Education to examine how assessment can be used most effectively to serve the educational and informational needs of students, teachers, and society.[2] Chaired by Edmund Gordon, the panel advocated a fundamental shift in thinking about the purpose of assessment. As it stated, "Throughout the long history of educational assessment in the United States, it has been seen by policymakers as a means of enforcing accountability for the performance of teachers and schools. For a relatively low outlay, assessment could expose academic weaknesses and make it possible to pressure schools and teachers to improve."[3] At their core, the commission continued, "educational assessments are statements about what educators, state policymakers, and, indirectly, parents want their student to learn and—in a larger sense—become. What we choose to assess is what will end up being the focus of classroom instruction."[4]

The Gordon Commission argued that going forward, assessments must advance competencies that are matched to the era in which we live. "Contemporary students must be able to evaluate the validity and relevance of disparate pieces of information and draw conclusions from them. They need to use what they know to make conjectures and seek evidence to test them, come up with new ideas, and contribute productively to their networks, whether on the job or in their communities. . . . At the most general level, the emphasis in our educational systems needs to be on helping individuals make sense of the world and how to operate effectively within it."[5]

As Heather Kugelmass, one of my graduate students at Princeton, wrote in a working paper about assessment, school impact tends to be measured in various ways. This often results in differing opinions about what is important to students and society, what outcomes should be valued by stakeholders, and what data can feasibly be collected.[6] Educational metrics not only measure educational effectiveness, she noted, they also can influence it, as reflected in the adage "What gets assessed gets addressed." Kugelmass continues: "Yet in education as elsewhere, metrics seem to emphasize what is easily measurable over what is valuable to measure. In the age of accountability, those two tendencies can form a dangerous combination—one that must be taken into consideration when evaluating options for improving education for the most disadvantaged students."[7]

To do justice to the academies I envision and, above all, to the youngsters who attend them, the mechanisms used for evaluating the intervention should be true to the vision, attuned to the mission, and calibrated to capture the impacts on the students' academic as well as social development. The dual mission of academic and social development requires nuanced assessment mechanisms that convey students' progress—and any lingering problems—along multiple, mutually reinforcing pathways. These assessments should also recognize that young people learn and develop at different rates. Care must be taken in defining the metrics, as conventional tests alone, while unquestionably important, will not suffice. Nor, as experience teaches us, are short-term tests and time horizons appropriate since the benefits, assuming they surface, may take time to materialize.

Let us begin with near-term indicators. The obvious place to start is measures of academic progress, stagnation, or regression. These metrics might include:

- Reading and math competency as reflected on state and district tests, as well as on NAEP or closely calibrated to it. Since many and perhaps even most students in these academies will start out performing way below par, it will be important to measure any gains in the proportion that climb from Below Basic up to Basic and beyond as defined by NAEP.

- Changes in students' grade point averages.

- "Freshman-on-track," an intriguing and potentially important metric employed by the Chicago schools to predict high school success and identify students at great risk for dropping out of school.[8]

- School engagement as measured by attendance, tardiness, and truancy rates.

- Grade-by-grade promotion vs. retention rates.

- On-time school completion and graduation rates.

- GED completion rates.

- Acquisition of skills needed to qualify for admission to community colleges, four-year colleges, and universities; postsecondary career training programs; and decent-paying jobs.

- Acceptance rates for two-year and four-year colleges, ranging from those using open enrollment to highly competitive institutions.

- Placement in postgraduation career-training programs and jobs.

Assessing students' social and emotional development obviously requires using different metrics and mechanisms for capturing impacts. Some of these "soft" skills may lend themselves to "testing" or formative assessment. Others could be gauged using surveys, interviews, and other feedback from teachers, school staff, parents, and youngsters themselves. Under acute pressure to improve test scores, underperforming school systems typically ignore or lack the resources to undertake this mode of assessment. Yet it is essential to the mission of these academies. Therefore, school districts and individual institutions that authentically embrace this mission must invest in calculating these nonacademic outcomes. Examples of those they should endeavor to capture include:

- Gains in such ChalleNGe-inspired core competencies as life-coping skills, health and hygiene, fitness, leadership and followership, and community service.

- Engagement in and assumption of leadership roles in student government and extracurricular activities.

- Development of work-related skills and habits such as teamwork, problem-solving, and productivity that are valued by prospective employers.

- Improvements in SEL skills and attitudes, such as social awareness, self-discipline, decision-making ability, positive relationships with adults and peers, and healthy sense of personal identity.

- Incidence of negative behaviors, such as gang membership, criminal activity, alcohol or substance abuse, or unwed pregnancy or fatherhood.

- Reductions in emotional distress and conduct problems triggering expulsions, suspensions, and lesser sanctions.

Beyond the conventional metrics for ascertaining school effectiveness, it is also relevant and important to assess how satisfied teachers, parents, and students are with the academies. Are these academies perceived by educators as safe and orderly? Are educators drawn to teach there and do they believe they are more effective there than in traditional schools? Do parents feel their children are well served and safe? Do the students feel supported and safe? Are they reengaged and recommitted to proceeding with their education?

Assessment of the academies should not cease when secondary schooling ends. Transition to adulthood is the crucial next step in the youngsters' development. MDRC has focused on this phase in many evaluations of program interventions, including ChalleNGe. After all, it is critically important to know whether and to what extent an intervention actually prepares young people for life after high school since this phase is the launching pad for the rest of their lives. As might be expected, the metrics would include education and employment experiences, such as:

- Enrollment in GED prep classes and receipt of GED certificates in the event they do not graduate from high school.

- Enrollment part-time or full-time in community college or four-year institutions.

- Receipt of associate or bachelor degrees and beyond.

- Participation in and completion of creditable job-training programs that prepare trainees for better than low-wage, entry-level jobs.

- Labor market experience, including success in obtaining employment, whether and to what extent their earnings exceed the minimum wage, and number of months employed in recent years.

Preoccupied with daily pressures and strapped for funds, school districts seldom keep tabs on the longer-term impacts of their efforts. Indeed, even the most sophisticated evaluations are unable to track participants well into adulthood, typically for want of funding. Yet as some long-term studies have shown, it is critically important wherever possible to capture longer-term outcomes to determine whether and to what extent investments in interventions pay enduring, significant dividends for participants and for society.

Significant impacts can surface in subsequent years. A telling example are the so-called career academies evaluated by MDRC over the course of 15 years.[9] Career academies are organized into small learning communities and offer a personalized learning environment. Unique among public schools, they combine academic, work-related, and technical curricula around career themes. The academic gains were unimpressive in the early going because the overall performance of career academy students on standardized tests was no higher than those of the controls.

These indifferent results could easily have tempted educators and policymakers with short-time horizons to abandon the intervention, or at least cease keeping track of the outcomes. Yet MDRC found that eight years after career academy alumni graduated, they had earned on average 11 percent more than the controls. Interestingly, the gains were concentrated among young men, 80 percent of whom were black or Latino.[10] Thus, thanks to the long duration of the evaluation, MDRC could report that career academies are one of the few youth-focused interventions found to improve the labor market prospects of young men of color. The evaluators also reported that young men were more prone to marry and serve as custodial parents.

These findings enabled Gordon Berlin, president of MDRC, to reach another key conclusion that bears on the curriculum of the public academy concept I am proposing. This study, he commented, provides the most rigorous evidence to date that investing in career-oriented programs and experiences for high school students can have a long-term payoff in the labor market.[11] In other words, the employment and earnings gains did not come at the expense of postsecondary enrollment and completion. Academy participants and students in the control group had similar levels of academic achievement. These findings, Berlin noted, suggest that pitting academic preparation against career development in high schools may be a false dichotomy.[12]

Since the academies I envision would address the academic and social development of their students, it would be important and instructive to track their experiences once they enter adulthood. Do they continue their formal educations to completion? Do they obtain "good" jobs and manage to remain employed? How much do they earn? Do they and their families attain economic self-sufficiency, partially or even entirely free of income supports provided by government? Do they indeed form families and support their children? Are they married to or at least cohabiting with the other parent? Do they stay out of trouble with the law? Do they vote and otherwise participate actively in the civic life of their communities and the country? Do they take appropriate care of their health?

Sophisticated assessments of program interventions can also examine such operational issues as quality of execution, fidelity of replication, and scalability. Since interventions for human beings must contend with the vagaries of human behavior, there is much to be learned from nuanced studies of program implementation, from conception to expansion.

14

Cost-Benefit Considerations

THE ACADEMIES I ENVISION may cost more to operate on a per-pupil basis than traditional schools. That is attributable to the unique ingredients associated with the dual mission of fostering the academic and social development of the youngsters who enroll, compounded by the unique challenges presented by adolescents who are struggling in school and in life. These young people cannot be steered back on track on automatic pilot.

Operating Costs

On the expense side of the ledger, the curriculum of the academies would cover those subjects mandated by the state as well as the local school district. Perhaps school districts that establish these academies could persuade the state education agency to waive or relax certain higher level course requirements in, say, science or social studies. After all, given where these academically troubled youngsters start out, it may not be realistic to expect all of them to make up so much lost ground and reach the finish line articulated by increasingly rigorous state graduation standards. In any event, sponsors of the academies should not count on concessions.

Drawing on the lessons of ChalleNGe, the mandatory curriculum should include coursework in such so-called nonacademic subjects as responsible citizenship, life-coping skills, health and hygiene, physical fitness, leadership and followership, and job skills and readiness. Conceivably, some of these elements could be incorporated in the curriculum in lieu of more traditional courses, thus reducing the incremental costs. For example, perhaps responsible citizenship and leadership and followership could incorporate elements of traditional social studies and government and be taught instead of those courses. Health and hygiene could take the place of science. Physical fitness belongs in every school. And life-coping skills and job skills/readiness could be bundled together. Some of these topics could be incorporated into the school day or substitute for elective courses and extracurricular activities. As in the case of ChalleNGe, community service can provide an outlet for experiential learning.

The point is, there may be opportunities for subject matter consolidation or substitution that reduce the incremental cost of the more expansive curriculum associated with academic and social development. This probably would require approval from the state. But it may be obtainable given the grim fate that otherwise awaits these youngsters who clearly have disengaged from school and are on the verge of becoming disconnected from society.

These academies will require teachers and administrators, just as other small schools do. For the dual mission to succeed, the teachers must be supplemented by the life coaches, namely the civilian equivalent of the cadre in ChalleNGe. In traditional schools, the counselor function is typically underfunded. Incorporating life coaches on staff will add costs compared with the customary budget of schools.

Drawing on Donohue's concept, the school day, week, and year of an enterprise like this would be lengthened to accommodate all of the elements, provide more time on task for learning and mentoring, and keep the youngsters out of harm's way to the maximum extent possible. Extended hours cost extra money. Since some school districts are already moving in this direction, the incremental cost is not an unaccustomed expenditure. If, as Donohue strongly recommends, institutions like these academies occupy their own buildings instead of co-locating in large facilities with other schools, this may be less cost-effective albeit considerably more desirable programmatically.

Other ingredients of the academies I envision may add to the cost. As Sloman observed, common attire, ribbons, material incentives, awards ceremonies, and all the activities for which students are honored will also add up.[1] Schools will have to make difficult decisions about how lavish to make the awards ceremonies. Pageantry and material incentives matter in communicating the importance of students' accomplishments. Lastly, community service projects and experiential learning that take students outside the building will cost extra.

Efficiencies

On the other hand, these academies may generate meaningful savings and efficiencies compared with traditional schools. Assuming the atmosphere is orderly and the students are focused on learning, the academies may actually get by with larger classes. They may need fewer administrators and no strictly security personnel since the life coaches who mentor students can also keep a watchful eye on them, as well as the corridors and grounds. It may be reasonable to expect the principal and other administrators to double up and teach one of the curricular components. The academies can hire life coaches who handle the leadership/followership and physical fitness components. In other words, it may be feasible in the current labor market to recruit staff who can multitask by performing administrative or mentoring roles while also carrying part of the instructional load.

Additional efficiencies may accrue from integrating technology-based instruction deeply into the curriculum. Intrigued by the potential cost savings, some of the nation's most prestigious colleges and universities have taken a cue from their for-profit counterparts and begun offering online courses. Public schools are getting into the act as well. Some states and school districts offer accredited online courses that can be taken in lieu of those offered in school buildings.

The State of Florida goes so far as to require that all ninth graders take at least one online course to graduate, with the expectation that the requirement will increase over time. The state recognizes an entity known as the Florida Virtual School (FLVS) as a public school authorized to provide web-based courses to middle school and high school students.[2] FLVS is accredited by several entities including the Southern Association of Colleges and Schools and other bodies. Fittingly enough, its slogan is "any time, any place, any path, any pace." Florida forbids school districts from limiting student access to FLVS courses. The proviso is that the school counselor must determine that the online course is suitable based on the student's academic record, grade level, and age. Courses are taught by certified instructors who know their subjects. Teachers interact with students through email, voice mail, and instant messaging. They are available from 8:00 a.m. to 8:00 p.m. daily and on weekends. FLVS is not a full-fledged school, however. It does not grant diplomas or GED certificates. Enrollment in FLVS courses surged from 1,100 students in 33 courses in 1998 to nearly 315,000 students in 120 courses as of 2011–12.[3]

Virtual instruction appeals to financially strapped states and school districts because of the anticipated cost savings. If, as this robust enrollment trend suggests, students and parents really take to virtual instruction, it could blossom into a viable and sustainable complement to traditional K–12 education. Some school systems are calling and raising the idea of online instruction by creating full-fledged virtual schools. For instance, the Fairfax County (Virginia) school system near Washington, D.C., offers online courses à la carte. Furthermore, the district is thinking of creating a virtual high school that allows students to take all of their courses online from home.[4] Assignments would be delivered on-screen and after-school clubs would meet online. The downside is there would be no sports teams or pep rallies for these youngsters.

Some assessments of virtual courses suggest that combining online instruction with face-to-face learning enables students to progress through the curriculum at their own pace. This requires that they take more responsibility for their own learning. A survey of students indicated that most of those who have taken virtual courses like the flexible scheduling, control of their own learning, and ability to work at their own pace.

A recent phenomenon worth noting—and understanding—is the steep 32 percent decline in FLVS enrollment since 2012, forcing the layoff of one-third of its workforce.[5] Evidently, the state has decided to introduce competition in virtual education and diversify the array of providers. According to *Education Week*, weak academic results in the early going at some virtual public schools and charter schools in Kansas and Tennessee confirm that they are not an instant success and may take several years to get their footing. One key may be the combination of classroom and virtual instruction in what's called blended learning, as opposed to exclusive reliance on virtual instruction that isolates youngsters from real-life instructors and peers. This obviously would be true of students who need substantial doses of social and emotional development, which surely cannot be taught online.

The push toward online learning triggers worries about whether low-income and minority youngsters who are likely candidates for the academies I envision would be handicapped by lack of familiarity with technology or access to it outside of school.

When I headed the National Urban League, we joined with the Federal Communications Commission and other civil rights and community-based groups in a concerted effort to close the so-called digital divide. By that we meant the yawning gap between white middle- and upper-income families, on the one hand, and low-income and minority families, on the other, in their comparative rates of computer ownership, utilization, and literacy, as well as Internet access. Although it is narrower now, there remains a gap between digital haves and have-nots. As *The New York Times* has reported, roughly two-thirds of all Americans have broadband access at home.[6] But for families earning less than $20,000 annually, that proportion falls to 40 percent. Half of all Hispanics and 41 percent of African-American homes still lack broadband.

As with technology, the nature of the digital divide has changed over time. There is a new unanticipated gap that is equally disturbing and detrimental. As the *Times* reported, a study by the Kaiser Family Foundation in 2010 found that youngsters whose parents do not have college degrees spend 90 minutes more per day exposed to media—TVs, computers, and other devices—than children from higher socioeconomic families.[7] Alarmingly, the difference little more than a decade ago was merely 16 minutes.

If the extra time was largely devoted to doing schoolwork and other enriching activities, the gap would be less worrisome. Unfortunately, the Kaiser study's coauthor, Vicky Rideout, discovered this was not the case. "Despite the educational potential of computers," she remarked, "the reality is that their use for education or other meaningful content creation is minuscule compared to their use for pure entertainment. Instead of closing the achievement gap, they're widening the time-wasting gap."[8]

A refreshingly frank 12-year-old from Oakland, California, named Markiy Cook acknowledged the academic damage. Even though money is tight, his family has two laptops, an Xbox, and a Nintendo. Plus, he has a phone. He uses these devices for Facebook, YouTube, texting, and playing games. Markiy admitted that on weekends he stays up all night, until 7 a.m. "It's why I'm so tired on Monday."[9] And probably why his grades are so dreadful that he ranks at the bottom of his class.

While I recognize the persistence of the digital divide, I wholeheartedly endorse the aggressive use of technology-driven instruction in the academies I envision. After all, the reality is that young people readily take to video games, computers, smartphones, and the Web as though they were second nature to them. Like it or not, ready or not, they must be technologically literate to survive and thrive in the information age economy of the twenty-first century.

This point about the direct connection between literacy, technology, employability, and economic competitiveness was driven home to me in a conversation with a corporate CEO some years ago. He told me that his company's factory workers would be required to use wireless hand-held computers that store all sorts of information about inventory supplies and assembly procedures. To use these computers, employees would have to be able to read. But this goes way beyond identifying the words in front of them on the screen. They must be able to follow the instructions, proceed from one step to the next, and find solutions to the problems put to them by their supervisors. So word recognition and reading comprehension are critically important.

Applicants who possess these new basic skills can qualify for good-paying jobs as twenty-first-century factory workers. Those who do not will be lucky to land a lowly job as a twenty-first-century janitor. The company's success in a global economy depends as never before on a workforce that can read and is technologically literate.

Online and technology-driven instruction permits a degree of personalized learning seldom seen in traditional classrooms. Technology also facilitates fresh configurations of the teaching corps that can measurably reduce personnel costs. As *Education Week* reported, a school in Eagle County, Colorado, cut three foreign language teaching positions and replaced them with online instruction.[10] Not surprisingly, the parents and teachers objected.

As online instruction gains momentum and financially strapped school systems search for savings, schools may be able to rely on fewer, more highly skilled and paid teachers who are supported by new technology and larger numbers of less expensive paraprofessionals.[11] Richard Murnane, an economist and professor of education at Harvard, observes that restructuring schools using technology would mirror changes wrought in other fields. The military has vastly more experience than public schools with technology-based instruction. The Army's March2Success program brings those benefits to the students who need academic support.

The academies I envision offer the opportunity to devise a staffing pattern on a clean slate with no preconceptions about instructional methods, class size, or pupil–teacher ratios. The efficiencies that could be realized from extensive use of virtual and technology-based learning may necessitate fewer classroom teachers and facilitate a staffing pattern and student–teacher–coach ratio that accommodates SEL staff within traditional per-pupil expenditure levels.

As appealing as virtual education may be, the approach is not free of controversy. Virtual education may not work for every student. Self-motivated youngsters might take to it, but low-performing students may falter if there is diminished personal supervision and encouragement from teachers as a result. Yet the academies may be able to compensate for both concerns because of the high level of personal support from the instructors and coaches and because of the heavy emphasis on motivating and monitoring the youngsters.

Additional savings may be in store for school districts if these academies succeed. For instance, school systems might save money by retaining fewer students in grade, scaling back summer school, and graduating more students on time. There would also be less need for other alternative programs and GED offerings for push-outs and dropouts.

The costs and efficiencies discussed here that are associated with operating the academies would be realized in the near term. Taking a cue from the RAND analysis of ChalleNGe, the academies I envision could generate significant intermediate and longer-term savings if it turns out they work.[12] RAND noted that the benefits of obtaining higher levels of education accrue over an entire lifetime. The gains from receiving a high school diploma and attending a year or more of college are substantial. By contrast, earning a GED generated little additional value, at least as narrowly estimated. The analysis by Bettina Lankard Brown pinpointed some valuable benefits, such as GED recipients encouraging their children to complete high school, which were not factored into RAND's calculus.[13]

ChalleNGe on average costs $15,436 per participant. Since participants are in residence only for five months, the annualized cost of one participant would be more than twice that amount, and appreciably higher than the typical expense of educating a youngster in a public middle or high school.

Notwithstanding the heftier price tag per participant compared with public schools, ChalleNGe generated an estimated $40,985 in total benefits and $25,549 in net benefits.[14] The gains that helped offset the costs included such factors as higher lifetime earnings along with reduced social welfare dependency and criminal activity. The net result was a benefit–cost ratio of 2.66 and a return on investment of 166 percent, for an internal rate of return of 6.4 percent.[15]

That was true of ChalleNGe. Since the academies I have in mind do not now exist, there is no way to predict whether they will work or, if they do, to project whether the economic and noneconomic benefits will appreciably outweigh the costs. Compared to ChalleNGe, these academies would serve an even more difficult population of young people who are drawn from a poorer, more densely minority pool and who may not volunteer. As a nonresidential intervention, there is a risk that academies may be a less intense and impactful intervention. The youngsters in these academies will be less insulated from negative forces since they will return to their homes and communities each day.

On the upside, however, the academy experience may actually be more impactful since the youngsters could attend throughout their middle school and/or high school years, instead of for merely five months. Academy staff would have considerably more opportunity to build stronger, more effective bridges to colleges, career-training programs, summer internships, and prospective employers. This might generate even stronger outcomes when it comes to education, employment, earnings, and self-sufficiency.

If they succeed, the academies could help stem the tide of school disengagement and dropping out that is costing our society dearly. As Sarah Burd-Sharps and Kristen Lewis have observed, more than 5.8 million young people nationwide—about one in seven teenagers and young adults between the ages of 16 and 24—are neither working nor in school.[16] "Rather than laying the foundation for a productive life of choice and value," they remarked, "these disconnected youth find themselves adrift at society's margins, unmoored from the systems and structures that confer knowledge, skills, identity, and purpose."

After a decade of relatively stable rates, the problem of disconnection grew significantly worse during the Great Recession. The combined bill for direct support and lost tax revenues associated with young people who are adrift cost U.S. taxpayers more than $93 billion in 2011 alone.[17] According to another estimate, high school graduates on average will earn $130,000 more over their lifetimes than high school dropouts. The dropouts from the Class of 2001 would have generated up to $154 billion in additional earnings over their lifetimes had they graduated from high school.[18]

If the academies I envision work, they will contribute other sizable savings to society. According to a report by the Alliance for Excellent Education, significantly reducing the number of high school dropouts would save society billions of dollars in health care costs because graduates of high school and college lead healthier lives and incur lower medical costs than dropouts.[19] Drawing on an analysis by Dr. Peter Muennig of Columbia University's Mailman School of Public Health, the alliance estimates that if half of the nation's high school dropouts over the age of 25 had graduated instead, the U.S. would have saved more than $7 billion in Medicaid expenditures in 2012 alone.[20] The savings accumulate with each subsequent year. Reducing the number of dropouts by half would save nearly $40 billion more in reduced incidence of heart disease, obesity, smoking, and alcoholism.[21]

Finding funds for the near-term incremental costs may be daunting, but it need not defeat the idea of these academies. Since this innovative model holds promise for boosting the achievement levels and social skills of youngsters who are struggling in school and in life, these academies may be eligible for supplemental federal and state funding and attract private funding as well.

Local school districts and states could finance these academies by

pooling funds from various sources. These might include the customary per-pupil expenditure allocated by the school district, as well as
funds that would otherwise be devoted to special education and alternative programs for these young people. It may be possible to persuade
states to invest some of their social service, juvenile corrections, and
criminal justice funding, at least on a pilot basis, to determine whether
the model works and to what extent. Another potential source could be
reprogrammed money that is not well spent. For example, Balfanz
notes that school districts spend roughly $2.4 billion annually on ninth
graders who are retained in grade, yet manage to promote only a quarter of them.[22] The academies I envision might be a smarter investment.
It may also be feasible to attract demonstration funding from various
federal agencies, foundations, and corporations that have a keen interest in improving the life prospects of these young people who are at
acute risk of being left behind.

15

From Idea to Implementation

EDUCATIONAL INNOVATIONS like the academies I propose seldom happen by osmosis. It will take vision, commitment, and initiative by educators, policymakers, and/or organizations to bring this new paradigm of public academies to fruition. Fortunately, there is a great deal of creative ferment in public education these days as schools systems in search of answers, or at least improved performance, are increasingly open to new approaches and players, and willing to take political risks by reconstituting or closing failing schools.

One potentially effective way to advance this idea is to establish an entity that serves as a repository of knowledge, best practice, technical assistance, and assessment, and in effect provides a repertory company of experts who can work directly with school districts interested in creating these types of academies. The kind of outfit I have in mind could be a newly minted "intermediary" organization that is available to assist districts in designing, establishing, and assessing the academies.

These organizations could call upon experts like Dan Donohue, former directors of successful local ChalleNGe units, experienced athletic coaches, counselors and social group workers, and other administrators or principals of schools who are genuinely devoted to the dual mission. An alternative scenario is for a national nonprofit group that is already deeply engaged in SEL programming in schools to expand its horizons and fulfill this role as a national intermediary organization.

Mind you, the intermediary's role would not be to operate these academies, but to facilitate their establishment and expansion by supporting school districts and/or states willing to take the initiative. The responsibilities and requisite capabilities of an intermediary would depend, of course, on whether it is the engine driving the national effort or else an indispensable source of support to help other entities propagate new academies across the country. Depending on its raison d'être, the intermediary could play the following roles:

- Seek out and negotiate relationships with states, local school districts, and other partners that add expertise, resources, and other value.

- Persuade those federal and state agencies that oversee education, labor, social services, criminal justice, and corrections to provide the supplemental funding needed above and beyond the annual per-pupil expenditures that participating school districts would be required to commit.

- Secure funding from corporations and philanthropies so that school districts will be assured the supplemental resources needed to operate these potentially costlier academies. One key to creating and then scaling up this model is for the intermediary to possess the authority to bring these supplemental resources to the table and to oversee whether they are awarded, extended, suspended, or rescinded. This leverage is essential for ensuring the fidelity, integrity, and durability of the academy model.

- Establish a national brand name that is copyrighted and bestowed exclusively by the intermediary on participating academies. For example, each might be called the Strivers Academy of (name of city, community, or neighborhood).

- Issue charters or licenses to the academies, officially anointing them as participants in the network overseen by the intermediary.

- Require that school districts and academies sign a memorandum of understanding or terms of affiliation, stipulating the respective obligations and expectations of the participants and the national intermediary.

- Promulgate operating protocols and performance expectations that participating academies must meet. Expectations include school reengagement, academic progress and achievement, high school graduation rates, and postsecondary outcomes, as well as metrics related to the effective and appropriate operation of the academy.

- Closely monitor whether the academies meet expectations. If they fall significantly short, the intermediary should ascertain what the game plan is for getting them back on course. Academies that persistently falter could be placed on probation, or, if it comes to that, dropped from the network and stripped of the supplemental funding that the intermediary dispenses.

- Bestow the highly coveted equivalent of a "Good Housekeeping Seal of Approval" upon soundly conceived and well-run academies that function in effect as the benchmarks for everyone else.

- Possibly treat all methods and material as proprietary, i.e., copyrighted and owned by the intermediary and offered only to academies that operate under the common brand name and adhere to the prescribed protocols. Proprietary content might include: curriculum content and materials; instructional methods; program components and structure; membership entity to which students belong; frequency, forms, and criteria for student recognition; and requirements and methods for recruiting, screening, and selecting the blend of lead administrator, teachers, life coaches, and other staff to run the academy.

- Provide on-site and virtual training for academy staff during the planning stage, start-up phase, and ongoing implementation. In addition, conduct ongoing monitoring, technical assistance, troubleshooting, and problem-solving to the participating school districts and academies.

- Specify the data that every site must collect and provide to the intermediary. This includes requiring that all students in the academies submit to the same assessment system so that there is consistency and transparency of reported outcomes across all sites.

- Report annually on the implementation, progress, and student outcomes to all funding sources, legislative bodies, parents and families of the participants, the media, and the general public.

National intermediaries, whether conducting demonstrations or taking promising ideas to scale, must proceed cautiously and respectfully in working with school districts, which have seen many an ostensibly effective reform and well-intentioned reformer come and go over the years. As Michael Casserly of the Council of the Great City Schools cautions, intermediary organizations should approach schools in an authentic spirit of collaboration.[1] Interventions need to be jointly developed and "owned" by local educators if they are to garner sustainable support locally. Otherwise, school administrators and educators may feel put upon by outside reformers, implement the intervention poorly or indifferently, and then exchange bitter recriminations over which side is to blame for disappointing results.

A rather different scenario is to establish the equivalent of a charter management organization (CMO), akin to the national KIPP organization, that is prepared to design and operate this kind of school at the invitation of interested districts. This could take the form of an entirely new CMO-like organization; or an existing, highly regarded CMO that "gets it" could expand into this line of work if there is sufficient demand from local school districts.

At the local level, school systems can invite an intermediary or CMO, if such exist, to establish new academies with this dual mission in their districts. Alternatively, they can invite their strongest principals and ablest teachers who are truly committed to this approach to design and establish prototype academies. Since the culture and structure would be so distinctive, ideally these schools should not be co-located as schools-within-schools. Perhaps the districts could designate closed school buildings that are not too large or even take over decommissioned parochial school buildings, which are increasingly available in cities.

School districts that are willing to glean lessons from the quasi-military programs, while hewing to the strictly civilian nature of the academy, could conceivably figure out how to move forward on their own based on available case studies, evaluations, and other literature. Alternatively or in addition, they could mine the nearest JROTC programs, ChalleNGe units, and public military academies for ideas about how to adapt their components and attributes without incorporating any military content.

In addition, host districts should seek waivers from the state to give the new academies breathing room to go through startup and growth pangs. And districts should seek exemptions from the rigid, state-imposed testing regimes and consequences to enable it to establish more sophisticated methods for assessing students' near-term and longer-term academic and social progress along the lines discussed earlier. Districts should endeavor to finance the schools by pooling their per-pupil expenditures and special education funding with supplemental funding from foundations as well as education, social service, labor, and criminal justice agencies at the state and federal levels.

For their part, state school boards and education agencies should grant interested districts the latitude to establish these schools and to institute assessment systems that are calibrated to their dual mission and longer-term goals. States should also help fund these schools, which may be costlier at the outset, by pooling resources from various sources.

Interested states could go even farther by establishing a variation of the special state-run districts for low-performing schools. Tennessee created the Achievement School District, which oversees the lowest 5 percent of public schools in the state. Michigan instituted the Education Achievement Authority to manage the poorest-performing schools in Detroit, an initiative that is encountering resistance from home rule advocates in that beleaguered city. In an approach that is even more akin to what I have in mind, Louisiana established the Recovery School District to create and manage new schools for children who returned to New Orleans after fleeing Hurricane Katrina.

In other words, instead of taking over low-performing schools, states could establish special purpose districts composed of newly created public academies devoted to the academic and social development of youngsters who are languishing hopelessly behind academically and clearly destined to fail and drop out of traditional schools. Of course, states would also be obliged to take lead responsibility for funding these schools, a prospect that is enhanced by the state's ability to assemble resources from various sources, such as the corrections and social services budgets. What's more, any state funding that would customarily go to local districts for educating these specific children should flow instead to the state-managed academies.

Governors with ChalleNGe units in their states could instruct the directors and staff of these programs to assist the special state districts and/or local school districts that want to create academies on their own. In fact, to ensure that the line of demarcation between this distinctive domestic role and other customary National Guard functions is crystal clear and impenetrable, governors might even go so far as to establish a separate administrative department under the aegis of the Guard whose sole mission is to collaborate with local districts and the special state district. This would help ensure access to emerging military research, best practice, and technology-driven training methods that are germane to young people served by public academies.

At the federal level, the U.S. Department of Education could establish a competitive demonstration program aimed at providing the supplemental funding needed to design and then operate these schools. Presumably the funding would be of long enough duration, say seven to ten years, to obtain a reliable picture of whether they are likely to benefit youngsters' academic performance and life prospects. This is necessary to insulate these schools from the frenetic testing pressure and annual frenzy over school grades and ratings. In addition, the DOE could form a dedicated program design group, composed of seasoned educators plus experts on SEL and quasi-military programs like ChalleNGe, to devise academy models that the DOE would be prepared to fund, presumably on an RFP basis. The DOE could also forge a strategic alliance with other federal agencies, such as Labor and Justice, as well as with the National Guard, the Army or other branches of the military that are willing to share their methods, models, and expertise for the purpose of helping interested states and school districts create these kinds of academies.

Since the lessons from these academies may have profound implications for the design and operation of public schools going forward, provision should be made for highly sophisticated and respected independent evaluators to assess them. In the early years, this could take the form of ethnographic and implementation studies. These could be coupled with "before and after" assessments, mainly to obtain a preliminary sense of whether these schools are gaining traction with their students.

As the academies mature, they should be subjected to more scientifically rigorous, random-assignment evaluations to help establish, as convincingly as research methods permit, whether and to what extent they make a genuine and enduring difference in the lives of their students.

Optimally, these evaluations should be conducted on an arm's-length basis. While it is conceivable for local districts, states, and/or the federal government to commission the assessments, these levels of government, as operators and/or funders, have a stake in the results. As was the case with the ChalleNGe evaluation, the optimal scenario is for a major foundation or, better yet, consortium of foundations to finance these studies.

These suggested next steps are neither prescriptive nor exhaustive. They are merely offered to illustrate some concrete ways for moving from idea to implementation. There may be other pathways that are more logical or compelling to educators who get the idea and want to go with it.

16

Conclusion

MILLIONS OF AMERICAN YOUNGSTERS are marginalized academically and destined for social and economic oblivion in the twenty-first century. They will be unable to uphold their obligations as citizens and providers. Their plight stems from many factors: family poverty and economic circumstances beyond their control; their own indifference to achievement and disenchantment with formal education as they have known it; and the inflexibility of public schools that fail to meet these troubled young people halfway.

My proposal to create these academies will not cure poverty or replace ill-equipped or inattentive parents. They will not revitalize ravaged communities, rejuvenate the economy, or create good, middle-class jobs.

But compared with the path of school failure that far too many youngsters are currently on, public academies devoted to the academic and social development of those youngsters may improve their inclination and capacity to achieve in school, steer them toward postsecondary schooling or training, prepare them to become coveted and productive workers, transform them into law-abiding and engaged citizens, and position them to be providers for their families and children.

The stubborn patterns of chronic school failure clearly show there is a profound mismatch between the mind-sets of millions of youngsters and the way their schools operate. This chasm will not be bridged by forcing more of the same on these frustrated youngsters or on their overmatched teachers, or by inundating these disaffected students with drill-and-kill testing that fuels more school failure.

We urgently need a new paradigm for adolescents who are struggling futilely in school and in life. For children who have clearly left the school building—attitudinally, emotionally, and/or physically—it is high time to think outside the box. The plain fact is, the U.S. military figured out how to nurture and unleash the potential of young people like these generations ago. By examining and adapting what the Pentagon knows about educating and developing aimless young people, we can transform these troubled and troublesome young Americans into a valued social and economic asset to our nation. As RAND discovered in its cost-benefit analysis of ChalleNGe, the dividend for the children and for society would amply justify the investment.

What a waste it is to write off these young people. Consider the staggering cost to society of maintaining prisons, welfare, and foster care. According to the U.S. Census Bureau, the average cumulative cost in lost productivity and wages for each high school dropout may total as much as $900,000. Think of the taxes they would have paid into the government's coffers and the fair share of baby boomers' Social Security benefits that they could have borne.

Some years ago a guest on the PBS show *NewsHour* commented that for World War II veterans from poor and working-class families, the GI Bill was their magic carpet to the American mainstream. The academies I envision could become the twenty-first-century magic carpet for young people who otherwise will surely never get a realistic shot at the American Dream.

Acknowledgments

MANY COLLEAGUES AND FAMILY MEMBERS have contributed importantly to this book. Let me begin, however, with more than 100,000 total strangers, namely the graduates of the National Guard Youth ChalleNGe Program, for demonstrating that investing in second chances for young people who are struggling in school and in life can pay handsome dividends for them as well as society at large.

As proud as I am of helping spawn the idea of ChalleNGe, the true founder and architect is Dan Donohue, former head of public information for the Guard, who designed the program and shepherded it during the critical formative years. Gratitude also goes to General Herbert Temple, former head of the National Guard, for enthusiastically embracing the idea at the outset. His successors as well as countless local ChalleNGe unit directors and leaders of the National Guard Youth Foundation have been critical to the program's success.

During the gestation period for ChalleNGe, William Taylor, of the Center for Strategic and International Studies, and Michael Bailin, of Public/Private Ventures, played pivotal roles in establishing the feasibility of a quasi-military youth corps for school dropouts. When I undertook the initial research in the mid-1970s that helped build the conceptual foundation for ChalleNGe, my indispensable partners in that task were Doris Zelinsky and Harry Wexler.

A generation later, Isabel Sawhill and Ron Haskins, codirectors of the Center on Children and Families at the Brookings Institution, provided the incubator that enabled me to examine the potential applicability of the methods and lessons from ChalleNGe for public education. Oliver Sloman, another colleague at Brookings, served as an invaluable research associate and sounding board. He enriched my thinking and wrote working papers that have contributed importantly to this book. Several benefactors have generously supported this work over the years, notably the Taconic Foundation, Goldman Sachs Foundation, and Abt Associates.

My research, thinking, and writing have been powerfully informed by Dr. James Comer, the guru of academic and social development, as well as by the important work of many scholars and educators who have advocated and authenticated the benefits of social and emotional learning. I am also grateful to MDRC and RAND for their rigorous assessments, which, happily, ended up affirming the worth of the intervention. I also thank the Rockefeller Foundation for providing a one-month residency at its magnificent Bellagio Center, where I researched and drafted significant portions of this book.

I am indebted to Professor Larry Mead of New York University for strongly encouraging me to write a book about ChalleNGe and its implications. Thanks to their curiosity and tough questioning, many of my students in the Woodrow Wilson School at Princeton University helped sharpen my thinking. Three in particular—Danielle Vildostegui, Caroline Hanamirian, and Bridget Bartlett—wrote term papers and, in the latter's case, a senior thesis that were immensely useful resources for this book.

Strugglers Into Strivers is my maiden voyage in self-publishing. Nevertheless, this book would not have seen the light of day without the wise counsel and able assistance of Fred Levine of Small Batch Books.

As always, I owe an unbounded debt of gratitude to my beloved wife, Marilyn, and the rest of our family for their enduring wisdom and support.

Notes

Chapter 1

1 National Commission on Excellence in Education, *A Nation at Risk: The Imperative for Educational Reform, A Report to the Nation and the Secretary of Education/United States Department of Education*, April 1983, datacenter.spps.org/uploads/SOTW_A_Nation_at_Risk_1983.pdf, p.5.

2 Condoleezza Rice and Joel Klein, *U.S. Education Reform and National Policy*, Council on Foreign Relations, 2012, www.cfr.org/united-states/us-education-reform-national-security/p27618.

3 Ibid., Overview.

4 Ibid.

5 Gregory Bangser and others, "Urban Education That Works: Moving Past School Type Debates and Embracing Choice" (unpublished report prepared by students in Woodrow Wilson School Graduate Policy Workshop WWS 591E, Princeton University, January 2012), p. 31.

6 Ibid., p. 11.

7 Alyson Klein, "SIG Effort Posts Promising Early Results: One-Year Improvements Seen in Many Schools, Ed. Dept. Finds," www.edweek.org, March 27, 2012.

8 Alyson Klein, "School Turnaround Push Still a Work in Progress," www.edweek.org, April 15, 2012.

9 *The Nation's Report Card: Trends in Academic Progress 2012*, Executive Summary, National Center for Education Statistics, Institute of Education Sciences, U.S. Department of Education, nces.ed.gov/nationsreportcard/pubs/main2012/2013456.aspx, 2012.

10 Ibid.

11 Erik W. Robelen, "Achievement Gaps Narrow on Long-Term NAEP," www.edweek.org, June 27, 2013.

12 Ibid.

13 *Beating the Odds: Analysis of Student Performance on State Assessments and NAEP: Results from the 2009–10 School Year,* (Washington, DC: Council of the Great City Schools, www.cgcs.org/Pubs/BTOX.pdf, March 2011), p.6.

14 Ibid., p. 1.

15 Ibid., p. 4.

16 Ibid., p. 5.

17 Howard S. Bloom, Saskia Levy Thompson, and Rebecca Unterman, *Transforming the High School Experience: How New York City's New Small Schools Are Boosting Student Achievement and Graduation Rates* (New York: MDRC, 2010), p. 5.

18 Caroline Preston, "Champions of 'Small Schools' Struggle in the Wake of Gates Foundation's Pullout," www.philanthropy.com, April 15, 2012.

19 Ibid.

20 Bangser and others, "Urban Education That Works," p.8.

21 Ibid.

22 Ibid.

23 Christina Clark Tuttle and others, *Student Characteristics and Achievement in 22 KIPP Middle Schools: Final Report,* Executive Summary (Washington, DC: Mathematica Policy Research, June 2010), pp. xi–xii.

24 Ibid.

25 Gary Miron, Jessica L. Urschel, and Nicholas Saxton, "What Makes KIPP Work: A Study of Student Characteristics, Attrition and School Finance" (paper jointly released by the National Center for Privatization in Education at Teachers College/Columbia University and the Study Group on Educational Management at Western Michigan University, March 2011), p. ii.

26 Ibid, p. iii.

27 Julian Betts and Y. Emily Tang, *The Effect of Charter Schools on Achievement: A Meta-Analysis of the Literature,* National Charter School Research Project (Seattle: Center on Reinventing Public Education), p. 1.

28 Center for Research on Education Outcomes, "National Charter School Study: 2013," CREDO at Stanford University, credo.stanford.edu/documents/NCSS%202013%20Final%20Draft.pdf., 2013.

29 Center for Research on Education Outcomes, "Multiple Choice: Charter School Performance in 16 States," CREDO at Stanford University, credo.stanford.edu/reports/MULTIPLE CHOICE_CREDO.pdf, 2009.

30 National Charter School Study: 2013, p. 3.

31 Ibid., p. 81.

32 Lisa Barrow and Cecilia Elena Rouse, "School Vouchers and Student Achievement: Recent Evidence, Remaining Questions" (Federal Reserve Board of Chicago Working Paper #2008-08, Abstract, ssrn.com/abstract=1267346., August 8, 2008).

33 Matthew M. Chingos and Paul E. Peterson, "The Effects of School Vouchers on College Enrollment: Experimental Evidence from New York City," Brown Center on Education Policy at the Brookings Institution and Harvard Kennedy School Program on Education Policy and Governance, August 2012, p. ii.

34 Alyson Klein, "SIG Effort Posts Promising Early Results: One-Year Improvements Seen in Many Schools, Ed. Dept. Finds," www.edweek.org, March 27, 2012.

35 Alyson Klein, "Ed. Department Analysis Paints Mixed Picture of SIG Program," www.edweek.org, December 4, 2012.

36 Alyson Klein, "School Turnaround Push Still a Work in Progress," www.edweek.org, April 15, 2012.

37 Christopher B. Swanson and Sterling C. Lloyd, "Graduation Rate Approaching Milestone," "Diplomas Count: Second Chances: Turning Dropouts Into Graduates," *Education Week* 32, June 6, 2013, p. 22.

38 Robert Balfanz and others, "Building a Grad Nation: Progress and Challenge in Ending the High School Dropout Epidemic: Annual Update 2012" (a report by Civic Enterprises, Everyone Graduates Center at Johns Hopkins University, America's Promise Alliance, and Alliance for Excellent Education, March 2012), p. 6.

39 *The Urgency of Now: The Schott 50 State Report on Public Education and Black Males: 2012* (Cambridge, MA: Schott Foundation for Public Education, www.blackboysreport.org/urgency-of-now.pdf, September 2012), p. 7.

40 Ibid.

41 Michael Hout and Stuart W. Elliott, eds., *Incentives and Test-Based Accountability in Education, Committee on Incentives and Test-Based Accountability in Public Education*, National Research Council of the National Academies (Washington, DC: National Academies Press), 2011.

42 Ibid., p. 4.

43 Ibid., p. 5.

44 Ibid., p. 16.

45 Ibid., pp. 62–63.

46 Sarah D. Sparks, "Panel Finds Few Learning Gains From Testing Movement," www.edweek.org, May 26, 2011.

Chapter 2

1 *What Matters Most: Teaching for America's Future*, Report of the National Commission on Teaching & America's Future (New York: Teachers College, Columbia University, 1996), p. 12.

2 Ibid.

3 Ibid, p. 19.

4 National Assessment Governing Board, "Achievement Levels," www.nagb. org, November 2006.

5 nationsreportcard.gov/reading_math_2013/#/student-groups.

6 Ann Flanagan and David Grissmer, "The Role of Federal Resources in Closing the Achievement Gap," *Bridging the Achievement Gap*, edited by John Chubb and Tom Loveless (Brookings, 2002), p. 213.

7 Nancy Kober, Naomi Chudowsky, and Victor Chudowsky, *Slow and Uneven Progress in Narrowing Gaps: State Test Score Trends Through 2008–09: Part 2* (Washington, DC: Center on Education Policy, December 2010).

8 Ibid., p. 15: Table 10: Hypothetical progress in closing achievement gaps in selected states, 2002–2009.

9 Leslie A. Maxwell, "D.C. Schools Post Strong Results on Common-Core-Aligned Tests," www.edweek.org, July 30, 2013.

10 Javier C. Hernandez, "Under New Standards, Students See Sharp Decline in Test Scores," *New York Times*, August 7, 2013.

11 Charles Kolb, "The Cracks in Our Education Pipeline," www.edweek.org, July 11, 2006.

12 Adam Kernan-Schloss and Bill Potapchuk, *Double the Numbers for College Success: A Call to Action for the District of Columbia*, (Washington, DC: Education Compact, DC State Education Office, DC Public Schools, and DC College Access Program, October 2006), p. 2.

13 Daniel J. Losen and Jonathan Gillespie, "Opportunities Suspended: The Disparate Impact of Disciplinary Exclusion from School," The Civil Rights Project/Proyecto Derechos Civiles, UCLA, August 2012.

14 Ibid., p. 6.

15 Tony Fabelo and others, *Breaking Schools' Rules: A Statewide Study of How School Discipline Relates to Students' Success and Juvenile Justice Involvement*, Council of State Governments Justice Center and Public Policy Research Institute at Texas A&M University (New York: Council of State Governments Justice Center), July 2011, p. ix.

16 Losen and Gillespie, "Opportunities Suspended."

17 Nirvi Shah and Leslie A. Maxwell, "Researchers Sound Alarm Over Black Student Suspensions," www.edweek.org, August 7, 2012.

18 Motoko Rich, "Suspensions Are Higher for Disabled Students, Federal Data Indicate," *New York Times*, August 7, 2012.

19 Ibid.

20 Shah and Maxwell, "Researchers Sound Alarm."

21 Ibid.

22 Losen and Gillespie, "Opportunities Suspended," p. 6.

23 Rich, "Suspensions Are Higher for Disabled Students."

24 Ibid.

25 Caralee J. Adams, Erik Robelin, and Nirvi Shah, "Civil Rights Data Show Retention Disparities," www.edweek.org, March 6, 2012.

26 Ibid.

27 Ibid.

28 Ibid.

29 Robert Balfanz and Nettie Legters, "Closing Dropout Factories," *Education Week,* July 12, 2006, 42.

30 Robert Balfanz and Nettie Legters, *Locating the Dropout Crisis: Which High Schools Produce the Nation's Dropouts? Where Are They Located: Who Attends Them?* (Baltimore: Johns Hopkins University, Report 70, Center for Research on the Education of Students Placed At Risk [CRESPAR], September 2004).

31 Ibid., vi.

32 Ibid., vi.

33 Ibid., v.

34 Ibid.

35 Schott Foundation, *The Urgency of Now,* p. 7.

36 Ibid.

37 Ibid.

38 Balfanz and others, "Building a Grad Nation," p. 7.

39 Lauren Weber, "Among Minorities, a New Wave of 'Disconnected Youth,'" www.wsj.com, November 7, 2011.

40 Ibid.

41 Sarah Burd-Sharps and Kristen Lewis, *One in Seven: Ranking Youth Disconnection in the 25 Largest Metro Areas,* Measure of America (Brooklyn, NY: Social Science Research Council, 2012), p. 1. www.measureofamerica.org.

42 Ibid.

43 Ibid.

44 Leslie A. Maxwell, "Growing Gaps Bring Focus on Poverty's Role in Schooling," www.edweek.org, March 16, 2012.

45 Greg J. Duncan and Richard J. Murnane, eds., *Whither Opportunity? Rising Inequality, Schools, and Children's Life Chances,* (New York: Russell Sage Foundation and Spencer Foundation, 2011), p. 2.

46 Maxwell, "Growing Gaps."

47 Ibid.

48 Ibid.

49 Ibid.

50 Balfanz and Legters, *Locating the Dropout Crisis,* 19.

Chapter 3

1 The comments cited here by black youngsters are drawn from Tracey Sparrow and Abby Sparrow, "The Voices of Young Black Males," www.edweek.org, February 3, 2012.

2 Ibid.

3 The survey results cited in this paragraph and the next were drawn from: John M. Bridgeland, John J. Dilulio Jr., and Karen Burke Morrison, *The Silent Epidemic: Perspectives of High School Dropouts*. Report by Civic Enterprises in association with Peter D. Hart Research Associates for the Bill & Melinda Gates Foundation, Washington, DC, March 2006.

4 Ruth B. Ekstrom and others, "Who Drops Out of High School and Why? Findings From a National Study," *Teachers College Record*, 87, Spring (1986): 362.

5 Ibid., p. 367.

6 Ibid.

7 Robert Balfanz, "What Your Community Can Do to End Its Drop-out Crisis: Learnings From Research and Practice," National Summit on America's Silent Epidemic," Washington, DC, May 9, 2007, p. 3.

8 Ibid., p. 3.

9 Ibid. p. 8.

10 Ibid., p. 5.

11 Robert Balfanz and others, "Preventing Student Disengagement and Keeping Students on the Graduation Path in Urban Middle-Grades Schools: Early Identification and Effective Interventions," *Educational Psychologist* 42 (2007): p. 225.

12 Ibid., p. 230.

13 Ibid.

14 Balfanz, "What Your Community Can Do," p. 5.

15 Ibid.

16 Ibid., p. 6.

17 Ibid., p. 15.

18 Balfanz and others, "Preventing Student Disengagement," pp. 223–235.

19 Ibid.

20 Bridgeland, Dilulio, and Morrison, *The Silent Epidemic*, p. 11.

Chapter 4

1 Dan Bloom, Alissa Gardenhire-Crooks, and Conrad Mandsager, *Reengaging High School Dropouts: Early Results of the National Guard Youth ChalleNGe*

Program Evaluation (New York: MDRC, February 2009), p. ix.

2 James P. Comer, "Our Mission: It Takes More Than Tests to Prepare the Young for Success in Life," www.edweek.org, January 5, 2006.

3 Ibid.

4 Ibid.

5 Maurice J. Elias and others, *Promoting Social and Emotional Learning: Guidelines for Educators* (Alexandria, VA: ASCD, 1997), p. 2.

6 Comer, "Our Mission."

7 "Teachers Call for Social and Emotional Learning in School" (press release accompanying CASEL report entitled "The Missing Piece," casel.org/the-missingpiece/, May 15, 2013).

8 CASEL, "What is SEL?" www.casel.org/why-it-matters/.

9 Elias and others, *Promoting Social and Emotional Learning*, p. 3.

10 Ibid.

11 Ibid.

12 Robert Sylwester, *A Celebration of Neurons: An Educator's Guide to the Human Brain* (Alexandria, VA: ASCD, 1995), pp. 72, 75.

13 Ibid.

14 Elias and others, *Promoting Social and Emotional Learning*, p. 5.

15 Ibid.

16 California Healthy Students Research Project, "Healthy Steps Toward Student Achievement: Research-based Recommendations for Policy and Practice," commissioned by the James Irvine Foundation, California Endowment, and William and Flora Hewlett Foundation, www.inpathways. net/bwlw2011_healthy_steps_synthesis.pdf, May 2011, p. 7.

17 California Education Supports Project, "The Critical Connection Between Student Health and Academic Achievement: How Schools Can Achieve a Positive Impact" (a brief developed jointly by WestEd and the Philip R. Lee Institute for Health Policy Studies, University of California San Francisco, 2009), p. 3.

18 James W. Pellegrino and Margaret L. Hilton, eds., *Education for Life and Work: Developing Transferable Knowledge and Skills in the 21st Century*, National Research Council (Washington, DC: National Academies Press, 2012).

19 Sara D. Sparks, "Experts Zero In on Nonacademic Skills Needed for Success," *Education Week*, January 12, 2011, p. 12.

20 Pellegrino and Hilton, *Education for Life and Work*, p. 4.

21 Ibid, pp. 4–5.

22 William C. Symonds, Robert Schwarz, and Ronald F. Ferguson, *Pathways to Prosperity: Meeting the Challenge of Preparing Young Americans for the 21st Century* (report issued by Pathways to Prosperity Project, Harvard Univer-

sity Graduate School of Education, February 2011), p.1.

23 Elias and others, *Promoting Social and Emotional Learning*, p. 7.

24 Ibid.

25 Ibid., p. 7.

26 Henry M. Levin and Carolyn Kelly, "Can Education Do It Alone?" *Economics of Education Review* 13 (1994): pp. 97–108.

27 Ibid., p. 97.

28 Ibid., p. 99.

29 Daniel Goleman, *Emotional Intelligence: Why It Can Matter More Than IQ; Tenth Anniversary Edition* (New York: Random House Publishing Group, 2006), p. xii.

30 Janice L. Cooper, Rachel Masi, and Jessica Vick, *Social-Emotional Development in Early Childhood: What Every Policymaker Should Know*, National Center for Children in Poverty, Mailman School of Public Health, Columbia University, August 2009, pp. 4–5.

31 *The National Survey of Children's Health*, U.S. Department of Health and Human Services, Rockville, MD, 2005.

32 Caroline D. Hanamirian, "Reforming School Curricula to Combat Chronic Poverty: How Integrating Social and Emotional Learning Into Academic Programs Can Benefit Low-Income Children" (final paper written for WWS 401f: Combating Chronic Poverty in an Age of Austerity, Woodrow Wilson School, Princeton University, January 10, 2011), p. 7.

33 Robert C. Pianta and Daniel J. Walsh, *High-Risk Children in Schools: Constructing Sustaining Relationships* (New York: Routledge, 1996), p. 117.

34 Ibid., p. 120.

35 Ibid., p. 123.

36 Ibid., pp. 133–4.

37 Ibid.

38 Elias and others, *Promoting Social and Emotional Learning*, p. 8.

39 Ibid., pp. 9–10.

40 Jennifer Dubin, "School Ties: A Psychiatrist's Longtime Commitment to Education," *American Educator* (Spring 2013): p. 21.

41 Comer, "Our Mission."

42 James P. Comer, *Leave No Child Behind: Preparing Today's Youth for Tomorrow's World* (New Haven, CT: Yale University Press, 2004), p. 17.

43 Comer, "Our Mission."

44 Ibid.

45 Elias and others, *Promoting Social and Emotional Learning*, p. 12.

46 Ibid.

47 Thomas Hanson, Gregory Austin, and Hong Zheng, "The Achievement Gap and School Well-Being" (brief #2 prepared for the California Healthy Stu-

dents Research Project, 2011), p. 4.

48 John Bridgeland, Mary Bruce, and Arya Hariharan, "The Missing Piece: A National Teacher Survey on How Social and Emotional Learning Can Empower Children and Transform Schools" (report prepared for CASEL by Civic Enterprises with Peter D. Hart Research Associates, casel.org/themissingpiece/, 2013).

49 Ibid., p. 5.

50 Nirvi Shah, "District Race to Top Will Consider Emotional, Behavioral Services," www.edweek.org, October 19, 2012.

51 Nirvi Shah, "Students' Well-Being a Focus of Race to Top," *Education Week*, May 8, 2013, p. 6.

52 Ryan Reyna, remarks offered at conference "America's Youth in Crisis: Understanding Why Adolescents Disengage and Drop Out," cosponsored by the Center for Strategic and International Studies and the National Guard Youth Foundation (held at CSIS in Washington, DC), June 19, 2013.

53 Goleman, *Emotional Intelligence*, p. x.

54 Nirvi Shah, "At S.C. School, Behavior is One of the Basics," www.edweek.org, October 25, 2012.

55 Catherine P. Bradshaw, Tracy E. Waasdorp, and Philip J. Leaf, "Effects of School-Wide Positive Behavioral Interventions and Supports on Child Behavior Problems," *Pediatrics* 130 (November 2012): pp. e1136–e1145.

56 Sarah D. Sparks, "A 'Neglected' Population Goes Back to School," in "Diplomas Count: Second Chances: Turning Dropouts Into Graduates," *Education Week* 32 (June 6, 2013): p. 3.

57 Ibid.

58 Collaborative for Academic, Social, and Emotional Learning (casel.org), casel.org/why-it-matters/what-is-sel/.

59 Ibid.

60 Elias and others, *Promoting Social and Emotional Learning*, p. 10.

61 Ibid., pp. 2–3.

62 Joe Nocera, "Addressing Poverty in Schools," *New York Times*, July 27, 2012.

63 Ibid.

64 Philip V. Robey, "Catholic Schools and Educating the Whole Child," www.edweek.org, October 5, 2011.

65 www.nuevaschool.org/sel-background.

66 Elias and others, *Promoting Social and Emotional Learning*, p. 10.

Chapter 5

1 Joseph A. Durlak and others, "The Impact of Enhancing Students' Social

and Emotional Learning: A Meta-Analysis of School-Based Universal Interventions," *Child Development* 82 (January-February 2011): p. 406.

2 Ibid, pp. 405–432.

3 Ibid, p. 413.

4 Ibid., p. 417.

5 Sarah D. Spark, "Study Finds Social-Skills Teaching Boosts Academics,"
www.edweek.org, February 4, 2011.

6 Durlak and others, "The Impact of Enhancing Students' Social and Emotional Learning," p. 417.

7 Ibid., p. 416.

8 Ibid, pp. 412–3.

9 Ibid., p. 417.

10 Ibid., p. 410.

11 Spark, "Study Finds Social-Skills Teaching Boosts Academics."

12 Durlak and others, "The Impact of Enhancing Students' Social and Emotional Learning," p. 418.

13 J. David Hawkins and others, "Preventing Adolescent Health-Risk Behaviors
by Strengthening Protection During Childhood," *Archives of Pediatric & Adolescent Medicine* 153 (March 1999): pp. 226–234.

14 Ibid., p. 226.

15 Ibid., p. 230.

16 Ibid., p. 231.

17 Ibid., p. 233.

18 Camille A. Farrington and others, "Teaching Adolescents to Become Learn-
ers: The Role of Noncognitive Factors in Shaping School Performance; A
Critical Literature Review," University of Chicago Consortium on Chicago
School Research, June 2012.

19 Ibid., p. 3.

20 Ibid., p. 78.

21 Ibid., p. 72.

22 Ibid., p. 74.

23 Ibid., pp. 75–76.

24 Ibid., p. 77.

25 Ibid.

26 Geoffrey D. Borman and others, "Comprehensive School Reform and
Achievement: A Meta-Analysis," *Review of Educational Research* 73 (2003):
p. 161.

27 James P. Comer and Christine Emmons, "The Research Program of the Yale
Child Study Center School Development Program," *The Journal of Negro Education* 75 (Summer 2006): p. 367.

28 Ibid.

29 "Close the Achievement Gap by Closing the Development Gap," School Development Program, Yale Child Study Center, www.schooldevelopmentprogram.org/news/asheville.aspx, 2011.

30 Ibid.

31 Thomas D. Cook, Robert F. Murphy, and H. David Hunt, "Comer's School Development Program in Chicago: A Theory-Based Evaluation," *American Educational Research Journal*, 37 (Summer 2000): p. 535.

32 Ibid.

33 Christine Emmons, "Academic Achievement for Selected Districts From the Dissemination Phase," School Development Program, Yale University Child Study Center, New Haven, CT, Spring 2002, pp. 3–17.

34 Ibid.

35 Comer and Emmons, "The Research Program of the Yale Child Study Center School Development Program," p. 361. See also: Cook, Murphy, and Hunt, "Comer's School Development Program in Chicago," p. 589.

36 Comer and Emmons, p. 361.

37 Cook, Murphy, and Hunt, "Comer's School Development Program in Chicago," p. 564.

38 Comer and Emmons, "The Research Program of the Yale Child Study Center School Development Program," p. 359.

39 Cook, Murphy, and Hunt, "Comer's School Development Program in Chicago," p. 590.

40 Hanamirian, "Reforming School Curricula to Combat Chronic Poverty," p. 16.

41 Ibid.

42 Nirvi Shah, "Why One Chicago School Won't Close: Social-Emotional Learning," www.edweek.org, May 23, 2013.

43 Hanamirian, "Reforming School Curricula to Combat Chronic Poverty," p. 18.

44 Ibid.

45 Ibid., p. 20.

46 Rachel Gordon and others, "Social and Emotional Learning for Illinois Students: Policy, Practice, and Progress," *The Illinois Report 2011* (University of Illinois Institute of Government and Public Affairs, 2011), p. 77.

47 Jonathan Zaff, remarks offered at conference on "America's Youth in Crisis: Understanding Why Adolescents Disengage and Drop Out," cosponsored by the Center for Strategic and International Studies (CSIS) and the National Guard Youth Foundation (held at CSIS in Washington, DC, June 19, 2013).

Chapter 6

1 Balfanz, "What Your Community Can Do," p. 5.

1 Ibid.

3 Anthony S. Bryk and others, *Organizing Schools for Improvement: Lessons from Chicago* (Chicago: University of Chicago Press, 2010).

4 Ibid., p. 179.

5 Ibid., p. 172.

6 Ibid., p. 181–2.

7 Bryk and others, *Organizing Schools for Improvement*, p. 194.

8 Robert Balfanz, "What Your Community Can Do," p. 8.

9 Ibid., p. 6.

10 Bryk and others, *Organizing Schools for Improvement*, p. 173.

11 Hawkins and others, "Preventing Adolescent Health-Risk Behaviors," p. 233.

12 Bryk and others, *Organizing Schools for Improvement*, p.196.

13 Ibid, p. 210.

14 Ibid., p.211.

15 Interview with Eddy Bayardelle, president of the Merrill Lynch Foundation, May 2, 2006.

16 Ibid.

17 Larry McClure, Susan Yonezawa, and Makeba Jones, "Personalization and Caring Relationships With Adults in Urban High Schools: Is There a Relationship With Academic Achievement?" (California Health Students Research Project, Brief #6, June 2010), p. 3.

18 Elias and others, *Promoting Social and Emotional Learning*, p. 10.

19 Ibid.

20 Balfanz, "What Your Community Can Do," pp. 13–15.

21 Robert Balfanz, "Why Are Achievement Gains So Difficult to Realize in High Poverty Middle Grade Schools: What Can Be Done About It? Conjecture from a Decade of Work," Johns Hopkins University, 2006.

22 Balfanz, "What Your Community Can Do," p. 15.

Chapter 7

1 Robert J. Sampson and John H. Laub, "Socioeconomic Achievement in the Life Course of Disadvantaged Men: Military Service as a Turning Point, Circa 1940–1965," *American Sociological Review*, Vol. 61 (June 1996): pp. 347–367.

2 Dirk Johnson, "High School at Attention," *Newsweek*, January 21, 2002, pp. 42–44.

3 Elizabeth Heneghan Ondaatje, "Policy Options for Army Involvement in Youth Development" (report prepared for the United States Army, RAND Corporation, Santa Monica, 1993), p. 24.

4 Lieutenant General Julius W. Becton Jr. (Ret.) and Colonel William J. Taylor Jr. (Ret.), *Using Military Capabilities to Help Young Adults in U.S. Inner-City Areas* (report by the CSIS Political-Military Studies Program and the National Urban League Joint Study Group, Washington, Center for Strategic and International Studies, March 1997), p. 9.

5 Johnson, "High School at Attention," pp. 42–44.

6 John Sibley Butler and Charles Moskos, "Lessons on Race From the Army," *Chicago Tribune*, July 26, 1998, p. C15.

7 Ibid.

8 Beth J. Asch, "Military Support for Youth Development: An Exploratory Analysis" (Santa Monica, CA: RAND Corporation, December 1994), p. 29.

9 Ibid.

10 Colonel William J. Taylor Jr. (Ret.), "Junior Reserve Officers' Training Corps: Contributing to America's Communities" (final Report of the CSIS Political-Military Studies Project on the JROTC, Washington, DC: Center for Strategic and International Studies, May 1999), p. xi.

11 David Goodman, "Recruiting the Class of 2005," *Mother Jones*, January/February 2002.

12 Ibid.

13 Presentation by Lieutenant Colonel Russell A. Gallagher (Ret.), director of Junior ROTC for the Philadelphia Public Schools, "What Does the Pentagon Know About Developing Young People? Examining the Effectiveness of High Schools Based on a Military Model," at Alliance for Excellent Education, Washington, DC, January 23, 2007.

14 Taylor, *Junior Reserve Officers' Training Corps*, p. 7.

15 Kim Harrell, "Connecting the World of the Military Model and Education," *The State Education Standard*, March 2010, p. 22.

16 Colonel John W. Corbett (U.S. Army) and Colonel Arthur T. Coumbe (U.S. Army Reserve), "JROTC: Recent Trends and Developments," *Combined Arms Center Military Review* LXXXI (January-February 2001): p. 40.

17 Taylor, *Junior Reserve Officers' Training Corps*, p. 18.

18 Ibid., p. 28.

19 Ana Beatriz Cholo, "New Military High School Planned for North Side," *Chicago Tribune*, July 17, 2004, p. 14.

20 Taylor, *Junior Reserve Officers' Training Corps*, p. 18.

21 Elda Pema and Stephen Mehay, "The Effect of High School JROTC on Student Achievement, Educational Attainment, and Enlistment," Graduate School of Business and Public Policy, Naval Postgraduate School, www.uf-

pj-dvn.org/ed-com/JROTC_Pema_Mehay.pdf, 2009, p. 2.

22 Taylor, *Junior Reserve Officers' Training Corps*, p. 29.

23 Ibid.

24 Ibid., p. 30.

25 Ibid., p. 35.

26 *Army Education News & Updates*, Issue #9, U.S. Army Accessions Command, www.ws-wr.com/Army/EdSpace_Newsletter/Issue9/2.html, November 2, 2011.

27 Ibid.

28 Ibid.

29 Gallagher, "What Does the Pentagon Know About Developing Young People?"

30 Bridget L. Bartlett, "The Public Military Academy: Building a Culture of Success for Inner City Youth" (senior thesis presented to the faculty of the Woodrow Wilson School of Public and International Affairs, Princeton University, 2010), p. 29.

31 Oliver W. Sloman, "Imagining Nonmilitary Public Schools in the Image of Public Military Academies: Creating Rigorous, Safe, and Supportive Schools for Students and Teachers Stranded in Dysfunctional Ones" (working paper prepared for Hugh Price of the Brookings Institution, October 1, 2008), p. 5.

32 Gallagher, "What Does the Pentagon Know About Developing Young People?"

33 Stephanie Banchero and Carlos Sadovi, "Reading, Writing, and Recruiting? Debate Rages as City's Newest Facility Is Dedicated," *Chicago Tribune*, October 15, 2007.

34 Dirk Johnson, "High School at Attention," pp. 42–44.

35 Sloman, "Imagining Nonmilitary Public Schools," p. 3.

36 Sloman, "Imagining Nonmilitary Public Schools," p. 4.

37 Bartlett, "The Public Military Academy."

38 Ibid., p. 36.

39 Ibid., p. 37.

40 Guy McCarthy, "Pulled Up by the Boot Straps: A New Perris School Reflects the Trend of Tackling Educational Challenges With Military-Style Discipline," *Press Enterprise*, September 27, 2003, p. A1.

41 Bartlett, "The Public Military Academy," p.2.

42 Kim Harrell, "Connecting the World of the Military Model and Education," *The State Education Standard*, March 2010, p. 22

43 The statistics in these three chapters are drawn from Bartlett, "The Public Military Academy," pp. 101–03.

44 Bartlett, "The Public Military Academy," p. 103.

45 Interview with cadet, California Military Institute, January 26, 2010, in

Bartlett, "The Public Military Academy."

46 Orquedia Price, "Guarded Optimism at OMI," *East Bay Express*, January 16, 2002, www.eastbayexpress.com/oakland/guarded-optimism-at-omi/Content?oid=1066785.

47 Nancy Trejos, "For Pr. George's Teens, New Marching Orders," *Washington Post*, December 22, 2002, p. A1.

48 Nancy Trejos, "A Md. School Tries an About-Face: Students and Teachers Brave a Military Campaign in Pr. George's County," *Washington Post*, November 30, 2003, p. A1.

Chapter 8

1 *National Guard Youth ChalleNGe Program: 2004 Performance and Accountability Highlights*, 2nd Edition (Arlington, VA: National Guard Bureau, 2004), p. 3.

2 Dan Donohue, "Designing a 'ChalleNGe-Like' Non-Residential Program for High School Dropouts and Students Who Are Drifting Through School, Disengaged, and Repeating Grades" (working paper commissioned by the Brookings Institution, Donohue Associates LLC, Fairfax Station, VA, June 2008), p. 4.

3 Megan Millenky, Dan Bloom, and Colleen Dillon, *Making the Transition: Interim Results of the National Guard Youth ChalleNGe Evaluation*, New York: MDRC, May 2010, p. ES-1.

4 Donohue, "Designing a 'ChalleNGe-Like' Non-Residential Program," p. 6.

5 Ibid., p. 10.

6 National Guard Youth Foundation, "Executive Summary" (undated document provided by the National Guard Youth Foundation to Hugh B. Price on October 4, 2005), p. 1.

7 Megan Millenky and others, *Staying on Course: Three-Year Results of the National Guard Youth ChalleNGe Evaluation* (New York: MDRC), p. 9.

8 Bloom, Gardenhire-Crooks, and Mandsager, *Reengaging High School Dropouts*, pp. 13–19.

9 Millenky and others, *Staying on Course*, p. 12.

10 Ibid., p. 19.

11 Ibid., p. 38.

12 Ibid., p. 56.

13 "National Guard Youth ChalleNGe Program," p. 5.

14 Millenky, Bloom, and Dillon, *Making the Transition*, p. 4

15 Bloom, Gardenhire-Crooks, and Mandsager, *Reengaging High School Dropouts*, p. 41 (see chap. 4, n. 117).

16 Ibid., p. 44.
17 Ibid.
18 Donohue, "Designing a 'ChalleNGe-Like' Non-Residential Program," p. 12.
19 Ibid.
20 Bloom, Gardenhire-Crooks, and Mandsager, *Reengaging High School Dropouts*, p. 46.
21 Donohue, "Designing a 'ChalleNGe-Like' Non-Residential Program," p.13.
22 Ibid., p. 12.
23 Bloom, Gardenhire-Crooks, and Mandsager, *Reengaging High School Dropouts*, p. 48.
24 Donohue, "Designing a 'ChalleNGe-Like' Non-Residential Program," p. 11.
25 Bloom, Gardenhire-Crooks, and Mandsager, *Reengaging High School Dropouts*, p. 48.
26 Ibid., p. 49.
27 Ibid., p. 22.
28 Ibid., p. 49.
29 Ibid., pp. 23, 49.
30 Ibid., p. 50.
31 Donohue, "Designing a 'ChalleNGe-Like' Non-Residential Program," p. 11.
32 Ibid., p. 15.
33 Ibid., p. 25.
34 Ibid., p. 27.
35 Ibid., p. 28.

Chapter 9

1 Bloom, Gardenhire-Crooks, and Mandsager, *Reengaging High School Dropouts*, p. ES-3.
2 Results of the initial survey were reported in Bloom, Gardenhire-Crooks, and Mandsager, *Reengaging High School Dropouts*.
3 Results of the second survey were reported in Millenky, Bloom, and Dillon, *Making the Transition*.
4 Results of the third survey were reported in Millenky and others, *Staying on Course*, p. ES-4.
5 Millenky and others, *Staying on Course*, pp. 15–29
6 Ibid., p. 23.
7 E-mails from Andrea Kane to author, July 8 and 26, 2013.
8 Ibid., p. ES-8.
9 Ibid., pp. 1–2.
10 Ibid., p. ES-8.

11 Francisco Perez-Arce and others, *A Cost-Benefit Analysis of the National Guard Youth ChalleNGe Program* (technical report, Santa Monica, CA: RAND Corporation, 2012).

12 Ibid., p. xii.

13 Ibid., p. xiii.

14 Ibid., p. 3.

15 Ibid., p. xiii.

16 Ibid., p. xiv.

17 Ibid., p. xv.

18 E-mail from Dan Donohue to the author, dated March 1, 2012.

19 The findings reported in these paragraphs are drawn from Millenky and others, *Staying on Course.*

20 Ibid., p. 39.

21 Ibid., p. 41.

22 Ibid., p. 47.

23 Ibid., p. 46.

24 Ibid., p. 50.

25 Ibid., p. 47.

26 Ibid., p. 39.

27 Ibid., p. ES-9.

28 Ibid., p. 45.

29 Ibid., p. 50.

30 Ibid., p. 51.

31 Ibid., p. 51.

32 Ibid., p. 47.

33 National Guard Youth ChalleNGe Program, "Parent Testimonials," new.ngycp.org/successstories_dependant_T15_R84.php, November 2006.

34 Ibid.

35 Ibid.

36 Ibid.

Chapter 10

1 Gordon served as a panelist at "Policy Forum on Quasi-Military Approaches to Educating Students Who Are Struggling in School and in Life," Center on Children and Families, Brookings Institution, Washington, DC, October 31, 2007.

2 "National Guard Youth ChalleNGe Program," p. 3.

3 Claude M. Steele, "Race and the Schooling of Black Americans," *Atlantic Monthly,* April 1992, p. 2.

4　Ibid, p. 6.

5　Ibid, pp. 12, 16.

6　Meredith May, "Out of Step; After 6 Months, Oakland Military Charter School Finds Students Must Do Double Time to Catch Up," *San Francisco Chronicle*, February 10, 2002, p. A21.

7　Alex Katz, "Charter School Stresses Academics, Discipline," *Alameda Times-Star*, January 31, 2002, p. 1.

8　Sloman, "Imagining Nonmilitary Public Schools," pp. 21–22.

9　Ibid., p. 21.

10　Donohue, "Designing a 'ChalleNGe-Like' Non-Residential Program," pp. 14–15.

11　Saul Lavisky, "Training Research for the Army," *Phi Delta Kappan* 48 (May 1967): p. 443.

12　Interview with Dan Donohue, chief, public affairs and special assistant to Chief National Guard Bureau, June 15, 2006.

13　E-mail message from Bella Rosenberg to the author, February 9, 2007.

14　Ibid.

15　Evelyn L. Parker, "Hungry for Honor," *Interpretation: A Journal of Bible and Theology* 55 (April 2001): pp. 148–160; and Jerome L. Blakemore and Glenda M. Blakemore, "African American Street Gangs: A Quest for Identity," *Journal of Human Behavior in the Social Environment* 1, (1998): pp. 203–223.

16　"When You're a Crip (or a Blood)," *Harper's,* March 1989, p. 51.

17　E-mail message from Colonel Norman Johnson (Ret.) to the author, January 22, 2007.

18　Carol Goodenow, "Classroom Belonging Among Early Adolescent Students: Relationships to Motivation and Achievement," *Journal of Early Adolescence* 13 (February 1993): p. 24.

19　Ibid, p. 25.

20　Ibid, p. 37.

21　Steven L. Rosenberg, "The Need to Belong," *American School Board Journal* 186 (September 1999): p. 26.

22　Ibid., p. 27.

23　Goodman, "Recruiting the Class of 2005."

24　Johnson, "High School at Attention," pp. 42–44.

25　Interview with General Colin L. Powell (Ret.), May 31, 2006.

26　Ibid.

27　Walter F. Ulmer Jr., *American Military Culture in the Twenty-First Century* (report of the CSIS International Security Program Washington, DC: Center for Strategic and International Studies, February 2000), p. 9.

28　These scholars include Geoffrey Schultz of Indiana University, Franzis Preckel of the University of Munich, Ericka Fisher of College of the Holy Cross,

Donna Ford of Peabody College at Vanderbilt University, Roslyn Arlin Mickelson of the University of North Carolina at Charlotte, and the late John Ogbu, noted anthropologist.

29 Bridgeland and others, *The Silent Epidemic*, p. 5.

30 Roslyn Arlin Mickelson, "The Attitude-Achievement Paradox Among Black Adolescents," *Sociology of Education* 63 (January 1990): p. 59.

31 Matthew Cullinan and others, *Forging a Military Youth Corps: A Military-Youth Service Partnership for High School Dropouts*, final report of the CSIS National Community Service for Out-of-School Youth Project (Boulder, CO: Westview Press, 1992), pp. 6–7.

32 McCarthy, "Pulled Up by the Boot Straps . . . ," p. A1.

33 Trejos, "Scholars First, Soldiers Second," p. B1.

34 Reva Klein, "Marching On—the Chicago Military Academy," *Young Minds Magazine,* May/June 2003, (www.youngminds.org.uk/magazine/64/klein.php [November 2006]).

35 Ibid.

36 Katz, "Charter School Stresses Academics, Discipline," p. 1.

37 Ibid., p. 1.

38 Steve Inskeep, "Analysis: Junior ROTC Program and Whether It Actually Helps," *Weekend All Things Considered*, NPR, January 30, 2000.

39 David Nakamura, "Students Drilled in Discipline, Leadership," *Washington Post*, January 25, 2001, p. T8.

40 Inskeep, "Analysis: Junior ROTC Program and Whether It Actually Helps."

41 Nakamura, "Students Drilled in Discipline, Leadership."

42 Trejos, "For Pr. George's Teens, New Marching Orders," p. A1.

43 May, "Out of Step," p. A21.

44 Rosalind Rossi, "School's Raisin Fight is Bad for the Bunch," *Chicago Sun-Times*, August 31, 1999, p. 8.

45 Ibid.

46 Trejos, "Scholars First, Soldiers Second," p. B1.

47 Katz, "Charter School Stresses Academics, Discipline," p. 1.

48 Ibid.

49 Tugend, "Public Military Academies Put Discipline in the Schools," p. B9.

50 Klein, "Marching On—the Chicago Military Academy."

51 Katz, "Charter School Stresses Academics, Discipline," p. 1.

Chapter 11

1 Ulmer, *American Military Culture in the Twenty-First Century*, p. xv.

2 Ibid, p. 7.

3 Brian Mockenhaupt, "The Army We Have," *The Atlantic*, www.theatlantic. com/magazine/archive/2007/06/the-army-we-have/305902/, June 2007.

4 Ibid.

5 Ibid.

6 Bettina Lankard Brown, "Is the GED a Valuable Credential? Myths and Realities No. 10," Center on Education and Training for Employment, College of Education, Ohio State University, 2000, pp. 3–4.

7 Ibid.

8 Ibid.

9 Caralee Adams, "High School Equivalency Test Gets a Makeover," "Diplomas Count: Second Chances: Turning Dropouts Into Graduates," *Education Week* 32 (June 6, 2013): p.8.

10 Danielle Vildostegui, "Femininity in a Masculine Model: Making Military Models Successful in Aiding At-Risk and Disengaged Female Students" (final paper written for Professor Hugh Price for WWS 401g, Applying Military Models to Aid Struggling Students and Schools, Woodrow Wilson School, Princeton University, January 5, 2010).

11 Ibid., p. 3.

12 Ibid., p. 13.

13 Millenky and others, *Staying on Course*, p. 10.

14 Ibid., p. 9, footnote 26.

15 Vildostegui, "Femininity in a Masculine Model," p. 5.

16 Ibid., p. 17.

17 Ibid.

18 Ibid., p. 19.

19 Ibid., p. 15.

20 Lawrence M. Hanser and Abby Robyn, *Implementing High School JROTC Career Academies* (Santa Monica, CA: RAND Corporation, August 2000), pp. xi, 8.

21 "Prince George's Enlisted in Military School Concept," *Washington Business Journal* 20 (July 2001): p. 36.

22 May, "Out of Step," p. A21.

Chapter 12

1 Bryk and others, *Organizing Schools for Improvement*, p. 195.

2 Ibid., p.196.

3 Ibid., p. 210.

4 Ibid., p. 211.

5 "Adapting Public Military Academies Into Purely Civilian Schools" (discus-

sion held at the Philadelphia Downtown Marriott with staff and students from the Philadelphia Military Academy at Leeds, June 12, 2008).

6 Donohue, "Designing a 'ChalleNGe-Like' Non-Residential Program."

7 Ibid., p. 31.

8 Sloman, "Imagining Nonmilitary Public Schools," p. 9.

9 Donohue, "Designing a 'ChalleNGe-Like' Non-Residential Program," p. 32.

10 Ibid., p. 33.

11 Sloman, "Imagining Nonmilitary Public Schools," p. 7.

12 Ibid.

13 Ibid.

14 Donohue, "Designing a 'ChalleNGe-Like' Non-Residential Program," p. 23.

15 Sloman, "Imagining Nonmilitary Public Schools," p. 8.

16 Ibid.

17 Sloman, "Imagining Nonmilitary Public Schools," p. 21.

18 Ibid., p. 22.

19 Ibid.

20 Liana Heitin, "Project-Based Learning Helps At-Risk Students," www.edweek.org, April 24, 2012.

21 Ibid.

22 Ibid.

23 Symonds, Schwarz, and Ferguson, *Pathways to Prosperity*, p. 1.

24 Ibid., p. 6.

25 Ibid., pp. 7, 24.

26 Ibid., p. 11.

27 Ibid., p. 24.

28 Ibid.

29 Ibid., p. 25.

30 Ibid., p. 28.

31 Ibid., p. 30.

32 Leslie A. Maxwell, "A Chicago Charter Network Staunches the Flow of Dropouts," "Diplomas Count: Second Chances: Turning Dropouts Into Graduates," *Education Week* 32 (June 6, 2013): p. 16.

33 Sean Cavanagh, "Philadelphia District Plans to Open Online School," www.edweek.org, April 19, 2013.

34 Sarah D. Sparks, "Online Providers Find a Market in Returning Dropouts," "Diplomas Count: Second Chances: Turning Dropouts Into Graduates," *Education Week* 32 (June 6, 2013): p. 12.

35 Ian Quillen, "L.A. School First in KIPP Network to Embrace Blended Learning," www.edweek.org, October 23, 2012.

36 Donohue, "Designing a 'ChalleNGe-Like' Non-Residential Program," p. 26.

37 Sloman, "Imagining Nonmilitary Public Schools," p. 10.

38 Ibid.
39 *The Philadelphia Military Academy Parent/Student Handbook 2007–2008* (Philadelphia: Philadelphia Military Academy at Leeds, 2007).
40 Sloman, "Imagining Nonmilitary Public Schools," p. 11.
41 "Adapting Public Military Academies," Philadelphia.
42 Sloman, "Imagining Nonmilitary Public Schools," p. 13.
43 Ibid., p. 13.
44 *Philadelphia Military Academy Parent/Student Handbook 2007–2008.*
45 Sloman, "Imagining Nonmilitary Public Schools," p. 13.
46 Ibid. p. 14.
47 "Adapting Public Military Academies Into Purely Civilian Schools" (discussion held at the Rickover Naval Academy with staff and students from the Rickover Naval Academy, Chicago, June 14, 2008).
48 Ibid.
49 Sloman, "Imagining Nonmilitary Public Schools," p. 14.
50 Ibid.
51 Ibid., p. 15.
52 Ibid.
53 Ibid.
54 "Adapting Public Military Academies," Chicago.
55 Sloman, "Imagining Nonmilitary Public Schools," p. 16.
56 Ibid.
57 Ibid., p. 19.
58 "Adapting Public Military Academies," Philadelphia.
59 Ibid.

Chapter 13

1 Hout and Elliot, *Incentives and Test-Based Accountability in Education* (see chap. 1, n. 41).
2 "A Public Policy Statement," The Gordon Commission on the Future of Assessment in Education, March 2013, p. 5, www.gordoncommission.org.
3 Ibid., p. 7.
4 Ibid., p. 9.
5 Ibid., p. 10.
6 Heather Kugelmass, "Metrics for Assessing School Effectiveness" (working paper prepared for Woodrow Wilson School Graduate Policy Workshop WWS 591E, Princeton University, November 13, 2011), p. 1.
7 Ibid.
8 Ibid., p. 8.

9 James J. Kemple, *Career Academies: Long-Term Impacts on Labor Market Outcomes, Educational Attainment, and Transitions to Adulthood* (MDRC, New York, June 2008).

10 Ibid., p. iii.

11 Ibid., p. ix.

12 Ibid.

Chapter 14

1 Sloman, "Imagining Nonmilitary Public Schools," p. 22.

2 Much of the information here about FLVS is drawn from its website, www. flvs.net.

3 "FLVS Legislative Report: 2011–2012," www.flvs.net/areas/aboutus/Documents/2011_12_Legislative _Report.pdf.

4 Emma Brown and Michael Alison Chandler, "Fairfax County Considers Creating Virtual High School," *Washington Post*, April 12, 2012.

5 Benjamin Herold, "Florida Virtual School, Other E-Schools Face Difficult Times," www.edweek.org, August 13, 2013.

6 Matt Richtel, "Wasting Time Is the New Divide in Digital Era," *New York Times*, May 30, 2012, p. A1.

7 Victoria J. Rideout, Ulla G. Foehr, and Donald F. Roberts, "Generation M2: Media in the Lives of 8- to 18-Year-Olds" (study prepared for Kaiser Family Foundation, Menlo Park, CA, www.kaiserfamilyfoundaton.files.wordpress.com/2013/01/8010.pdf, January 2010), p. 37.

8 Richtel, "Wasting Time."

9 Ibid.

10 Ian Quillen, "Can Technology Replace Teachers?" www.edweek.org, August 7, 2012.

11 Ibid.

12 The statistics in this paragraph and the next are drawn from Perez-Arce and others, *A Cost-Benefit Analysis of the National Guard Youth ChalleNGe Program.*

13 Brown, "Is the GED a Valuable Credential? Myths and Realities No. 10," pp. 3–4.

14 Perez-Arce and others, *A Cost-Benefit Analysis of the National Guard Youth ChalleNGe Program*, p. 32.

15 Ibid.

16 Sarah Burd-Sharps and Kristen Lewis, *One in Seven: Ranking Youth Disconnection in the 25 Largest Metro Areas*, Measure of America, Social Science Research Council, www.measureofamerica.org, 2012, p. 1.

17 White House Council for Community Solutions, "Community Solutions for Opportunity Youth," June 2012, p. 8.

18 Balfanz and others, "Building a Grad Nation," p. 5.

19 Bill DeBaun and Martens Roc, *Well and Well-Off: Decreasing Medicaid and Health-Care Costs by Increasing Educational Attainment*," Alliance for Excellent Education, Washington, DC, July 2013, www.all4ed.org/files/Well&WellOff.pdf.

20 Ibid., p. 2.

21 Ibid., p. 5.

22 Robert Balfanz, remarks offered at conference "America's Youth in Crisis: Understanding Why Adolescents Disengage and Drop Out," cosponsored by the Center for Strategic and International Studies and the National Guard Youth Foundation, Washington, DC, June 19, 2013.

Chapter 15

1 Interview with Michael Casserly, executive director of the Council of the Great City Schools, February 6, 2007.

About the Author

HUGH B. PRICE is currently a nonresident senior fellow at the Brookings Institution, the nation's oldest think tank. His interests include education, equal opportunity, civil rights, and urban affairs. From 2008 until 2013, he was the John L. Weinberg/Goldman Sachs visiting professor of public and international affairs in the Woodrow Wilson School at Princeton University. Price served as president and chief executive officer of the National Urban League from 1994 to 2003. Founded in 1910, the National Urban League is the oldest and largest community-based movement empowering African Americans to enter the economic and social mainstream. The league is a nonprofit, nonpartisan organization headquartered in New York City, with nearly one hundred affiliates in thirty-six states and the District of Columbia.

After graduating from Yale Law School in 1966, Price began his professional career as a legal services lawyer representing low-income clients in New Haven, Connecticut. During the turbulent late 1960s, he served as the first executive director of the Black Coalition of New Haven. In 1978 Price and his family moved to New York, where he served until 1982 as a member of the editorial board of *The New York Times*. He wrote editorials on an array of public policy issues, including public education, welfare, criminal justice, and telecommunications. He then served for six years as senior vice president of WNET/Thirteen in New York, the nation's largest public television station. In 1984 Price became director of all national production. Notable series developed or produced for PBS under Price include *Nature, Great Performances, The Mind, American Masters, Dancing, Art of the Western World, Childhood,* and *Global Rivals.*

Price was appointed vice president of the Rockefeller Foundation in

1988. He oversaw its domestic investments to improve education for at-risk youth and increase opportunities for people of color. He was instrumental in conceiving and launching such innovative initiatives as the National Guard Youth ChalleNGe Corps, the National Commission on Teaching and America's Future, and the Coalition of Community Foundations for Youth (now known as Community Foundations Leading Change).

Taking the helm of the National Urban League in 1994, Price led the way in tripling the league's endowment; restructuring and strengthening its board of directors and staff; defining a new mission and strategic vision for the twenty-first century; conceiving and launching the league's historic Campaign for African-American Achievement; establishing the league's new research and policy center, known as the National Urban League Institute for Opportunity and Equality; reviving *Opportunity*, the league's landmark magazine; and establishing its new headquarters on Wall Street in New York City.

Following the National Urban League, Price served for two years as senior advisor and co-chair of the nonprofit and philanthropy practice group at the global law firm of DLA Piper. In 2006–07, he co-chaired the Commission on the Whole Child for the Association for Supervision and Curriculum Development.

Price is the author of three books—*Mobilizing the Community to Help Students Succeed, Achievement Matters: Getting Your Child the Best Education Possible,* and *Destination: The American Dream,* a compilation of his speeches and position papers published by the National Urban League. The league has also published collections of his "To Be Equal" newspaper columns. Brookings published his working paper entitled "Demilitarizing What the Pentagon Knows About Developing Young People: A New Paradigm for Educating Students Who Are Struggling in School and in Life," which gave rise to this book.

His articles have appeared in numerous newspapers and journals, including the *New York Times, Wall Street Journal, Washington Post, Los Angeles Times, San Francisco Chronicle, Phi Delta Kappan, Chronicle of Philanthropy, Education Week, Chronicle of Higher Education, Educational Leadership, American Legacy, New York Times* Sunday travel section, and *Review of Black Political Economy.*

In February 2010, the Carl A. Fields Center at Princeton University staged an exhibit entitled "Commemorating the 20th Anniversary of the Birth of the New South Africa: A Personal Account of Cape Town in 1990." The exhibit was based on photographs Price took and local newspaper articles he collected during a visit to Cape Town that coincided with the historic speech on February 2, 1990, by South African President F.W. de Klerk, freeing Nelson Mandela from prison and proclaiming the end of apartheid.

Price's article published in *Washingtonian* magazine entitled "Jackie and Me," about growing up as an ardent baseball fan in the nation's capital, won first place for magazine sports writing in the 2006 Dateline Awards presented by the Washington, DC, chapter of the Society of Professional Journalists. The article was cited as one of the notable essays of 2005 in *The Best American Essays 2006*.

Over the years, Price has appeared on many television and radio programs, including *Meet the Press, The NewsHour with Jim Lehrer, Charlie Rose, The O'Reilly Factor, Hannity & Colmes, Crossfire, On the Record with Greta Van Susteren, CBS Evening News, Lead Story, BET Tonight, The Montel Williams Show, Tom Joyner Morning Show*, and many national and local NPR broadcasts. While at the National Urban League, he distributed a weekly radio commentary and wrote a weekly column, "To Be Equal," for African-American newspapers across the country.

Currently, Price chairs the board of the Jacob Burns Film Center. He was formerly on the boards of Metropolitan Life Insurance Company, Verizon, Georgetown University, Sears Roebuck, Mayo Clinic, the Committee for Economic Development, the Educational Testing Service, and the Urban Institute. He was a member of an advisory committee established to formulate recommendations for improving the governance of the United States Olympic Committee.

Price has received honorary degrees from Yale University, Amherst College (his alma mater), and Indiana University-Purdue University, as well as the Medal of Honor from Yale Law School, the President's Medal from Hunter College, and honorary degrees from numerous other colleges and universities. He is a member of the American Philosophical Society, a fellow of the American Academy of Arts and Sciences, and an honorary member of the Academy of Political Science.

Price and his wife have three grown daughters.

CPSIA information can be obtained at www.ICGtesting.com
Printed in the USA
BVOW05s1807281014

372692BV00001B/13/P